FRANK & AVA

Also by John Brady

The Craft of Interviewing

Bad Boy: The Life and Politics of Lee Atwater

Craft of the Screenwriter

FRANK & AVA

IN LOVE AND WAR

John Brady

THOMAS DUNNE BOOKS
St. Martin's Press
New York

THOMAS DUNNE BOOKS.
An imprint of St. Martin's Press.

FRANK & AVA. Copyright © 2015 by John Brady. All rights reserved. Printed in the United States of America. For information, address St. Martin's Press, 175 Fifth Avenue, New York, N.Y. 10010.

www.thomasdunnebooks.com
www.stmartins.com

Designed by Kathryn Parise

The author is grateful for permission to reprint lyrics to the following songs:

"No One Ever Tells You" (Carroll Coates–H. Atwood).
Copyright © Carroll Coates D/B/A Micana Music. All Rights Reserved.
International Copyright Secured. Used by Permission.

"I Wanna Be Around" (Johnny Mercer–Sadie Vimmerstedt).
Copyright © Warner-Chappell Music, Inc. *The Complete Lyrics of Johnny Mercer*, Robert Kimball, ed., and The Johnny Mercer Foundation. All Rights Reserved.
International Copyright Secured. Used by Permission.

LIBRARY OF CONGRESS CATALOGING-IN-PUBLICATION DATA

Brady, John Joseph, 1942–
    Frank & Ava: in love and war / by John Brady.
        pages cm
    ISBN 978-1-250-07091-3 (hardcover)
    ISBN 978-1-4668-8157-0 (e-book)
    1. Sinatra, Frank, 1915–1998. 2. Singers—United States—Biography. 3. Gardner, Ava, 1922–1990. 4. Motion picture actors and actresses—United States—Biography.
I. Title. II. Title: Frank and Ava.
    ML420.S565B73 2015
    782.421640922—dc23
    [B]
                                                                    2015025547

Our books may be purchased in bulk for promotional, educational, or business use. Please contact your local bookseller or the Macmillan Corporate and Premium Sales Department at (800) 221-7945, extension 5442, or by e-mail at MacmillanSpecialMarkets@macmillan.com.

First Edition: October 2015

10 9 8 7 6 5 4 3 2 1

For TESS & ROSS,
with love

❧ CONTENTS ❧

No one ever tells you what it's like to love and lose,
How it feels to waken and have breakfast with the blues . . .
Someone tells you later all is fair in love and war,
But no one ever tells you before.

—"No One Ever Tells You,"
by Carroll Coates and Hub Atwood
Recorded by Frank Sinatra, Los Angeles, April 9, 1956
Capitol Records *A Swingin' Affair*
Arrangement by Nelson Riddle

FRANK & AVA

◁ PROLOGUE ▷

This is a story of love and war that begins in the 1940s, Hollywood's so-called golden age, when celebrity and stardom were different from what they are today. It is a story about a love that was real, not a publicist's arrangement, love between two of the biggest stars in the world. It was a time when no paparazzi lurked around corners—until these two stars came along.

It was the era of flight, but not jet flight. It was a time when there was no Internet, no television, and all phones had cords. News, if you heard or read it, was usually received the next day, or the day after that, and by then it hardly mattered.

The Depression was winding down, but it had left devastating scars. Poverty and struggle were evident everywhere. Kids signed up for the military, lying about their age, because it was at least something to do. It was work.

For relief, there were radio and the movies. If you wanted to see a movie, you went to a theater, which 95 million people in a nation of 132 million did at least once a week.

There were some exceptions, but movies weren't really that good.

They didn't have to be—they were the only game in town, and because the studios that produced films also owned the theaters, they could smugly guarantee that none would do badly. Movie making was a billion-dollar business, the sixth-largest industry in the United States.

In Hollywood, the studios were called "dream factories," emphasis on *factories*. Stars were like factory workers—certainly well paid, but not celebrities the way they are today. There was no actors union then. Even the big stars were treated like studio property. In one four-year period at Warner Bros., Humphrey Bogart acted in twenty-nine gangster films. It was work.

Sex was different then. It was a powerful motivator—people often married for it, and marriages lasted longer. There was no birth-control pill. For many, there was only abortion, and that was illegal. Families were often large. Only one in six marriages ended in divorce.

In Hollywood, though, the marriage rules were different, and lightly enforced. It was an era when the Caddy was king and nighttime glamour was an evening in a dinner club with a band and dancing. Sex was everywhere. Hollywood was where promiscuity prospered, long before the love-in sixties and the swinging seventies. On location, nothing counted.

Onto this playground came Ava Gardner and Frank Sinatra. In Hollywood, their ambitions and sex drives found their place. "Everybody was fucking everybody," said Ava. "Maybe it was the war." Frank was married at the time, which made her a home wrecker, and so there was notoriety and shame and all of the things that tabloids and fan magazines quickly learned to exploit.

Their affair became America's first reality show, with photographers and reporters pursuing Frank and Ava, filing photos and stories from hotels and movie sets around the world.

Their affair led to a tempestuous marriage and a lifelong relationship that was either the best or the worst thing that ever happened

to them, depending on how you interpret events. This is the story—
for better and for worse—of their remarkable lovers' quarrel as
they battled their way toward what they hoped would be a Hollywood
ending.

৵ 1 ৶

She Can't Act, She Can't Talk,
She's Terrific

When Ava Gardner arrived in Los Angeles in the summer of 1941, all she knew about Hollywood was what she had read in the fan magazines back home in Smithfield, North Carolina, where her mother had taken her to the Howell Theatre, at age nine, to see reigning heart-throb Clark Gable and "blonde bombshell" Jean Harlow in *Red Dust*. After three scorching days of travel, Ava stepped off the Super Chief in a cheap summer dress and white wedge sandals, carrying a cardboard suitcase with most of her possessions. The eighteen-year-old beauty did not smoke, did not drink, and was a virgin. She was a stranger in a strange land.

Earlier that summer, in the Manhattan offices of the MGM publicity department, Ava laughed about her chances of fame and fortune before the train started its trip across the continent to Hollywood. "Well, if I make it big there," she told the staff, "I'll marry the biggest movie star in the world."

"Would you like to see the biggest movie star in the world?" a publicist asked. He had a photo behind his back, and it wasn't of Clark Gable, as Ava had anticipated. It was of Mickey Rooney.

Six months after this playful exchange, Ava Gardner would indeed marry MGM's biggest moneymaker, Mickey Rooney. When the marriage failed, Ava would marry (and divorce) bandleader Artie Shaw, and have numerous affairs on and off the set, and star in movies with Burt Lancaster, Robert Taylor, and, yes, Clark Gable, in *Mogambo,* a remake of *Red Dust,* the movie she had seen with Mama.

In the midst of it all came Frank Sinatra, the most popular singer on the planet, the entertainer of the century, the womanizer of the ages—in full pursuit of Ava, a brunette bombshell, the Jean Harlow of her time.

How quickly and easily everything had unfolded. Before the age of thirty, Ava had three brief, wild marriages, and had become a major film star as well as an international sex symbol. It was like one of those breathless stories you might read in a fan magazine.

....

Ava Lavinia Gardner was born a farmer's daughter on Christmas Eve, 1922, in a house without water or plumbing in a tiny crossroads hamlet called Grabtown, not even on the map, seven miles east of Smithfield, North Carolina, population 5,574. Because of the proximity of her birthday and Christmas, two cakes were baked to celebrate that day—one chocolate, for the family, and a white coconut cake, for baby Ava, both according to mother Mollie's recipe. It became a custom that would continue through the years.

Ava was the youngest of five daughters and two sons of Jonas and Mollie Gardner, tobacco sharecroppers who also operated a boardinghouse for teachers. The family was poor. At school, Ava rotated two sweaters, one to wear and the other in the wash.

Jonas Gardner, a lean man of Scots-Irish ancestry, died when Ava was fifteen. "He did everything slowly, so deliberately and so well," Ava later remarked. He was her idol. "There wasn't an impulsive bone in his body," she said. "He used to make us lemonade and I can see him now, sitting at the kitchen table, rubbing the lemons hour after hour so they'd be soft and the juice would literally pour out of them when he finally got around to that part of the operation. I've never tasted anything like it. No booze was ever so good." Ava grew up playing in the tobacco fields, and assisting her father when the tobacco was aging in barns, where the furnaces had to be stoked to maintain a steady temperature for six or seven days until the leaves were cured. "I used to love it," she said. "I would stay the night with Daddy, sleeping with him."

At home, she remained the family baby. As her older sisters were married or nudged out of the house to get jobs after high school, Ava was cuddled and coddled. Her sisters bought her special bras to save her breasts from the fate of theirs—strapped against their chests in the Jazz Age style of the day. "I'd get out of doing the dishes," Ava said years later. "I can see Mama now, cleaning every room every day as though she were expecting Sunday visitors. But I never offered to help her. I should have, I suppose, and now I wish I had."

Mother Mollie was a woman of strict Baptist principles, who did not, or could not, bring herself to explain the facts of life to her daughters. When Ava had her first period and thought she was bleeding to death, it was not to her mama she rushed, but to the warmhearted black lady who worked in the Gardner household, who comforted her and explained what was happening. Mama had instilled in Ava a fear of the consequences of sex. On Ava's first date, a school prom, the lad tried to kiss her at the doorstep, and Mama came out of the house, scaring him away.

After a year at secretarial school, Ava came under the influence of her eldest sister, Beatrice, the family rebel, who lived in New York City with her second husband, a professional photographer. Beatrice was called "Bappie," a name Ava bestowed on her when the youngster could not pronounce her given name. Bappie, nineteen years older than Ava, had movie stars in her eyes. When she won a pair of green shoes—once worn by movie star Irene Dunne!—in a charity auction, she gave them to Ava, who kept them on a shelf in her bedroom to look at, but never to wear.

Ava talked Mollie into letting her visit Bappie in New York during the summer of 1939. Bappie's husband, Larry Tarr, took photos of the sixteen-year-old beauty and displayed one in his Fifth Avenue studio window as a sample portrait. A young clerk in MGM's New York office saw the photo and—hoping for a date—pretended to be a talent scout for the studio. He inquired about the model's name, and Larry Tarr used the occasion to send an array of photos to the MGM office. Ava soon found herself doing a screen test for the studio, including an audio sample, for Ava sang in the church choir and knew all of the old spirituals. She had a sweet singing voice, but her southern drawl was so heavy that few could understand her, so the technician sent the screen test to Hollywood—without audio. "She can't act, she can't talk," said studio chief Louis B. Mayer after viewing it. "She's terrific." He rose to leave the screening. "Give her to Gertrude and Lillian and let her have a year's training," he said. "Then test her again." A contract was issued. Beauty carried the day.

Milt Weiss, a young MGM publicist, and sister Bappie accompanied Ava on the train to Los Angeles, because that was how ladies traveled in those days, and that was what Mama wanted for her baby. When Bappie learned that Hedy Lamarr, MGM's reigning goddess, would arrive on the same train, she proclaimed, "That makes two movie queens on board!"

....

The drinks were strong and the conversations lively at Ruth Waterbury's home when Ava walked in on the arm of Milt Weiss. The publicist had called ahead and asked Ruth—the editor of *Photoplay* magazine—if he could stop by and show the new starlet off. "Naturally, the moment Ava walked in, the party was ruined," Waterbury wryly recalled. "The men were knocked speechless. They had never seen so much young beauty before, and I doubt if they ever will again. The women were kayoed, too, not only by Ava but also by the men's reaction to her." Ava was shy, but knew how to be slightly flirtatious in her charming southern way. This was her first night in Hollywood, and she was learning to operate on a mixture of instinct, charm, and looks. Tomorrow would be busy, said Milt, and they made a quick exit. "We were all relieved when Ava and the agent left," said Waterbury. But the conversations suddenly died. "Everybody else left right after them. There was no putting that party together again."

. . . .

No other lot in Hollywood knew a more spectacular and storied history than MGM, the celebrated real estate where *The Wizard of Oz* and most of the outdoor scenes in *Gone With the Wind* were filmed. It was where Myrna Loy and William Powell sipped martinis and walked their dog, Asta, where Katharine Hepburn met Spencer Tracy, where Judy Garland sang and danced down the yellow brick road. It was where Mickey Rooney said, repeatedly, "Let's put on a show!" Here Mama's favorite, Clark Gable, reigned as King of Hollywood for twenty-seven years.

The studio was a loose collection of buildings and soundstages, a self-contained entertainment factory that measured some five square miles in Culver City, south of Los Angeles, with its own police and fire departments, bank, post office, hospital with a physician and nurses on call, a swimming pool, commissary, a blacksmith's shop, city streets, western scenes, several lakes, and a fifteen-acre jungle. There were dozens of lavish dressing rooms, bungalows for the big stars, and a little red schoolhouse for child actors. One longtime publicist who was a former circus barker kept four elephants—from his circus days—as pets.

MGM produced the biggest films, paid the biggest salaries, and grossed the largest revenues. Walking through the commissary in that vintage year of 1941, you could have seen, picking at their salads, Jimmy Stewart, Hedy Lamarr, Greer Garson, Lionel Barrymore, Katharine Hepburn, Irene Dunne, Red Skelton, William Powell, Wallace Beery, Spencer Tracy, Walter Pidgeon, Robert Taylor, Lewis Stone, Gene Kelly, George Murphy, Van Johnson, Marsha Hunt, Robert Benchley, Spring Byington, Gladys Cooper, Barry Nelson, Desi Arnaz, and many others—including Louis B. Mayer, the founding father, who was in his fifties now, but still very much in power.

"L.B." was a short, barrel-chested man with thin white hair, round glasses, and an owlish, gruff expression that someone said made him look like a small-town high school principal. At fifty-six, he still worked until

8:30 P.M., minimum, with three secretaries. His birthday, celebrated on the Fourth of July, was a *real* holiday on the lot, with a huge party and entertainment by some of the top actors in the commissary, an event that everyone was commanded to attend.

Mayer had come out of a Russian ghetto, and he felt a great debt to the America that had permitted him to grow so powerful. He fancied himself a guardian of American family values. His favorite product was the Andy Hardy movie series, idealized sagas of small-town life, with Mickey Rooney as the devilish but good-hearted kid, learning life's lessons with his mom and pop and his wise old grandpa. L.B. truly believed the myth—and he loved the money it made for the studio, and for himself. At one million dollars a year, Louis B. Mayer was regularly named the country's highest-paid executive.

His office was cavernous, "about half as large as the lounge of the Radio City Music Hall," reported *New Yorker* journalist Lillian Ross. Mayer presided behind a huge creamy white desk covered with four creamy white telephones, overlooking a vast expanse of creamy white carpet. The walls were paneled in creamy white leather, and there was a bar, a fireplace, leather chairs, couches, and a grand piano, all creamy white. His desk, on a raised dais, was positioned so that the visitor, always looking upward, was made to feel like a recalcitrant child in the principal's office. L.B. got the idea from Harry Cohn, who ran Columbia Pictures (the salt mine of studios), who got the idea from Italian fascist dictator Benito Mussolini. "It made L.B. the prophet and all those sitting before him the disciples," said Jerry Lewis. "A great device for his need to dominate."

Mayer insisted on absolute punctuality on the part of visitors, who had to be impeccably dressed. Men were required to wear a jacket and tie. Joan Crawford came from a set in a swimsuit and bathrobe, and was sent home to change. Most of Mayer's top executives—Eddie Mannix, Benny Thau, and Sidney Franklin—were also short. Esther Williams, the gorgeous five-foot-eight swimming star, said that she felt like Snow White with the Dwarfs whenever she was in Mayer's office for a meeting. A story, probably apocryphal, was told of a somewhat proper actress entering the office one day and asking, "Don't you usually stand when a lady enters the room?" "Madam," replied the diminutive L.B., "I am standing."

Mayer was like a Jewish father (or mother, perhaps) who kept a vigilant eye on his film family. When Lana Turner's nights on the town elicited the wrong kind of publicity, he summoned her to his office—and demanded that she bring her mother. In an emotional, disappointed tone, he told the young star that keeping late hours and making the papers endangered her wonderful future. "He actually had tears in his eyes at one point, so I started crying, too," recalled Lana. Then L.B. jumped up and shouted, "The only thing you're interested in is . . ." and he pointed crudely to his crotch.

"How dare you, Mr. Mayer!" said Lana's mother righteously as they marched out. "In front of my daughter!"

Mayer was a micromanager, a stickler for details. One had to be a demagogue on little things if you wanted to have your way on the big things. He was also the best actor on the lot. He asked director John Huston to come to his house one Sunday for breakfast. A script in progress wasn't what L.B. wanted. He told Huston about Jeanette MacDonald and how he had instructed her to sing "Ah! Sweet Mystery of Life" by singing the Jewish "Eli, Eli" for her. "She was so moved," recalled Huston, "that Mayer said she wept. Yes, wept! She who had the reputation of pissing ice water!"

By way of demonstration, Mayer sang the song for Huston. Mayer said that if Huston could make the script into that kind of picture, he would crawl to the director on his knees and kiss his hand, which he then proceeded to do. "I sat there and thought, this is not happening to me," said Huston, who left in a cold sweat, with Mayer's words echoing in his ears: "You can only try! Try, John! Try!"

Nepotism ruled. Mayer's relatives and friends of relatives were everywhere. George Sidney, who directed Ava's screen test, was the son of Louis K. Sidney, pioneer producer and vice president of MGM. His wife was Lillian Burns, who worked in the drama department. Actress Norma Shearer's husband, legendary producer Irving Thalberg, had died in 1936, but he was still an influence at the studio. Her brother Douglas was head of the sound department. "We are a business concern and not patrons of the arts," said obsessive memo dictator David O. Selznick, who earned L.B.'s esteem (and his daughter Irene in marriage) by making two Westerns concurrently, with two scripts and two leading ladies, shooting all action material at the same time, "making two of them for the price of about one and one-eighth," memo'd Selznick. Such stratagems advanced Selznick's standing among producers, but it didn't hurt that there was reportedly an inscription in the commissary men's room: "The son in law also rises." The studio was like a Jewish resort in the Catskills.

....

Shortly after Ava's arrival, Milt Weiss took her for a tour, including a visit to the set of *Babes on Broadway,* where Mickey Rooney was dressed for his Carmen Miranda number, bedecked in a skirt, a fruit hat larger than his head, and platform-soled shoes, which added some height to his diminutive stature. When he espied Ava behind the cameras, it was lust at first sight.

"She had narrow ankles, perfect calves, full thighs, a tiny waist, a bosom that rose like two snowy mountain peaks, an alabaster throat, a dimpled chin, full red lips, a pert nose, wide green eyes beneath dark, arched brows, a wide, intelligent forehead and chestnut-colored hair that looked as if it had been stroked a thousand times a night ever since she was old enough to handle a brush," he recalled approvingly in his memoir, *Life Is Too Short*. At lunchtime that day, as Ava walked into the studio commissary, Rooney told his cronies that he was going to marry that girl.

Rooney, two years older (and four inches shorter) than Ava, was the biggest box-office attraction in the world, and—at twenty—still a convincing teenager in the studio's Andy Hardy movies. He was also a relentless womanizer—Lana Turner called him "Andy Hard-on"—and a regular at a brothel called T&M Studios, off Santa Monica Boulevard, where young women were made up to look like Greta Garbo, Jean Harlow, Norma Shearer, and other stars of the era.

When Mickey asked Ava for a date, though, she said no. He continued to pester, and she continued to turn down his requests. "That only made me want her more," he said, "not just so I could go to bed with her. I wanted to make her the mother of my children."

············

Ava drew a low salary, even by entry-level standards: At fifty dollars a week, plus acting, speech, and grooming lessons, she was a steal. Her salary was actually thirty-five dollars, because a clause in the contract gave MGM the right to stop payment for a twelve-week layoff period. "If Bappie hadn't come to Hollywood with me . . . and she hadn't gone downtown and got a job at I. Magnin's, we'd have starved to death," Ava later recalled. "As it was, we lived in one crummy room with a pull-down bed, and a kitchenette as big as a closet. Film star! More like slave laborer."

There was no equity among the starlets in residence. Esther Williams— who had an agent—signed on, shortly after Ava's arrival, for $350 a week. Of course, both lasses' salaries paled beside the one thousand dollars a week that Lassie earned as top dog around the studio, where *he* was known as "Greer Garson with fur."

Beyond salary inequities, contracts gave the studio the right to rule on all professional decisions in an actor's life. The studio decided which film she or he would make, who else would be in it, who would produce and direct it. The studio had the right to "loan" an actor out to another studio for any film that the other studio wanted to make. The loan-out fee went entirely to MGM, which paid the actor his regular salary out of its profits on the loan.

The studios used promotional films and stories in cooperative magazines and newspapers to create an image of themselves as exciting workplaces, with wardrobe and makeup departments for pampering the stars in their dressing rooms or at tables in the commissary. It was like a big game of pretend. Except for the small handful of top stars, working at MGM was like being part of an assembly line in a robber baron factory where the product was "pictures," as they were then called. Movie theaters in those days offered a double bill from Thursday to Saturday and another from Sunday to Wednesday. MGM supplied their chain of movie houses with four B movies—or "program pictures"—every week, along with the occasional big-budget picture. "I don't think you sat around just looking pretty at MGM," said Ava ruefully. "They worked you hard eight until five."

Director Elia Kazan termed the men who created Hollywood "marvelous monsters." He knew them all—Mayer and his enforcer, Eddie Mannix; B. P. Schulberg; the Warner brothers; Darryl Zanuck; Spyros Skouras; Harry Cohn; David Selznick; and Samuel Goldwyn. The front office and the producers had the power; the rest of the lot—writers, actors, directors, composers—were mere employees. The execs were responsible for artistic decisions, not the artists. "They were industrialists," said Kazan.

Recruited from Broadway in 1946, Kazan arrived in Hollywood with high hopes. "I'd be working at the greatest film studio in the world," he wrote, "Metro-Goldwyn-Mayer, the home ground of 'more stars than there are in the heavens.' I'd be a director among many famous directors whom I admired. I'd made it." Instead, he found himself "dumped into a perfectly structured organization . . . an industrial compound" where a "relentless conveyor-belt style of productivity depended on a constant ingestion of new creative talent, but the artists counted for little or nothing apart from their ability to deliver the goods."

MGM movies originated on the lot—rarely on location—where the studio had a special large stage and staff for rear projection. The powerful art department designed, built, painted, and put up backgrounds for scenes that were staged, just barely directed. Other scenes were shot with a process screen behind the actors, showing moving traffic on a street so that it looked, unconvincingly, like they were traveling down it. This was the cost-efficient way that Metro made movies, with control of lighting and other conditions, no matter what time of year.

The cost-accounting cynicism at MGM was so thorough that the studio brandished it on the lion's head logo, where the motto was *Ars Gratia Artis,* art for art's sake, very loosely speaking. Spencer Tracy recalled producer/director Mervyn LeRoy, at lunch in the commissary, raving about a book he'd bought. "It's got everything," he said. "Surprise, great characters, an important theme, fine writing! But," he added, "I think I can lick it."

....

The popular press exploited the Hollywood glamour game, and collected fat revenues for movie ads in their pages. Ava was part of the annual crop of what *Life* magazine, in a 1940 cover story, called "the world's most envied of girls." Starlets, usually discovered by roving talent scouts, had little or no acting experience. "At all times they are told what to do, what to say, how to dress, where to go, whom to go with," reported the weekly. "Only if they obey implicitly and only if, in addition, by some magic of beauty, personality or talent, they touch off an active response in millions of movie fans, will a few of them know the full flower of stardom, with its fabulous rewards of fame and wealth."

Of course, stardom could happen. Lana Turner was discovered, according to studio lore, as she sipped a soda in a Hollywood ice-cream parlor while cutting a secretarial class at her high school. This led to an interview with MGM director and producer Mervyn LeRoy, who began guiding her career. In her first movie, *They Won't Forget,* Lana spoke not one line, and was murdered in the first reel. She removed her blouse beneath a skintight sweater, however, and jiggled along a street, thus becoming the original "sweater girl." Stardom followed.

"It was all beauty and it was all power," Lana explained. "Once you had it made, they protected you; they gave you stardom. The ones who kept forging ahead became higher and higher and brighter and brighter and they were *stars*. And they were *treated* like stars." The star system was big business. When the actor or actress didn't personally own the appropriate clothes, the studio stepped in and provided what was needed to maintain the glamour and glitz—and protect its considerable investment.

Stars had drivers, bodyguards, and were accustomed to having assistants, valets, cooks, maids, servants, houseboys, secretaries, lackeys, toadies, hangers-on, all ready to run for cigarettes, speak only when spoken to, mind the pets, run for popcorn at previews, take notes, sign autographs (when no one was looking), bring the car around, do their hair, and answer their phones.

For every Lana success story, hundreds of starlets struggled for supporting roles; countless others never appeared in front of a camera. "The studio was full of them, sexy young women who wanted to make it in Hollywood," said Mickey Rooney. "Most often," he recalled, "Hollywood ended up making *them* because some of the women were there, first and foremost, as potential pussy for the executives at MGM."

The casting couch? It was real. Thanks to studio publicity, unknown starlets often became celebrities in their hometowns and would do almost anything rather than return home. L.B.'s office featured a private elevator for transporting secret visitors to the Mayer of Hollywood, who fell in love often. Benny Thau, the top casting producer at MGM, made directors cast the women he was sleeping with in their films. "He couldn't fire us if we said no because we had long-term contracts," said producer Gottfried Reinhardt, "but we never wanted to alienate him. He was too powerful."

Elia Kazan said that the studio heads "thought of every film they made, no matter how serious the theme, as a love story." Consequently, they cast by an elemental rule: Does the actress arouse me? "I believe this rule of casting is not only inevitable but correct, and quite the best method for the kind of films they made," said the director. "The audience must be interested in a film's people in this elemental way. If not, something essential is missing. If the producer wasn't interested in an actress this way, he was convinced an audience wouldn't be and that this actress wouldn't 'draw flies.'" Thus, when it came to actresses, said Kazan, "They went by a simple rule and a useful one: Do I want to fuck her?" They often put actresses to such a test.

The story circulated of a onetime New York glove salesman named Sam Goldfish, who was now a big-shot studio mogul named Samuel Goldwyn, attempting to mount Madeleine Carroll on the office sofa one day, and the actress—very poised, very British—twisted her body and threw Sam on the floor. As he adjusted his clothing, Goldwyn drew himself up to his most dignified posture, absorbed the novelty, and proclaimed, "I have never been so insulted in my life!"

. . . .

For Ava, MGM comprised a finishing school. She was put through the assembly-line gauntlet, where experts in make-up and hairdressing clinically examined her teeth, studied her figure, and experimented with her hair. They monitored her demeanor. One day, as she sat reading a magazine, a voice startled her. "Stop chewing that gum, will you?" It was Sydney Guilaroff, Metro's top hairdresser. "Take it out of your mouth this minute." (He would eventually become her best MGM friend.)

They scrutinized her walk, posture, everything. Ava was a tall, sensuous brunette with chestnut-colored hair that had a reddish glow. Her height (5'6") separated her from the smaller starlets—Lana claimed to be 5'3"—and endeared her to the wardrobe department as she carried stylish outfits with flair. She had a face of classical proportions and balance, a radiant smile, green almond-shaped eyes, a dimpled chin, and a long-legged figure of perfect proportions, 36-20-36, with high, firm breasts, prominent nipples, and skin like white jade.

MGM employed an elaborate makeup system, which included a chart of a generic face that was used by every makeup man, who marked it according to corrections he felt should be made on each actress. "Shading here, shading there, eyes made up this way, throat made up that way, and so on," recalled Betty Garrett. "Each picture then became completely different depending on the woman's natural coloring and contours. This line over Lana Turner's eyes, this direction for Ava Gardner's eyebrows. Everybody had her own chart so it did not matter which makeup man you got. He just looked at the chart and knew exactly what to do."

Ava had some social mannerisms that troubled Howard Strickling, the studio's legendary publicity chief. By her own description, Ava was a barefoot country girl who could be one of the boys—earthy, unpretentious, and capable of cussin' with the worst of them. "Strick" asked singer/actor Allan Jones and his wife, Irene Hervey, to invite Ava to their home so that she would note how people entertained. During the meal, Ava startled her hosts and guests by picking up her napkin between courses to wipe her knife and fork. There was still a residual amount of hillbilly in the starlet.

Ava cultivated table manners quickly, and her drawl diminished (except when she had a few drinks) in Gertrude Fogler's elocution class. MGM girls learned dance and movement from instructor Jeanette Bates, who had them walking down stairs, in heels, without ever looking at their feet. "We studied simple movements, such as getting up out of a chair, keeping your knees together, making exits and entrances, and how to tuck your bottom in when you walked," recalled Esther Williams.

MGM girls were beautiful, serene, poised, and deadly sure of themselves when making an entrance, or an exit. Posture was serious to acting coach Lillian Burns, who taught the *dramatic* exit—chin up, shoulders up, head thrown back. "Ava Gardner snapped her neck; so did Lana Turner and Janet Leigh," said Esther. "It's a wonder we all didn't end up at the chiropractor's."

. . . .

And Mickey? Gradually, he began to wear down Ava with his entreaties. The deal maker came out when Ava declined dinner one night because Bappie was with her, you see, and—

"Well, I'm inviting you *and* Bappie," said Mickey, making nice with Cinderella's older sister.

That evening, there was dinner for three at Chasen's—and the courtship of Ava Gardner began in earnest. Mickey Rooney was everywhere, driving her from her Franklin Avenue apartment to the studio, driving all over the lot, shouting to everybody he knew on the studio streets. "Hey, this is my new girl. She's going to be a big star. Isn't she gorgeous?"

They became a couple. They went to baseball games, auto races, and the track. In October, Bappie may have blabbed, for the *Smithfield Herald* was reporting to the hometown folks in North Carolina, "Pretty Ava Gardner in Limelight as Mickey Rooney's 'Latest' Girl Friend."

This was a new world for Ava, one she quickly became accustomed to. Movie stars liked to travel in the fast lane. Maître d's welcomed them with a smile and escorted them to good tables. Moreover, Ava was able to sidestep the perilous route taken by many wannabes in the hands of predatory producers—as Mickey's date, she was that rarest of starlets: a girl who *could* say no.

Hardly a day went by that Mickey didn't propose. Gradually, Ava's replies drifted from "You're crazy, Mick, I hardly know you" to "Marriage is a serious thing, Mick." She asked Bappie for guidance. What would Mama think? Bappie and Mama both approved. Eventually, her reply to Mickey was, "What'll our life be like?"

On Ava's nineteenth birthday, Christmas Eve 1941, Mickey Rooney asked Ava Gardner to be his wife, this time with a big diamond ring. Ava said yes.

L. B. Mayer summoned the couple. This was Ava's first encounter with L.B. "It would break my heart to see you unhappy," he told Mickey. "I've always been like a father to you. Believe me, this is not the girl for you. You're so hot for her you can't think straight." Ava squirmed in embarrassment. Later, with Rooney out of earshot, he warned her, "He just wants to get in your pants."

Mickey faced L.B. down, and when Mayer realized he couldn't prevent the marriage, he arranged a stag party for Mickey in his private dining room. There, Metro male stars rose to offer ribald advice to the young groom, including how to explain lipstick marks on his fly when he came home from a busy day at the studio. "During the first year, every time you make love, put a pebble in the sink," intoned Spencer Tracy. "The second year, every time you make love, you take a pebble out of the sink. You know what, Mickey?" he said. "You'll never empty the sink."

. . . .

On January 10, 1942, Mickey and Ava married, in a small Protestant church in the village of Ballard, in California's Santa Ynez Mountains. The bride wore a navy blue suit and a corsage of orchids. Bappie, Mickey's parents, and Les Peterson, the number-two gun in MGM publicity, attended the ceremony.

Hedda Hopper headlined her Sunday column with her exclusive on the wedding of the Mighty Mite to MGM's sexiest starlet. Mickey, standing on a stool, appeared as tall as Ava in the pictures. The couple took off on a working honeymoon (Mickey was promoting the latest Andy Hardy movie), with Les Peterson tagging along as MGM's chaperone.

Ava was apprehensive about losing her virginity on her wedding night. "Relax, you're going to do fine, honey," said Bappie. "Nature will take its course. Just open wide!"

Mickey, apprehensive in his own way, got so drunk that evening that Ava was still a virgin the morning after. Coitus interruptus number two occurred when Mickey pulled golf clubs out of the trunk of his car the next day. "Golf?" said Ava. "But I don't play golf."

Long after that marriage collapsed, long after several other marriages and divorces had transpired, Mickey Rooney, in his memoir, recalled how Ava had watched him play a round of golf that he found quite exciting that first married day—"and she saw me card a confident seventy-nine," he reported, quite pleased with himself. (Ava took up tennis.)

On evening number two, they had sex. "I was, by turns, alternately tender and tremendous," said Mickey, who could now return his undivided attention to playing thirty-six holes. "It was an ideal honeymoon: sex and golf and sex and golf," he said. "It never occurred to me to ask Ava what she wanted."

What Ava wanted—and she was good at it—was more sex. "Once Ava got into the spirit of things, she wanted to do it all the time," said Rooney. She quickly learned how to arouse a man with a smoldering look, kicking off her shoes as soon as she entered the house, or coming to breakfast in only a pair of shorts. "In the feathers," as she phrased it, Ava was exciting and could be starkly demanding. "Let's fuck, Mickey," she would say. "Now!"

Rooney—who, in addition to being short, could be small on occasion—

reported that "Ava's breasts were full, with large brown nipples that, when aroused, stood out like enlarged California golden raisins. And at the center of her femininity she had this little rosebud that seemed to have a life of its own. It was almost like a little warm mouth that would reach up and grab me and take me in and make my, uh, my heart swell."

············

One portentous evening, the newlyweds were enjoying drinks at the Mocambo on Sunset Strip when Frank Sinatra approached, all smiles.

"Hey, why didn't I meet you before Mickey?" asked Frank, clasping the Mick's hand and giving Ava what came to be known as "the look." "Then I could have married you myself!"

What a strange thing to say, thought Ava. She smiled but said nothing. She had seen Frank around the MGM lot, and pianist Skitch Henderson even introduced them one day between soundstages. She also told a friend that, as a teen in Newport News, Virginia, she had seen the singer perform with Tommy Dorsey. He was her dream idol, she said.

There were few kept secrets in Hollywood. Everyone knew Frank's wife, his kids, and his proclivities. Mickey and Frank chatted some—they were pals—and when he returned to the band, Frank Sinatra dedicated his first number to Mrs. Ava Rooney. What would Mama say about that? she wondered.

~ 2 ~

Frankie Comes to Hollywood

When Frank Sinatra arrived in California in the summer of 1943, the Super Chief had to stop in Pasadena—not downtown L.A.—to keep the mass hysteria to a minimum. Still, Frankie required a cordon of police for a crowd estimated at five thousand, mostly young women who had been coached by publicist George Evans to weep, scream, and swoon as the original American idol stepped off the train. Evans wanted to make absolutely certain that, for his star client, it would be a grand entrance in Hollywood.

In 1943, Sinatra was everywhere. He was the singing sensation of the era, due largely to impeccable career timing as musical tastes were shifting from big bands to boy singers with bands *behind* them. You could hear his records in music stores, on his own radio program and on "Your Hit Parade," and on jukeboxes in bars and restaurants. You could see and swoon over him at stage shows. He was the highest-paid concert performer in the country, making even more than Louis B. Mayer, America's highest-paid business executive.

Frankie's popularity coincided with America's late entry into World War II. "I'll Be Seeing You" took on a hymnlike significance for women uncertain they would ever see their boyfriends, brothers, sons, or husbands again. The war also brought talent shortages to the movie industry, including leading men. Tyrone Power, Robert Taylor, Henry Fonda, and now Mickey Rooney joined the armed forces. Clark Gable and Jimmy Stewart flew missions over Europe. Even Lew Ayres, a conscientious objector, served as a stretcher-bearer, transporting wounded marines in the Central Pacific.

In the vacuum, a highly vocal (and lucrative) segment of the population—known as bobby-soxers, for the ankle-length socks they wore with saddle shoes—had created a new leading man, Frank Sinatra. The singer had played himself in a couple of modestly successful films with the Tommy Dorsey Orchestra—*Las Vegas Nights* and *Ship Ahoy*—but now he was going to star in his own movies at RKO.

Of course, RKO was no MGM, but with proper care and handling, this deal could be a stepping-stone to a huge screen career. To George Evans, the contract must have been the equivalent of the legendary telegram Herman J. Mankiewicz sent Ben Hecht from Hollywood in 1925: "Will you accept three hundred per week to work for Paramount Pictures? All expenses paid. The three hundred is peanuts. Millions are to be grabbed out here and your only competition is idiots. Don't let this get around."

In Hollywood, where lies are bought and sold, Frankie was no stranger in paradise. This was like New Jersey, only with more girls. He luxuriated in North America's Gomorrah.

. . . .

George Evans planned Frank's life as if it were a movie, beginning with an imaginative Frank Capra–style narrative that would follow the singer for a lifetime. According to Evans's bio sheet, Frank was a graduate of Demarest High School in Hoboken, New Jersey, where he "was on the championship basketball team, won a trophy in swimming and was an outstanding member of the track team. He sang with his school band at proms and assemblies and helped form the school glee club. . . . Upon graduation he got a job with the *Jersey Observer* as a copy boy and studied short hand and journalism for a year at Drake Institute hoping to further his newspaper ambitions." Evans listed Frank as "five-foot ten and one-half inches tall, and weighing 140 pounds." About the only thing Evans got right was his client's eye color: blue.

The publicist told lies so beguilingly—to a conspiring Hollywood press (there was no "media" then)—that the tall tales were being recycled in a "news release" about "the new Sinatra" from the Rogers & Cowan PR firm in 1958, in which the singer's height had grown to five feet, eleven inches. By 1985, however (after his fourth marriage), Frank was down to five feet, ten and a half inches in his daughter Nancy's memoir. (The eyes remained blue throughout.)

According to Selective Service files, in December 1943, when he was classified 4-F, Frank Sinatra was five feet, seven and a half inches and weighed about 130. Frank certainly wasn't tall (the height of the average U.S. fighting man in World War II was five nine), but he was manly, craved being the center of attention, and having things his way at all times. "Frank was not like a band vocalist at all," said Harry Meyerson, the RCA Victor A&R man who supervised an early session when Frank recorded "Night and Day." "Frank came in self-assured, slugging. He knew exactly what he wanted. He started out by having a good opinion of himself. On that first date he stood his ground and displayed no humility, phony or real."

....

In later years, Frank's slender physique was a puzzlement. He weighed thirteen pounds at birth, on December 12, 1915, in a tenement at 45 Monroe Street in Hoboken, New Jersey—nearly killing his tiny mother, who weighed just under one hundred pounds. Initially, the doctor—thinking the baby was stillborn—concentrated on saving the mother as *her* mother took baby Francis Albert to the kitchen sink and revived him with cold water, and for the first time was heard the voice.

Natalie Catherine Garavente (called "Dolly"), from Genoa, would become a dominating mother with, yes, piercing blue eyes. She was busy, ambitious, a wife, mother, midwife, abortionist, and a ward captain for the

Democratic machine in Hoboken, where she delivered five hundred votes for the party—this, in an era when women did not yet have the vote.

There was no way to avoid Dolly. She was jovial, outgoing, and a terror to nearly everyone she encountered. Her marriage to Anthony Martin Sinatra (called "Marty"), from Agrigento, Sicily, was similar to the relationship between Penn and Teller. Dolly did all of the talking, all of the bossing. Marty just sat there, nodding. Through her political connections, she got him a position with the Hoboken Fire Department, where he worked his way up to captain and kept his mouth shut. Some speculated Marty could not speak English.

Watching the kind of man his father was—and how he related to his mother—would have lifelong effects on young Sinatra. It has been said that men who rail against women are railing at one woman only. For Frank, that would be Dolly.

After she recovered from the traumatic birth, Dolly relegated Francis Albert, at six months, to *her* mother for rearing. In 1974, Frank remembered those early years. "I hope you'll consider having another baby," he said to his daughter Nancy after the birth of her first child. "It was lonely for me," said Frank, who often came home to an empty house. "Very lonely."

. . . .

At Demarest High, early in his freshman year, Frank and two pals smuggled pigeons under their jackets into the auditorium for a school play. On cue, during a serious point in the production, they let the birds fly. That was the end of the play. Kids screamed and ducked the pigeons. It was also the end of Frank's high school career after forty-three days.

Thereafter, he spent most of his time on the street of big or broken dreams in Hoboken, where he took the occasional job and started singing for his supper in Italian social clubs and at his father's bar, called Marty O'Brien's, the name he used during a very brief career as an unsuccessful prizefighter. Frank's childhood pal, the diminutive Tony Consiglio, watched Marty fight in New Haven one night. "He stumbled around the ring, swinging at the air," he recalled. "If Marty had stayed in boxing, he would have spent more time on canvases than Picasso. He wisely packed it in."

The only thing Frank Sinatra ever wanted to be was a singer. He started riding the bus into New York, where he and Tony Consiglio went to the Horn & Hardart Automat for two French rolls and two cups of hot chocolate, a nickel apiece. Broadway had dozens of theaters, and it was safe for a teenager to wander around, go to a movie, watch the stage show, and spend the whole day being entertained. They took in a movie and band performance at the Paramount in Times Square, hiding out in the back row to stay for another show and hear a big band over and over.

In late November 1932, Frank, almost seventeen, took Nancy Barbato, a pretty dark-haired, brown-eyed girl from Jersey City, to see Bing Crosby, who was singing at Loew's Jersey Theatre, located in Jersey City's Journal Square. Watching Bing onstage, performing with the band, playing that wonderful music, afforded Frank the inspiration he needed. "Some day I'd like to sing like that guy," he told Tony Consiglio (who would become his assistant and traveling companion for thirty years). Music promised a ticket out of Hoboken.

In September 1935, Frank sang "Shine," in imitation of the Crosby–Mills Brothers recording, with the Three Flashes (renamed the Hoboken Four, with Frank as lead) on Major Bowes's "Original Amateur Hour," a popular weekly radio show that was an avatar for *American Idol*. Listeners phoned or sent postcards with the name of their favorite performer, and the Hoboken Four won. (Voting records do not indicate how many callers and postcards Dolly rounded up in Hoboken wards.)

The foursome went on the road with Major Bowes and his traveling show. One day, the major (his army reserve title) took Frank aside. "You've got the talent, and you're carrying this group," he said. "If you're smart, you'll go out on your own." Saying he was homesick, Frank left the group, and that was the last anyone heard of the Hoboken Four.

On February 4, 1939, Frank and Nancy married. He was earning fifteen dollars a week waiting tables and singing at the Rustic Cabin, a small club in New Jersey where trumpeter Harry James heard and hired him at seventy-five dollars a week for a band he was forming. In late August, Frank made his first recordings with James, including "All or Nothing at All," which sold six thousand copies and was forgotten. "He considers himself the greatest vocalist in the business," Harry told a *DownBeat* magazine staffer. "Get that! No one ever heard of him. He's never had a hit record. He looks like a wet rag. But he says he's the greatest!"

Tommy Dorsey liked what he heard on those early records, and, when his boy singer Jack Leonard left to join the army, he hired Frank and doubled his salary. Sinatra considered the bespectacled trombonist one of the most colorful and dynamic musicians in the trade. Three years earlier, Frank was dancing with Nancy at a Dorsey band show and pointed up to where Jack Leonard was sitting on the stand. "See that singer guy?" he said. "One day I'll be sitting where he's sitting." That day had come. "Tommy was like a god," said Frank. "We were all in awe of him."

Dorsey had a huge musical effect on Frank. As jazz historian and cornetist Richard Sudhalter observed, "When the autodidact looks around and sees a way of doing things, or a way of expressing himself that appeals to him, he makes it his own . . . And I think that Sinatra as a working-class kid from Hoboken learned that way." When the disciple is ready, the master will appear.

Frank observed Dorsey's phrasing techniques on the trombone and applied them to his own singing, building long, fluid lines on ballads. "Instead of singing only two bars or four bars of music at a time—like most of the other guys around—I was able to sing six bars, and in some songs eight bars, without taking a visible or audible breath," he later explained. "This gave the melody a flowing, unbroken quality and that—if anything— was what made me sound different. It wasn't the voice alone; in fact, my voice was always a little too high, I thought, and not as good in natural quality as some of the competition." Frank also learned something else from Dorsey: "Sing each song like it was my last."

Frank imitated Tommy's militarylike gait with its quick, graceful movements and his "bigger than life" physical presence, which was enhanced by the elevator shoes that Tommy (at five ten) wore to seem even taller.

Frank, too, started wearing Adler elevators—shoes that "lifted the spirits of small men."

Tommy's family lived at Tall Oaks, a twenty-acre homestead in Bernardsville, the heart of New Jersey horse country. Tommy bought the estate in 1935, at the age of twenty-nine. Tall Oaks became more than a home; it was his Graceland, a refuge for having fun, and a symbol of his success and position, "two things that were very important to him," wrote Dorsey biographer Peter Levinson. Dorsey was telling the world he came from a working-class background (his father labored in the coal mines of Pennsylvania), but he was a self-made millionaire in a time when a million meant something. "He also wanted to have the best clothes and the best car, and he wanted to be seen dining at the best restaurants in New York," said Levinson. "Tom was a great patron of excellence," said Jo Stafford, the band's girl singer.

Tommy brought guests and band members to Tall Oaks to enjoy the tennis courts and the swimming pool on weekends. It was an Olympic-size pool, identical to Crosby's in California, for Tommy had brought in the guy who did Bing's pool to build it. An electric remote was installed at the gate, and one of the first high-fidelity sound systems was installed on the third floor, which he had turned into a dormitory to accommodate the band, with bunk beds, five showers, and a wet bar. One year, Dorsey had the band play a benefit for the Bernardsville Fire Department. He bought enough half-inch tongue-and-groove planking to form a crude dance floor almost an acre in size, installed a huge tent, and built a bandstand so that the entire town could dance to his music.

Frank loved playing with an elaborate electric train set that Tommy had installed, ostensibly for his teen boys. In the basement, there was a roundhouse and a huge collection of Lionel trains with different engines, all overseen by a boyhood friend when the chief engineer was in residence. In many of the bedrooms, there was a ledge below the ceiling, with a track for long electric trains that entered through an opening in the wall, and a recorded voice announcing destinations—"All aboard! Philadelphia!" or "All aboard! Milwaukee!"—depending on the point of origin for guests in the rooms. "Those were tough years for the country," recalled a friend of the Dorseys, "but that place really jumped."

. . . .

Life on the road was intense. Dorsey forbade spouses to travel with band members, and few marriages survived, because there was no home life. Tommy, Frank, and the boys played cards and drank till early morning. Dorsey introduced Frank to golf—his way. He hired an extra caddie to push a baby carriage behind them, filled with ice and beer. "We'd have a beer after each shot," recalled Frank. "After nine holes, imagine—we were loaded."

Frank and drummer Buddy Rich started out as travel pals, sharing a seat on the band bus. Then they became roommates. The band members referred to Frank as "Lady Macbeth" because he was so meticulous, always showering and changing his clothes. The odd couple had their first falling-out when the clicking sounds made by Frank, who was cutting his toenails at two in the morning, awakened Buddy, who couldn't get back to sleep. There was a fight. The roommates split. One hot August night, as Frank was crooning a ballad, Buddy vengefully shifted from the feathery beat of brushes to a loud thumping of his sticks, throwing off Frank's delivery and destroying the romantic mood.

Afterward, at the door of the musicians' room, Sinatra threw a pitcher of ice water at the drummer. Rich ducked and the pitcher crashed into the wall as pieces of glass flew. The next day, Dorsey put his boy singer on leave. "I can live without a singer tonight, but I need a drummer," he said. A few nights later, two thugs approached Buddy as he left the hotel. "Is your name Rich?" they inquired. The September 1, 1940, issue of *Down-Beat* magazine reported, "Buddy Rich Gets Face Bashed In," adding that it "looked as if it had been smashed in with a shovel."

The 1940 Halloween night opening of the new Hollywood Palladium was a gala event. Dorsey's orchestra drew an overflow crowd of 6,500 who jammed the eleven-thousand-square-foot dance floor. That week, Tommy had the number-one record in the country, "I'll Never Smile

Again," with Frank doing the vocal. Frank wanted to leave the band, however, as he was suspected of having arranged Buddy's beating. When he saw Artie Shaw, Frank asked the bandleader if he would like to hire a new singer. "But I don't use boy singers," said Artie, known for only hiring singers with great legs. Artie, who rarely met a musician he didn't dislike, didn't think much of Frank. Let Tommy, who was more showman than bandleader, keep this sensitive young singer. Artie Shaw just wanted to make music.

By the fall of 1941, Frank was making $250 a week with the band, and his confidence and cockiness expanded with his newly found status at shows. In December of that year, the band was in Hollywood to film *Ship Ahoy* at MGM, where Lana Turner—fresh from a fast marriage and faster divorce from Artie Shaw—was queen of the lot. Lana invited Frank to come up and see her sometime at her new Westwood home, complete with a white grand piano. Starlets Susan Hayward and Linda Darnell would be there on Sunday, December 7. Frank and Buddy were friends again, so the drummer came along, as did Tommy Dorsey, and everyone was having a good time until Lana's mother, Mildred, returning from a trip to San Francisco, seemed astonished that the oblivious partyers hadn't heard the news. "Turn on the radio, for heaven's sake!" Pearl Harbor had been bombed. The country was about to go to war.

....

America entered World War II three weeks before Tommy Dorsey and the orchestra would be opening at the Palladium for the New Year. While it was truly a desperate hour in American history, the war did not dampen enthusiasm for entertainment events, especially the sounds of the big bands. This would continue unabated throughout the war years.

While making the movie at MGM, Dorsey received an offer for three one-nighters back in the Midwest, starting on Christmas Day. The band flew out of L.A. and encountered such stormy weather that the United Airlines charter made an emergency landing in Davenport, Iowa. The band then took off for Fremont, Ohio, but had to make another emergency landing in Moline, Illinois. The Fremont concert was canceled, but Dorsey was resourceful and hard-driving. He doubled up the one-nighters, playing Fremont the next afternoon, then going over to Cincinnati that evening to play at a private party. The following evening, they played in Flint, Michigan, and then the band flew back to Hollywood on the afternoon of the twenty-ninth for a film session on the soundstage at MGM. "It was a wonderful life, they were great days," said Frank. "But it was hard work. . . . No warm-up even; I had real strong pipes in those days." Jo Stafford had it about right when she said, "You had to be young."

....

After two years with Dorsey, Frank opted to go solo. In February 1942, he gave the bandleader notice of his planned departure backstage at the Golden Gate Theatre in San Francisco. Dorsey was angry; he barely spoke to the singer for months. With the war depleting the ranks, Frank was one of the few boy singers around, and Tommy had turned Frank into a star—even supplementing the orchestra with strings at the singer's insistence. He owned Frank's contract, and the crowd reactions whenever Sinatra stood at the microphone convinced him that he would be able to make more by using his singer as a single than by keeping him as a member of the band. And he wasn't going to make the exit easy. Frank owed him, big-time.

Meanwhile, Frank had signed with Columbia Records, where producer Manie (pronounced Manny) Sacks hired lawyers to break the contract. It was the start of a lifelong friendship. "There were stories about the mob moving in, paying Tommy a visit, and holding a gun to his head," recalled Tony Consiglio. Frank had, in fact, an uncle who drove the getaway car in a robbery/murder in Jersey. There were some shouts and threats. Tommy received some ominous phone calls at Tall Oaks, where there was now barbed wire atop the surrounding walls. "I was there," said Consiglio. "It happened in Room 215 at the Hotel Astor. Frank's uncle did pull a gun on Tommy, but getting out of the contract was more involved than that."

Eventually, the lawyers and agents worked out a cash settlement that pacified Tommy and freed Frank, who recorded his last song with Dorsey on July 2, 1942. At his farewell concert with the Dorsey orchestra, September 3, 1942, Frank introduced baritone Dick Haymes as his replacement. Onstage, the performance seemed friendly enough, but as Frank departed, Tommy was overheard to say, "I hope he falls on his ass."

In 1942, the American Federation of Musicians called a strike, which would last two years, banning musicians from making recordings. Manie Sacks reissued one of the recordings that Frank had made with Harry James back in 1939—and, suddenly, with Frank riding high, "All or Nothing at All" became his first million seller.

....

Buddy Rich also decided to leave the Dorsey band and join the Marine Corps, where he was quickly "drummed out," as one wag said, for emotional reasons. He returned to Dorsey. In 1946, Frank gave his old battling roommate $25,000 to fund a band of his own. Rich couldn't believe that Frank would give him the money. "He was so grateful, but, of course, with Buddy on the road, Frank could spend time with Buddy's wife, who had a serious thing for Frank," recalled Tony Consiglio. "There was no one who wanted the band to succeed more than Frank, unless it was Buddy's wife."

....

On December 30, 1942, Frank Sinatra, listed as an "Extra Added Attraction," made his first solo appearance at the Paramount Theatre with the Benny Goodman Orchestra, featuring Peggy Lee, plus a showing of the movie *Star Spangled Rhythm,* with Bing Crosby and an all-star cast. Goodman was unfamiliar with this new singer on the program, who was introduced by Jack Benny. As Frank walked to the microphone, the screaming began. "I couldn't move a muscle—I was as nervous as a son of a bitch," said Frank. "Benny had never heard the kids holler before and he froze too—with his arms raised on the upbeat. He looked around over one shoulder and said, 'What the fuck was *that?*!'"

The reaction from the teenage girls as Frankie began to sing "For Me and My Gal" was unprecedented. This was mass hysteria. Bedlam reigned as the singer tried, in vain, to soar above the din.

Originally booked to play for one month, Frank ended up staying ten weeks, changing bands every two weeks. The kids started arriving at 4:30 A.M. By 5:00, the lines were six abreast, going around the block. By 9:30, there were hundreds of cops in front of the theater, including patrol cars, mounted police, and ambulances parked in front of the theater (hired by George Evans for effect). Girls were passing out, some because of the anticipation of seeing and hearing Frank, others from standing for hours in the cold. The bobby-soxers would squeal through hundreds of shows and Sinatra would become a cultural phenomenon.

Frank sang with a band in seven shows each day, beginning at eleven o'clock in the morning and ending eleven at night, with the movie playing between shows. The kids stayed on and on. Some watched the movie, while others fell asleep, saving their energy for the next show. Frank was imprisoned inside the theater. Food was brought in from Sardi's, pushed under the dressing room door. "I won't be able to get out of here all day!" Frankie said. "You'd be killed, you'd be torn limb from limb," George Evans told him. Sinatra had superb performance skills. During one show, he sang a love song and kept staring at one girl, until she suddenly passed out. Other girls started screaming, and some of them started passing out, too. "It was the strangest chain reaction I've ever seen," recalled Tony. "Frank felt so bad that after that he tried to avoid focusing on any one person while he was singing."

"When Sinatra appeared solo at the Paramount Theatre," recalled Barbara Walters some fifty years later, "my mother, sister and I stood in line to get tickets to see him. His appearance created such hysteria among young girls, including fits of swooning, that newspapers turned to psychiatrists for explanations." Psychologists would warn parents about his mesmerizing powers over the young, sociologists would struggle to understand why this skinny man had become the object of such worship from millions of girls throughout the country, and the original American idol was in a stratosphere very few performers would ever know. Over the next three years, he would rake in more than eleven million dollars, sell a ton of records, and become a major radio personality and movie star. And to some it all started that December night at the Paramount in 1942.

In Boston, two girls stayed in the RKO Theatre for nearly a week to watch Frank. Their parents reported them missing as runaways. When the Boston police traced them to the theater, they asked Frank to interrupt the show and announce that the girls had won a prize—please come claim it. They screamed with excitement and jumped up. Frank signed record albums as they left.

"Psychologists tried to go into the reasons with all sorts of deep theories," said Frank. "I could have told them why. Perfectly simple; it was the war years and there was a great loneliness, and I was the boy in every corner drugstore, the boy who'd gone off to the war. That's all. It's directly in the troubadour tradition of the old days. Forget all this nonsense about everyone wanting to 'mother' me—they more likely wanted to jump on my bones."

....

George Evans had a label (today it would be a brand) for his prize singer: the Voice. Indeed, Frank had a remarkable vocal instrument, a clear and pliable voice that glided over both the baritone and tenor ranges. It sounded even better on radio than in performance. The mike conveyed a mixture of coolness and intimacy. He didn't have to raise or project his voice operatically, or try to seduce a crowd. While other singers sang to the heavens, Frank, with a mike, sang to one person at a time. He couldn't read music, but he had a retentive memory for song lyrics, melodies, and arrangements. (He also could recall hundreds of names and phone numbers, and used his memorative powers to create the impression that he was educated far beyond that freshman year of high school.)

There always loomed a touch of arrogance, even hubris, of course. Frank didn't heed anyone more than he had to. Apart from his mother, Frank never knew a restraining hand. "Sinatra is so belligerent that the squared shoulders of his coats sometimes seem to be built up largely with chips," wrote E. J. Kahn, Jr., in a 1946 *New Yorker* profile. Anyone who got to know or work with him for even a short while soon heard the cross Sinatra mantra: "Don't tell me what to do," he would say. "*Suggest.*"

Frank was sartorially obsessive: no starch in his shirts, soft collars and cuffs, on hangers, never folded. He had between eighteen and twenty-four shirts ready at a time, wearing six or seven a day, custom-made, with wide collars to go with his big floppy bow ties, which George Evans said were made by his wife, Nancy. (They were from Cy Martin's.)

He showered and changed his clothes fully three or four times a day. ("Frank was the cleanest man I ever knew," Ava would later say. "If I'd caught him washing the soap, it wouldn't have surprised me.") He did not use deodorant, and disliked the smell of men's cologne and women's perfume. "Frank didn't want to be the one to tell women about their perfume," said Tony. "He had me do it instead. I would say as politely as possible, 'Frank loves to have you around, but if you want to socialize with him, get rid of the perfume.' I would suggest that she take a shower, and show her to my room where she could have some privacy. I hate to mention some of the women I made this suggestion to, because a lot of them were famous."

....

Dorsey's boy singer had not fallen on his ass. "My gamble in leaving Tommy paid off," said Frank. "The first year on my own I made $650,000; the second, $840,000; the third, $1,400,000."

California, here he came.

❧ 3 ❧

The Education of a Femme Fatale

Although Ava had not yet been in a movie, she was enjoying the perquisites of a starlet on the rise. She was on the town with Mickey, who was huge, drinking and dancing at Ciro's until closing time, and seeing her name in the gossip columns. "Ava was undergoing the classic Hollywood transformation from small-town simplicity to big-city sophistication," said Rooney. "She found she had a tremendous capacity for liquor. Wine, cocktails, beer—alcohol in any form." She was also on her way to becoming a heavy smoker, thanks to Lana Turner, the studio bad girl, who, Ava thought, looked so cool with her gold lighter and cigarette case.

Mickey was an accomplished dancer, but Ava also liked to dance with young actors, who could become quite sensual with her after she'd had a few drinks. When Mickey questioned her about their innocence, tension began to mount between the newlyweds, and Ava was direct: She would dance with anyone she damn well pleased. After a late supper at Chasen's one night, they had a little spat when Ava wanted to leave, but Mickey had just bought a round of drinks for the bar and wanted to extend the evening. Ava took a cab home, and when Mickey arrived in the wee hours, the living room looked like the set of a horror movie. Stuffing was everywhere. Ava, in a drunken rage, had slashed their furniture with a carving knife.

Things reached a squalid crisis when Ava came home from the hospital, after undergoing an emergency appendectomy, and discovered that someone had been sleeping in her bed—and using her douche bag. She kicked Mickey out of the house, and he spent a month at his mother's place. They patched up things, sort of, because the sex had always been great. "We told ourselves that we were very much in love, and our sex life helped us in that particular piece of self-deception," said Mickey. But the end was near. One evening, after a few drinks, Ava, in full vindictive force, exploded: "You know, Mick, I'm goddamned tired of living with a midget!"

The marriage had lasted seven months.

....

In May 1943, shortly before the divorce proceedings, Eddie Mannix called Ava into his office. Mannix, who began his career as a bouncer at Palisades Amusement Park, was Louis B. Mayer's enforcer. (In June 1959, he would become a prime suspect in the mysterious death of *Superman* star George Reeves.) L.B. did not want Mickey to lose "his little treasure" to this starlet in the making. If she "took Mickey to the cleaners," cautioned Mannix, things would not go well for Ava at the studio.

While southern gals may seem soft on the outside, they can be very hard from within. Mannix probably thought he was dealing with the sweet, innocent ingenue he had met shortly after her arrival at MGM. Hardly. Ava was a few years older, a few years tougher, and she wasn't in Carolina anymore. After touring with the Mick for one of the Andy Hardy movies, she was developing a taste for traveling first-class, staying in good hotels, being transported in limousines, and even getting cash advances for travel and wardrobe.

Ava agreed pragmatically to waive her claim to half of Mickey's little treasure in exchange for better roles and speaking parts. Deal. As for the property settlement, in court she requested and was granted a car (a red Lincoln Continental convertible), the jewelry and furs Mickey had given her, and $25,000—the equivalent of $400,000 today—a hefty payout for a barefoot pilgrim who had been clearing thirty-five dollars a week when she arrived at the studio less than two years earlier.

The same week that Ava went to divorce court, Mollie Gardner died after battling breast cancer for a year. Ava and Bappie missed plane connections and arrived a day late for their mother's funeral in Smithfield, North Carolina. A graveside service was held the next day.

....

That summer, Ava encountered Howard Hughes, the wealthiest man in the world. Howard loved freshly divorced or separated starlets—"wet decks," he called them, and was infamous for having women stashed in bungalows and apartments all over Hollywood. "I didn't know anything about him," said Ava. "I didn't know about his reputation or his great wealth or his thing about airplanes and jetting around the world. I just knew that as soon as I got divorced from Mickey, Howard entered my life and I couldn't get rid of him for the next fifteen years, no matter whom I was with or whom I married. He was Johnny on the Spot."

Born on December 24, 1905 (like Ava, a Christmas Eve baby), Hughes was orphaned at the age of eighteen and took charge of the company his father had created, the Hughes Tool Company (aka Toolco), which collected massive licensing fees for a dual-cone rotary drill bit patented in 1909 and used for most of the oil drilling in the world. Howard's uncle, Rupert Hughes, was a successful screenwriter, and so young Howard decided to invest in film production. He spent three years (and $3.75 million) on *Hell's Angels,* launching Jean Harlow, the "blonde bombshell," in the process. Though the movie was unprofitable, it was a sensation and established Hughes as a player in Hollywood.

In the 1930s Hughes shifted to aviation, designing and testing airplanes. In 1938, he flew a Lockheed Super Electra around the world in ninety-one hours, for which he was honored at a ticker-tape parade in New York. He bought a controlling interest in Trans World Airlines (TWA), and then returned to moviemaking in 1941, producing *The Outlaw,* a movie starring the voluptuous Jane Russell (for whom, with his aeronautical skills, Howard designed a bra), which was deemed so sexual, it would not be released for another five years.

In 1943, he took to courting Ava in earnest. "He kept on and on and on, wanting to marry me, promising me anything in the world," she said. "But I never loved him. It just never clicked." Hughes was erratic and distrustful and shy, to the point of being reclusive. "He simply didn't want a lot of other people around," said Ava. "He was not much of a drinker—he drank tall rum drinks—and he didn't smoke. But he loved to dance." Howard would take Ava to a club after hours and grandiloquently take over the place, retaining the orchestra.

One evening, Hughes returned from a trip to Washington, and Ava wasn't at the Burbank airport to meet him. He always had his informants on duty, and he was certain that she was with someone else. She was. It was Mickey, home on leave from the service, and, yes, the sex was still great. When Howard confronted her, she said it was none of his business, and he flew into an abusive rage, knocking her across the face.

"This was the first time anybody had ever hit me," she said. "When he finally stopped and went to leave, I looked for some weapon to attack him. There was a bronze bell on the bar with a very long handle. I picked it up and walked toward the living room as he was going out and yelled at him. 'Howard!' I screamed, because he was very deaf and I knew he couldn't hear. As he turned I let go with this bell and conked him in the temple, splitting his face open and knocking out two teeth." Hughes went down, and Ava, furious, picked up a chair and went at him again. "He was scared, cowering in the corner as I lifted the chair over my head," she said. "I was going to kill him."

Ava's maid appeared and halted the battle just as Ava was about to smash another chair over Howard's skull. "If she hadn't come in, I'm sure I would have continued," she said. "Thank God I didn't because I'd probably still be in jail."

. . . .

In 1945, Ava met Artie Shaw, the bandleader and clarinetist, and one of Hollywood's presiding womanizers. He was twelve years older than Ava, tall, with dark slicked-back hair and a broad smile on a handsome sun-burned face.

Born Arthur Arshawsky in New York City, he changed his name to Art Shaw, but friends told him it sounded like a sneeze, so he became Artie, a highly successful musician whose reputation as one of America's top swing bandleaders was sealed in 1938 by his recording of Cole Porter's "Begin the Beguine," a number-one hit for six weeks. In the late 1930s, no musical performer was more famous than Artie Shaw.

Ava had heard plenty about Artie from Lana Turner, whose break-through movie was *Dancing Co-Ed* in 1939, a film that also featured Shaw. They clicked off-camera, and a few days after Lana's nineteenth birthday, in February 1940, they eloped to Las Vegas. Louis B. Mayer made a house call on the happy couple. After a few pleasantries, he asked if they were planning on having children. "Gee, I don't know," said Shaw. "They could come. I'm not taking any precautions. Why?" Mayer said that MGM had made a considerable investment in Lana, and that she was going to be one of their biggest stars. "It would be disastrous if she had a child," he said. "She's a love goddess. And love goddesses don't have children."

Lana called Artie "my college education." Artie wanted Lana to im-prove her mind by reading Nietzsche and Schopenhauer, but he would not explain the more abstruse passages. In public, he humiliated her in front of friends. He also wanted her to prepare meals, which he then sniffed at and refused to eat.

The marriage was brief, but by the time Lana filed for divorce after eight months, she was pregnant. Her agent told her that if she still wanted a ca-reer, she would either have to go back to Shaw or have an abortion. Lana was soon hospitalized for "exhaustion," and her career moved forward.

"Artie wasn't a hustler," said Ava. "The quick jump into bed, that's just for the common people. Oh boy, what a line he had! Every night we talked and talked. I just sat there wide-eyed and listened. After about eight months with Artie softening me up with his brainy bulldozing, he decided we'd better get on with the common thing and go to bed. That worked terribly well."

....

Artie Shaw's band members thought him snooty. "He had a tendency to look down on musicians, not for reasons of musicianship (although he was quite a perfectionist), but for their lack of intellectual interests," said big-band historian George T. Simon. "Artie was an avid reader, a man interested in many arts and many causes, and he liked to mingle with people who could discourse with him on the many subjects that interested him." He claimed to have spent time with Ernest Hemingway, F. Scott Fitzgerald, Thomas Mann, Sinclair Lewis, and other authors, names available on request. Many thought he was a pseudointellectual—like someone who goes through the Bible making the penciled notation "How true!" in the margins.

Did Ava love him from the time they first met? "Totally," she said. "The chemistry was right. He was a famous bandleader. That exerted big leverage. Remember . . . we were out of our minds with adoration for the big bands—Duke Ellington, Glenn Miller, Tommy Dorsey. I grew up on those sounds."

To mitigate gossip that had become malicious, the couple married on October 17, 1945, and with much trepidation. Ava, twenty-two, would wear the same blue suit she had worn for her first wedding, and her first divorce—just a thrifty Carolina gal, she liked to say—with white gloves, and a corsage of white orchids. Shaw was thirty-five—this was the fourth marriage for him (there would eventually be eight). Bappie was there, as always, though Ava's matron of honor was Frances Neal (wife of Van Heflin).

Ava traveled around with Artie and the band, sitting backstage and drinking bourbon and going to all of the big ballrooms in Chicago and New York. Artie was the first man to treat Ava as an intelligent person rather than a sex symbol, which had turned her off about Howard Hughes, who was still stalking her. Under Artie's tutelage, she took extension courses at UCLA and proudly earned A's and B's in literature, psychology, and philosophy. Artie gave her a heady reading list—*Babbitt* (by Artie's pal Sinclair Lewis), *The Brothers Karamazov, On the Origin of Species, Das Kapital, Madame Bovary, The Sun Also Rises, The Magic Mountain,* and *Tropic of Cancer* (of which Ava said, "Holy shit, what a dirty book!").

With Shaw, it was more about control than about knowledge. There was also a touch of buyer's remorse: As soon as Artie married someone, he started picking her apart, saying what a bad deal he'd made. "She never got *near The Magic Mountain,*" he said of Ava years later. "*The Sun Also Rises, maybe;* but—never finished it." He paid a Russian grand master to give Ava chess lessons, but grumbled after she defeated him in their first match. He no longer wanted to play.

Artie called her "Avala," a Yiddish variant, and their sexual relationship was "absolutely glorious," he said, until it stopped being absolutely glorious. Artie couldn't keep up. He told a joke to his psychiatrist about the guy lying in bed with his wife, and he's trying to get aroused, but nothing is happening. "What's the matter?" asks the wife. "I can't think of anybody tonight," he says. Then Artie said to the analyst, "What happens if you're lying in bed with a *goddess* and you can't think of anybody?"

He called marriage "a woman's racket," and had no respect for anyone who made her living as a movie actress. "They're aiming at a kind of fame that very rarely has anything to do with *abilities,*" he said. "It's cheekbones."

Ava did little to discourage him; she had begun referring to herself as a "dumb broad." Esther Williams recalled the young Ava from their starlet days at MGM: "She was the most beautiful girl you ever saw in your life, with naturally curly hair and a perfect figure. She was also the sweetest person you could meet, but she had such low self-esteem for a woman who was considered one of the most beautiful of the MGM roster... there was a kind of infinite sadness about her, as if everything good that came her way was undeserved. It made her easy prey for bad relationships. . . . I tried to chat with her at the parties at Louis B. Mayer's, but if she was a little tipsy she'd say, 'You don't want to talk to me, Esther. I'm just trailer trash.'"

Marriage to Artie brought out Ava's homebody streak. "At that period in my life I really did want to settle down and have a child," she said. "Artie shook his head very profoundly, saying, 'You are too young.'" Years later, in powder rooms, she and Lana Turner would discuss husbands and lovers—they had shared a few. "We agreed that we were absolutely madly in love with Artie," she said, "but he treated all his women about as generously as Scrooge." Artie certainly knew how Ava had handled herself in the settlement with Mickey. "The Bedford Drive house was worth a fortune. He sold the house because he thought if we got divorced, I might get a piece of it. We moved to a little ratty house, out in the valley."

That spring, Ava left Artie. "I was in a bad state," she said. "I was still crazy about Artie and when he called me one day I was thrilled. I went flying over to his office like a damn fool to see him. He wanted to see me, too—to ask me if I minded if he went to Mexico to get a quick divorce so he could marry Kathleen Winsor. I was crushed."

. . . .

As a newspaper columnist, Mark Hellinger was legendary for writing short stories that were very brief—one a day every day, seven days a week from 1925 to 1937. They were sob stories written in the style of O. Henry, about babes and bighearted hustlers on the fringe of Broadway.

"Be callous when you write a sob story," he said. "Be unfeeling. The reader will do the crying." The column attracted more than 22 million readers in syndication. Hollywood called.

Hellinger became an associate producer at Warner Bros., where his productions included *The Roaring Twenties*; *High Sierra,* which established Humphrey Bogart as a box-office attraction; and *They Drive by Night,* another Bogie hit. One night, Hellinger and Bogart went to a cabaret along Sunset Boulevard for a nightcap and were informed that Bogie was barred from the club. Hellinger became indignant and demanded to see the manager. He was finally allowed to slip inside the door, while Bogart was told to wait outside. The manager said that Bogart started fights and was undesirable, but when Hellinger vouched that he personally would be responsible for his colleague's behavior, the manager opened the door. Outside on the sidewalk, Bogart was slugging it out with two men.

Hellinger was a short, stout man with darting brown eyes, slick steel gray hair, and a puckering smile. He lived in the Hollywood Hills with Gladys Glad, a beautiful Ziegfeld showgirl, in an enormous house on a thirteen-acre country estate with electric gates, nine servants, and a lodge across from the main house that he used as a projection room. Despite doctors' warnings and a congenital heart condition (he was repeatedly rejected for active service during World War II), Mark Hellinger drank with both hands, downing a bottle of brandy most evenings. W. C. Fields, no light tippler himself, had profound respect for Hellinger's capacity. "I got Mark Hellinger so drunk last night," he said, "it took three bellboys to put me to bed."

Hollywood liked the work of Ernest Hemingway because, like Dickens, he bridged the gulf between high literature and popular fiction. Hemingway, however, did not like Hollywood. Although he had taken its money over the years, that was back when he was struggling in the thirties. Now, belatedly, he refused to sell anything to the movies because he could not bear to look at what they had done to his work.

Hellinger was a bigger-than-life character who delighted in the adventure of the deal. He wore a dark blue shirt and white silk tie, resembling a bookmaker from one of his own Broadway stories. When Mark was dealing around town, he drove a black Cadillac town car that still carried his old New York license number—MH-1—at terrifying speeds. How could he get the attention of Ernest Hemingway?

Hellinger's publicist, Al Horwits, urged him to fly to Havana, hang out in the Floridita bar, and wait for the great American drinker to show up. It worked. Over drinks, Hemingway began to like the slick-haired onetime Broadway columnist. One drink led to another, and, after two days of drinking, Hellinger said he would give his buddy Ernest fifty thousand dollars for the movie rights to all his pal's short stories. Papa extended his ponderous paw. It was a deal.

Hellinger didn't know what he was buying, and Hemingway had no idea what he was selling. Afterward, the deal was modified—one story only, "The Killers," for 50K, and Hellinger enlisted John Huston—who had coauthored the screenplay for *High Sierra*—to transform Hemingway's twelve-page story into a 120-page script; then he struck a deal with Universal for a budget of $809,000—very little money—to make his first picture as an independent producer. Next, he was casting the movie.

"Wherever possible, he wanted unknowns, or has-beens, or almost-wases," said Hellinger's secretary (and ghost columnist) Jim Bishop. One of Hellinger's "finds" was a former circus acrobat named Burt Lancaster. At MGM, Ava had worked her way up in walk-ons and bit parts, and Hellinger knew her from Universal, where she'd played opposite George Raft in a United Artists crime drama *Whistle Stop*. "She had worked in pictures, but no one remembered much about her except that she was one of Mickey Rooney's ex-wives," said Bishop. "Also, she lacked confidence in herself. Hellinger changed all that."

Hellinger liked what he saw, "a big, bosomy girl with long dark hair," said Bishop. MGM agreed to the loan-out, and Ava was cast as Kitty Collins, the costar and femme fatale of *The Killers*. And the girl could sing!

Ava had a lovely untrained alto voice, and when Kitty is introduced in the movie, she is leaning against a piano, singing. Ava was a smoldering presence. The producer instilled a confidence that would establish her as an important new talent among Hollywood starlets. For Ava, this was her first real chance at a dramatic role, with dynamic newcomer Burt Lancaster, who had most of the lines. One reviewer said she was the greatest silent star in the talkies.

....

In July 1946, a few days after previewing *The Killers* in Los Angeles, Ava was at a dinner party at John Huston's ranch. Huston had cowritten the screenplay for *The Killers* (with Anthony Veiller) without credit, as a favor to Hellinger. Huston was somewhat informally engaged to Evelyn Keyes, best known as Scarlett O'Hara's younger sister in *Gone With the Wind*. Ava was twenty-three, separated from Artie Shaw, and radiant.

After a few drinks, they went outside, and Huston could not contain himself. He moved toward Ava and she began to run. Huston, thinking she was being playful, ran after her. Ava ran among the trees, laughing, and then circled the swimming pool, with Huston in full pursuit. As he drew near, she dived into the pool fully clothed. Huston stood there laughing.

"We both had too much to drink," Ava later told Huston biographer Lawrence Grobel. "I knew if I didn't dive in I would have been in trouble. John was a great womanizer and I wasn't the kind of gal who liked to be womanized. I knew he wasn't serious; he was just looking for a good time."

Huston told Grobel, "The next day I went off to Las Vegas and married Evelyn Keyes. But I doubt that would have happened had Ava not jumped in that pool."

....

The publicity tour, devised by Hellinger, started a month before the picture was released. The newspaperman called in all his favors. There were parties in key cities with plenty to eat and drink, plus a private showing of the movie—not for critics, but for fellow reporters and editors. Soon writers and columnists—even sports columnists—were praising *The Killers.* Walter Winchell (best man at Hellinger's wedding) plugged the movie steadily. *Life* magazine gave it a seven-page layout.

At 9:00 A.M. on August 28, 1946, *The Killers* opened at the Winter Garden in New York. The theater ran the movie twenty-four hours a day, and it set a house record. Hellinger had a smash hit, and Ava made such a stunning impact as Kitty Collins, the sensual, deceitful gangster's moll, that MGM cast her as the other woman in *The Hucksters,* a searing tale of the advertising world, with Ava's old heartthrob Clark Gable. Ava had become the screen's most beautiful emerging femme fatale. Her salary at MGM quadrupled from $350 to $1,250 a week.

....

On October 24, 1946—one week after what would have been their first wedding anniversary—Artie and Ava divorced. The marriage had lasted eight months, slightly longer than Artie's marriage to Lana. "None of them were real marriages," Artie said afterward. "They were legalized affairs. In those days, you couldn't get a lease on an apartment if you were living in sin."

As for what love goddesses saw in him, he said, "I wasn't a bad-looking stud. But that's not it. It's the music; it's standing up there under the lights. A lot of women just flip; looks have nothing to do with it. You call Mick Jagger good-looking?" Artie, with eight ex-wives, admitted, "I know nothing about marriage, but I'm an expert on divorce. . . . These love goddesses are not what they seem, especially if you're married to one. They all think they want a traditional marriage, but they aren't married for that sort of thing. Somebody's got to get the coffee in the morning, and an Ava Gardner is not going to do that. So you get up and get it, and then you find you're doing everything."

Trying to meet Professor Shaw's marital standards, Ava lost ten pounds in the process. "He was always quoting Plato or Proust," she told reporters. "He told me I was dumb so often that I finally got smart and scrammed."

For Ava, that was two divorces within a three-and-a-half-year period. Gossip columnist Hedda Hopper later observed that Ava "was made to love and be loved," which would become Ava's sad mantra as she moved from the arms of one lover to another in the turbulent decades to follow.

. . . .

Ava spent her birthday that year—Christmas Eve 1946—on a plane grounded by a storm in Los Angeles. Earlier that month, Benjamin "Bugsy" Siegel, of lamentable renown, had been in L.A., trying to recruit Lana Turner, Jimmy Durante, Frank Sinatra, and other stars for the purpose of attending the opening of his Flamingo Hotel in Vegas.

The hotel opened that Christmas Eve—with a blackjack dealer named Dean Martin in the pit—but Ava and her party never made it to the festivities from L.A., as the flight was canceled. Frank Sinatra, who had a passing acquaintance with Ben, as he called Bugsy, never showed.

. . . .

Singer Mel Torme met Ava in early 1946 at the Bedford Drive home she shared with Artie Shaw. Torme was there to discuss an album of Cole Porter tunes they would be recording. "Ava sat quietly reading a book in a corner of the comfortably appointed music room," the singer recalled. "Sometimes she would put the book down and watch us. Occasionally, I would glance in her direction. I would have to have been superhuman to have been able to avoid looking at her."

Later that year, after *The Killers* was released, Torme bumped into Ava at a party. She was slightly tipsy, but she smiled, and he invited her to his New Year's Eve party. "Already have a date," said Ava. "Lawford. He's taking me to several parties."

Well, who should stop by Mel's party on New Year's but Peter Lawford and Ava, looking radiant. They departed after fifteen minutes—on to other parties—but at 2:30 in the morning, as stragglers were leaving Mel's place, the phone rang. "Lawford's still here, but he's leaving any second," said Ava. "I want to see you. Come on over."

As Mel arrived at Ava's apartment, Peter Lawford opened the door and handled the situation with typical English aplomb. "Come on in," he said. "I'm just leaving." Ava kissed Peter on the cheek, and he was gone. It was four o'clock in the morning.

Ava led Mel down to the garage and her dark green Cadillac convertible. "Howard Hughes gave me this car," she said. "He does things like that." She drove while Mel dozed, going north on the Pacific Coast Highway, top down. At 5:20, he awoke. "She was wide awake with the wind blowing her hair, the lapels of her suede coat flapping, and the scarf trailing behind her," he said. "Ava's classic profile stood out in relief against the faint twilight of the winter morning. God, this woman is astonishingly beautiful."

After breakfast at a pancake house in Santa Barbara, they returned to

Ava's apartment, where they spent New Year's Day and weekends for the next six months.

When Ava learned (from Marilyn Maxwell) that Mel was making overtures to Marilyn Maxwell, she asked the singer to come see her—and delivered lines that could have been right out of *The Killers*. "We're through, Melvin," she said. "Finished. Kaput." The femme fatale had moved from the screen and was now in residence at Ava's place. "You lied to me and I won't take that from anyone. Out!"

....

During his ten years in Hollywood, Mark Hellinger had fought just about every studio boss in town, and now he looked forward to the big payoff. At the end of 1947, he would become an independent producer with David O. Selznick, which would mean his own company, his own cameramen, directors, writers, his own front money for a picture, his own budget to spend as he saw fit—and his own bungalow on the lot.

In addition to *The Killers*, Hellinger had produced *Brute Force*, another successful film noir starring Burt Lancaster; and he had just completed *The Naked City*, his personal salute to New York, which he narrated. He was earning $3,500 a week, plus another thousand from Hearst for the syndication of his Sunday column.

Two weeks before *The Naked City* premiere, Hellinger suffered a heart attack. He was told to rest for six weeks, but he returned to the set. "The film was his responsibility and he felt he had to be there," said Miklós Rózsa, composer of the score for *The Killers*. "He looked drawn and old, a good ten years in excess of his real age." On December 21, 1947, Hellinger suffered another attack and died in Cedars of Lebanon Hospital in Los Angeles. He was forty-four.

....

In 1947, as Howard Hughes came courting again, Ava was mentally better prepared for the erratic aviator, who had crashed an XF-11 in a Beverly

Hills neighborhood in a 1946 test flight, and would be addicted to pain-killers for the rest of his life. Now he was in the process of purchasing RKO Radio Pictures. He told Ava he wanted to marry her, and showed her an old shoe box filled with thousand-dollar bills, $250,000 in all, which would be hers if she would make a picture with him.

"I told him to lump it," said Ava, "that if he wanted to make a deal with me he'd have to talk with my agent like everybody else. That I wasn't touching that kind of money—not now—not ever."

Still, Ava enjoyed Hughes because "for one thing he'd never given up wanting to marry me, and that's very flattering for a girl." There were other advantages, of course. Ava loved the pampered life. If you want to go shopping in Mexico City, for instance, all a gal needs to do is call Howard, "and within minutes there's a chauffeur outside waiting to take you to the airport, where there's an airliner standing by to take you to Mexico City. And when you get there, you're met by another chauffeured limousine and driven to the best hotel in town, where there's a suite waiting for you. If you want to be quiet and left alone, he arranges it. He's just the right ticket for a girl like me, from the Deep South and lazy."

Howard Hughes arranged for Ava and Bappie to have a small two-bedroom bungalow in Palm Springs, the little town that the legendary "two-hour rule" had put on the map as a perfect hideaway when actors had to be able to reach the studio within two hours for last-minute shoots and retakes. In the late 1940s, there was only one paved road in Palm Springs (population five thousand), though it was starting to sprout a few hotels to accommodate tourists in season, when the population jumped to eight thousand. There were a few lavish homes around town for the Hollywood A-listers, Gable and Lombard, Gary Cooper, Errol Flynn, Bette Davis, and Bing Crosby. There was even a social crowd that actually played polo at the Zanuck estate, Ric-Su-Dar, named after the mogul's kids.

When Hollywood columnist Joe Hyams visited Ava in Palm Springs for an interview, she cooked him supper—pan-fried chicken, her specialty.

"It was more like the home of a secretary than that of a movie star," he said, not "grand enough for the reigning sex queen of Hollywood." Ava loved it.

The modest house was perched on the edge of the town's airport, which was a crudely mowed field in those days. At night, cars lined up in the grass and turned on their headlights so that Howard Hughes could fly in and out to visit her with ease. The house had a carport by the side with Bappie's battered old Chevy, which Ava gunned around town. She drove a car as if she'd stolen it.

There was talk at the studio that Frank Sinatra had purchased some property on Alejo Road in the Springs, where he would be building a house, and that was only a few minutes from the airport, too.

❧ 4 ❧

More Stars Than There Are in Hoboken

In 1944, the Sinatras departed from Hasbrouck Heights, New Jersey, and relocated to the former home of actress Mary Astor, a slightly modest mansion at 10051 Valley Spring Lane, on Toluca Lake in the San Fernando Valley. Nancy was happy. It was a beautiful homestead, and, while Hollywood was no Hoboken, her five married sisters would follow. When Nancy's relatives began to use the Sinatra name for small businesses in the area—dry cleaner's, a restaurant with photos of Frank on the walls and a jukebox with his records—Frank told Tony Consiglio, "It looks like I've got a little city of my own here—everything's Sinatra." He shrugged. "Didn't want to cause a problem," said Tony.

George Evans persuaded Nancy to undergo some cosmetic enhancements—a nose job, capped teeth—so that she could hold her own in the cosmetic world of Hollywood. Except for a close friendship with Barbara Stanwyck, however, Nancy preferred to stay home with the kids while Frank kept up social obligations, rarely alone. He went to the Academy Award dinner that year with Gloria DeHaven, joined by Lana Turner and her new husband, Steve Crane. Hollywood was a different world, filled with beautiful young women who wanted to emerge from the crowd on the arm of a star, and Frank was surely the guy whom Oscar Wilde had in mind when he said he could resist everything but temptation. Or, perhaps another Wilde thought: Each man kills the thing he loves.

"Nancy was so maternal to Frank, she seemed like his mother rather than his wife, and I could see how the bull-in-a-china-shop boy in him could get tempted by the sirens of the movie business," said Frank's long-time valet George Jacobs. "It was what the Catholics call a Madonna/whore thing. . . . I sensed absolutely no resentment on Nancy's part over having lost her husband to the sleazy lure of showbiz, only resignation to the reality of the situation." Nancy Barbato Sinatra knew that Frank had a long-standing problem keeping his zipper up. Back in Jersey, when Frank was singing at the Wedgwood Room in the Waldorf-Astoria, his pal Tony—who was sleeping over at the house in Hasbrouck Heights—showed up alone one night. Nancy asked, "Where's Frank?"

"He's got a meeting with people tomorrow and he wanted to stay in the city," said Tony.

"Were the people blond or brunette?" she asked wearily.

. . . .

That first Christmas, Frank and Nancy started an annual tradition, transforming their living room into a "theater" for a New Year's Eve musical review, with complete score and sketches. Songwriters Jimmy Van Heusen and Sammy Cahn and comedian Phil Silvers were key performers. On one occasion, Van Heusen and Silvers presented the Sinatras with the song/tribute to their daughter, "Nancy (With the Laughing Face)." One year, Frank gave Nancy a convertible, which he used for some holiday shopping himself. When Nancy discovered a diamond bracelet in the car's glove compartment, she said nothing, thinking it was a surprise gift from Santa. Which it was—for Marilyn Maxwell, who walked into the New Year's Eve party, brazenly wearing the bracelet. Nancy called Frank out, and Marilyn made her MGM-style exit.

. . . .

Frank was footloose in a town where beautiful women vastly outnumbered single men (not to be confused with available men). He could seduce a vulnerable woman with tales of his troubles, real or imagined; with his attention to details, his star power and desire to make things easier for her in a competitive business. For Frank, adultery wasn't really about sex. It was about control and power. The lure was the hunt itself, not the prize. His coconspirator in the hunt was often songwriter Jimmy Van Heusen, whom George Jacobs described as Frank's "dear friend, favorite composer, and whore wrangler." One of his jobs involved procuring young ladies.

Sinatra called Van Heusen "Chester," after his real name, Edward Chester Babcock. Jimmy had adopted his professional name from the shirt company that ran those classy ads. He had a house in Palm Springs (called the Rattlesnake Ranch), and he was a pilot who could take Frank to romantic places on short notice.

Frank had something else motivating him: He was Italian. Stella Adler, the great theater teacher, coached and cautioned her young actress students, saying, "It's wonderful and almost necessary to have an Italian lover, but you must not marry them." "Frank was an Italian man," said Hollywood biographer Scott Eyman. "He wouldn't leave his wife and family for just a piece of ass. It would have to be a big cataclysmic event for him to do that. He was getting laid all the time, but he was going home to his wife. It was two separate things. He had that Joe Kennedy duality. He was very loyal to his family, emotionally if not physically. However, when Ava came along, it blew the top off his head."

· · · · · · · · · · · ·

Frank appeared at a Jewish charity benefit at the Earl Carroll Theatre one evening, attended by the Hollywood elite, including Louis B. Mayer. When Frank sang "Ol' Man River," it brought a tear to Mayer's eye. He turned to one of his associates and said, "We could use that boy over on our lot." Whatever you say, L.B.

Louis B. Mayer, titular guardian of family values, thought that Frank would fit right in at MGM. "If you worked for MGM, you automatically became whatever they wanted. And what Louis B. Mayer wanted was for Frank to go on with the fan-magazine version at its most simpleminded," said Wilfrid Sheed. Thus, Frank came across as "an Italianate Andy Hardy, everybody's kid brother who had stayed home with the girls while the grown-ups were off fighting."

MGM cast him to costar with Gene Kelly in *Anchors Aweigh,* where he came into his own as a film personality, not just a singer. Frankie had never danced a step in his life when Gene Kelly—one of the greatest dancers in film history—stayed up all night working on various routines with Frank, who turned out to be a gifted dancer in spite of himself. They went on to perform in *Take Me Out to the Ball Game* (1949), where Frank got top billing, and then *On the Town.*

Frank loved the lush, sprawling MGM facilities, the commissary, and dressing rooms—with settees and coffeemakers and a record player—and the way the studio treated stars. No phones were allowed; a ringing phone could spoil a scene. Well, Frank wanted a phone, so they made one with a silencer on the bell and a light that indicated a call was coming in. "It was almost like a womb," he said. "Everything was done for you."

He also loved making an entrance. On the night of July 20, 1946, Arthur Freed produced a lavish memorial concert to Jerome Kern at the Holly-wood Bowl, an event that sold out weeks in advance to an audience of eighteen thousand. The program, narrated by Robert Walker, was a reprise of *Till the Clouds Roll By,* with songs sung by the film's MGM stars. Frank would close with "Ol' Man River," complete with white tux. The third and final segment of the concert was under way, yet Frank hadn't shown up. Everyone's nerves were at the breaking point when, dramatically, during the eight-bar introduction to "Ol' Man River," Sinatra suddenly appeared, sashayed to the microphone, and began to sing.

. . . .

Frank occupied a plush Hollywood bachelor's pad in the Sunset Towers, where many single and separated guys dwelled. According to a report in

Playboy, Frank put up in his dressing room a list of the most desirable actresses, and was working his way through the MGM harem. "It is doubtful that anyone, anywhere makes out any better than Sinatra," said jazz writer Robert Reisner. "And that is partly because 'the broads,' as he calls them, are an obsession with him. He is as intense in his pursuit of a better broad as he is of a better song or better part in a picture."

He was linked romantically with Lana Turner, Marilyn Maxwell, and numerous lesser-known starlets. From his bachelor pad, Frank could see the little house down the block and across the street where Ava Gardner lived with her maid Mearene ("Reenie") Jordan, who would serve Ava for more than thirty years. (Bappie had an apartment of her own now.) Reenie had come to L.A. from New Orleans as a seamstress, and a friend of a friend told her about Ava, who was looking for a maid. Reenie was black, southern, and was born the same year as Ava. They clicked.

Frank's pals and fellow residents at Sunset Towers included Jimmy Van Heusen and Sammy Cahn. In his memoir, Sammy wrote, "If you looked down from Frank's terrace you'd see, across the street, a series of little houses, one of them owned by Tom Kelly, a noted interior decorator; the occupant of that house was Ava Gardner. Just for mischief, Frank and I would stick our heads out the window and lean down over his terrace and call, 'Ava, can you hear me, Ava? Ava Gardner, we know you're down there. Hello, Ava?' She couldn't know, of course, that one of the voices yelling her name would someday make international headlines with her."

....

Despite the backstage efforts of George Evans, the first public breach in the Sinatras' "perfect marriage" occurred in October 1946, when Frank abandoned Nancy and the kids for two weeks, during which he was seen with "home wrecker" Lana Turner at the Mocambo and elsewhere around town. *Time* reported that Frank gave "at least $100,000 worth of gifts in only six months" to an unnamed star (that would be Lana), who was startled to read in a newspaper that he had returned to his wife and kids.

"For you to do this to me, a famous picture star, is unforgivable!" bleated the famous picture star. "*Nobody dumps Lana Turner, mister.*"

....

FRANKIE GOES TO HOLLYWOOD was the *Variety* headline when the cocky singing phenomenon came to MGM with second billing to Gene Kelly in *Anchors Aweigh,* which was a smash hit. It received rave reviews, was the second-highest-grossing film in 1945–1946, was nominated for five Oscars, including Best Picture, and was an auspicious debut for Frankie at MGM. But after that promising start, Frankie's movies did not do well. The "Ol' Man River" performance, so effective live in the Hollywood Bowl concert, seemed gauche and ridiculous on-screen in *Till the Clouds Roll By*—a 1946 movie of Jerome Kern's songs set in a phony reenactment of his life. Frank, wearing a white suit, standing on a fluted pillar, and crooning a song about the plight of blacks in the South, was declared "the worst moment in movies for the year" by *Life* magazine, which commonly read like a house organ for MGM.

Foundering now as a movie star, Frank "tended to give his most dramatic performances off-screen," said journalist Frank Rose, "singing for Charlie Luciano, Meyer Lansky, Frank Costello, Vito Genovese, and the rest of the boys at the Hotel Nacional in Havana in February 1947." There had long been rumors that Frank's career in the early days was helped along by friends in the mob. He accepted the invitation to go to Havana from Joe Fischetti, who ran a Chicago club where Sinatra had played—and who was the youngest of the infamous three Fischetti brothers, who ran the Chicago rackets established by Al Capone during Prohibition.

Frank was photographed getting off a plane with Fischetti. "Both men were wearing sunglasses and carrying attaché cases; they definitely looked like a pair of gangsters," said Pete Hamill in his *Why Sinatra Matters.* At the Hotel Nacional, then the grandest hotel in the Cuban capital, the host was Meyer Lansky, and the guest of honor was Lucky Luciano, just back from his deportation to Italy (for nine months). Lansky invited all of the Mafia barons to Havana to welcome Lucky back—Frank Costello and Joe Adonis from New York; Vito Genovese and Joe Bonnano; Carlos Marcello from New Orleans; Santos Trafficante from Florida, "the whole lot," said editor and author Otto Friedrich. It was at this meeting that the chieftains learned that Bugsy Siegel's venture in Las Vegas had gone from one million dollars to more than four million, and that some of their Flamingo money might be going to Switzerland.

Robert Ruark, a newcomer to journalism, shook up Hollywood with the first column revealing that Sinatra had been seen in the company of Charles "Lucky" Luciano. It was reported that everyone brought envelopes of cash for Lucky, and that Frank had carried a suitcase containing two million dollars in cash. "This curious desire to cavort among the scum is possibly permissible among citizens who are not peddling sermons to the nation's youth," said Ruark. "But Mr. Sinatra seems to be setting a most peculiar example for his hordes of pimply, shrieking slaves." Cuban authorities arrested Luciano and shipped him back to Naples.

"Any report that I fraternized with goons and racketeers is a vicious lie," said Frank. "I was brought up to shake a man's hand when I am introduced to him without first investigating his past." Louis B. Mayer called Frankie in for a scold, and MGM responded by announcing that Sinatra would play a Catholic priest in *The Miracle of the Bells.* His $100,000 salary would be donated to the church.

This disaster followed *The Kissing Bandit,* a movie so bad that Frank turned to Tony Consiglio at the premiere and said, "I think only my relatives are going to see this one." Finally, there was the humiliation of having the studio switch his billing from number one to number two when *On the Town,* his final picture at MGM, was released.

. . . .

On the evening of June 21, 1947, barely four months after the conference in Havana, there was a change of management at the Flamingo. Bugsy

Siegel was killed in his Beverly Hills home when someone fired nine bullets from a .30-30 carbine into him as he sat on his living room couch.

....

Hoboken declared a Frank Sinatra Day in 1947, and, on the surface, everything looked fine—it was a year in which he recorded nearly seventy songs. Nancy was pregnant again in the fall, and Tina was born on June 20, Father's Day, 1948.

Six months later, the Sinatra family relocated to 320 North Carolwood Drive in Holmby Hills, an upscale community where neighbors included Bing Crosby and Walt Disney, the latter just across the street and up three houses. The Disney place featured a scaled-down model train on three-foot-wide tracks that circled the perimeter of his property. At one o'clock on Saturdays, Walt, in his engineer's cap, straddling the locomotive, gave rides to neighborhood kids.

While Beverly Hills was flat, Holmby Hills felt like the country, with streets snaking through rolling hills, and houses set back like fortresses. The Sinatra house was long and low, made out of adobe, with a red-tiled roof, aged beams supporting the ceiling of the porch, and bougainvillea climbing all over it. There was also privacy, which Frank was looking for. The home, on three acres with a large pool, was surrounded by a high wall of Mexican masonry, with a wooden gate that opened (if you were invited) to a courtyard complete with a wishing well and a large olive tree.

Actress Betty Garrett visited and said the walls were decorated with paintings by Rouault and Utrillo—Frank's favorite painter—along with some of Frank's own paintings. Nancy took her upstairs to little Nancy's bedroom, with its canopied bed, ruffled bedspread, and dozens of dolls sitting on it, wearing dresses decorated with flowers.

North Carolwood Drive was a shorter commute to Frank's workplace, MGM Studios, but it would not be Frank's address for long, as his career continued to dip. "And within a year after that," wrote Tina Sinatra, "my father would leave us to be with Ava Gardner."

············

There were occasional encounters on the lot, and one summer when Ava was cheerleader for the Swooners, Frank's softball team that played in a studio league. And there were those lads up in the balcony at Sunset Towers, hollering to Ava as she made her rounds (she had very good ears). And so it was inevitable that Frank and Ava would meet for real at the entrance to Towers one day, and Frank asked Ava to dinner. She said yes.

"Frank wants to take me to dinner," she told Reenie back at the apartment.

"Great, when?"

"Tonight," said Ava. "I know he's still married to Nancy, but that's broken up a long time ago."

"He's still dating Lana," said Reenie.

"Who isn't?"

············

On May 1, 1947, Frank Sinatra, wearing a sailor's hat and holding an ice-cream cone, wandered into the offices of Williams, Williams & Williams, an architectural firm, and said he had purchased some land in Palm Springs and he wanted them to design and build a home for him in the desert. He spoke with E. Stewart Williams, who had just joined his father's firm. Frank wanted the home to be ready by Christmas, for a party he was hosting. Eight months. Williams had never designed a private residence. He said yes.

Williams concocted designs in the mid-century-modern style, for which he would become famous. Construction began that summer on the four-bedroom, five-bathroom, 4,500-square-foot home with a circular drive on Alejo Road that Frank would call Twin Palms, after the two large palm trees flanking the piano-shaped swimming pool, and a likely reminder of Tall Oaks, the Tommy Dorsey estate back in Jersey. It was built fully air-conditioned at a cost of $162,000, astounding for the time, and completed in time for Frank's party.

One bedroom had bunk beds for the kids, which gave Sinatra fans temporary hope that the marital troubles were over. But the home soon became Frank's getaway *from* his family. "I wouldn't live anywhere else in the world," Frank said. "It is hot in the winter and hotter in the summer, which discourages the tourists, so we kids can play by ourselves."

············

Ava came home very late from her dinner date with Frank. Reenie didn't wait up. In the morning, Ava said, "Reenie, nothing happened, and I bet you're disappointed." She laughed.

"No, I'm not disappointed," said Reenie. "Was the dinner any good?"

"We had a lot to drink."

············

During the Springs social season of 1948, Darryl F. Zanuck hosted a party at his estate, where the chemistry was almost immediate between Frank and Ava. They had a lot more in common now. In addition to the smoking, drinking, cursing, and partying they so enjoyed, they also had careers at MGM to wonder and worry about.

"Frank and Ava were a lot alike in that regard—they were both insecure as actors, which was unusual at MGM, a studio with a lot of pros who knew what they were doing," said Hollywood biographer Scott Eyman. "At MGM, if you didn't know what to do, the studio's acting school would teach you. But Sinatra wouldn't do that kind of thing. And Gardner was terribly insecure about her acting. She gravitated toward guys who knew what they were doing. Mickey Rooney and Artie Shaw—both of them, total pros. They are just huge talents. And here's this scared little girl from North Carolina, Tobacco Road, really.

"She wanted some of their certainty to rub off on her," said Eyman. "I think that was part of what drew them together, a sense of, hey, everybody here is topnotch.... Lionel Barrymore, Clark Gable, Jimmy Stewart ... total pros. And here we are, we don't know what we're doing. And so, once they got the sex thing out of the way, they clung together."

That evening, Frank told Ava it had been over with Nancy for years but that he was committed to the kids. "I suppose we were rushing things a little the last time we met," he said, smiling.

Gone was the cocky bastard Lana had warned her about. "*You* were rushing things," she said.

On this night, he seemed vulnerable. She came under his spell. "Let's start again," he said.

They roared off in Frank's Cadillac like two kids on a joyride, with a bottle from Ric-Su-Dar, and two Smith & Wesson .38's in the glove compartment. Some thirty miles and many rounds later, they shot up the little town of Indio, California, and were arrested.

At three o'clock in the morning, Frank called George Evans's associate Jack Keller in Los Angeles. Keller later made a tape recording with his recollection of what came to be known as the "Indio Incident."

"Me and the kid here, we got a little loaded," said Frank, "and we drove down here from Palm Springs and we thought we'd have a little fun and we shot up a few streetlights and store windows with the thirty-eights, that's all."

Keller asked if they hit anybody.

"Well, there was this one guy, we creased him a little bit across the stomach. But it's nothing. Just a scratch."

"Have you been booked at the police station? Do the newspapers know anything about it?"

"No, the chief here is a good guy. He knows who I am and all, and he ain't doing nothing until you get down here. You better make it fast, Jack."

Keller chartered a plane and flew into Indio with a briefcase fattened with money—between twenty and thirty thousand dollars (reports vary)—and made the rounds, negotiating deals so that what happened in Indio stayed in Indio.

....

The morning after, Bappie wondered where her sister had been.

"I went out with Frank Sinatra," Ava said. "We had a blast!"

....

And so *It* began, the destructive, tumultuous saga that would define and measure out their lives in terms of "before" and "after." Ava had an exalted feeling. It had been like great theater, a glorious first act.

She called him Francis. He called her Angel.

"Oh, God, it was magic," said Ava. "We became lovers forever—eternally."

❧ 5 ❧

Hollywood Department of Public Affairs

Ava Gardner, wearing a familiar blue tailored suit, eased the dark green Caddy into midmorning traffic on Sunset Boulevard and headed west to La Cienega, where she turned south toward Culver City, a drive that could take ten minutes if she was lucky, twenty-five if she was not. It was Thursday, February 10, 1949, a balmy and overcast day in the brief, subtropical Los Angeles winter. The temperature would reach seventy-four that afternoon.

Ava usually passed through the Metro gates by 6:00 A. M., was in makeup by 7:00, and on the set by 8:30. After rehearsals, filming began before noon and continued until everything was completed to the director's satisfaction, which could mean midnight or even later. Today was different.

Today the stars would be arriving in the morning for a luncheon on soundstage 29, where Louis B. Mayer was launching the silver anniversary for MGM, the studio that had "more stars than there are in the heavens." The event was being covered by *Life* magazine and film highlights would be shown on thousands of Loew's theater screens around the world.

Suddenly, a black Cadillac Brougham sped past Ava, then swung in front of her car and slowed down so that she had to pass it. The car overtook her again, and repeated the careening maneuver. As she pulled alongside the Caddy, she could see the grinning driver raising his hat. It was Frank. With a burst of speed, he zoomed off on his way to the same luncheon date at MGM.

That Sinatra, thought Ava. He could even flirt in a car.

....

The menu featured the usual chicken and matzo-ball soup à la Louis B. Mayer—made according to the studio head's mother's recipe—followed by stuffed squab, and ending with chocolate ice cream in the shape of Leo the lion. After lunch, fifty-eight stars, including Lassie, sat on a tiered dais set against a sky blue backdrop, posing for the famous twenty-fifth-anniversary group portrait. The stars were arranged in alphabetical order, which placed the G's in the second row—and there, seated between two of MGM's biggest stars, Clark Gable and Judy Garland, in the middle of the portrait was Ava Gardner, laughing and joking.

A few seats from Ava, actress Jennifer Jones thought that Ava, wearing no makeup, looked as though she hadn't slept in a week. Everyone knew she was having a torrid affair with Frankie, now sitting in a back row, next to comedian Red Skelton, who had broken up the group earlier by walking across the front of the stage, raising both hands in the air, and saying, "Okay, kids, the part's taken, you can go home now."

Frank wasn't laughing lately. His bank account was dwindling; his career was faltering. He owed thousands in income tax. He worried that he'd overspent on the house in Palm Springs. "Some columnists gloated about his tailspin and said the little bobbysoxers had now grown up and gotten some sense," said columnist Earl Wilson. "Music tastes were changing. Whatever Frank did was wrong, and whatever he rejected was brilliant if somebody else did it." Two songs that Mitch Miller wanted him to record (and which he rejected) became big hits by Al Cernik, renamed Guy Mitchell.

Frank had also gotten into a dispute with a UPI correspondent over an interview. "Pictures stink," Frankie told Hal Swisher. "Most of the people in them do, too. I don't want any more movie acting." Frank said he was misquoted, and he threatened to sue. Swisher stood by his story, saying that Frankie said that—and more. MGM insisted that the struggling actor quit talking about suing UPI and make it clear that he regretted his words.

Frank's liberal politics didn't sit well with Louis B. Mayer, the most Republican of Republicans. Frank supported FDR publicly, visiting him in the White House—even naming his son Franklin after the president! In her monthly *Photoplay* column, Louella Parsons warned that he was going to be dropped by MGM for being difficult on the lot, adding that Frank "isn't a well boy."

....

No matter how one looked at 1949, it was going to be terrible. Although Louis B. Mayer put on a brave face that day, major changes were under way at MGM. The studio system was imploding and the stars were starting to hear the rumors. "When MGM was formed in 1924, we had six stars and forty acres of land," Mayer told the audience. "Today we have thirty-one modern soundstages, sixty stars and five lots covering 176 acres.

"The motion picture industry will go forward in the years to come just as it has at this studio in the past 25 years," said Mayer. "It is to entertainment what the game of baseball is to American sports."

Although profits were still huge, the box-office receipts were dwindling. Nearly one-third of the studio's stars ducked L.B's command luncheon, and many who did were near the end of contracts that would not be renewed. It was the twilight of the Hollywood gods, and the gods were exiting Valhalla.

This new preposterous thing, television, once viewed as a novelty item—with its ten-inch screen—was the most rapidly expanding industry in the country, with casting under way for weekly shows. A program called *I Love Lucy* was in development at Desilu Productions.

As television cut into box office receipts, studios' profits sagged. From 1946 to 1950, motion picture stocks had declined 40 percent, whereas television stocks rose 243 percent. To show profits, without the risk or expense of making new movies, the studios would resort to selling off their back-logs of old films to the television networks. "Probably never in the history of industry has any group committed such efficient suicide," said Jesse L. Lasky, Jr., son of the movie pioneer. "The Christians, feeding their own children to the lions, thus gave the lions greater strength to devour them all the more! People began to stay home to watch old movies on television instead of paying to see new ones in the theaters. The writing was on the walls of the great sound stages. One might go and live—or stay and die."

More ominously, the Justice Department was dismantling the lucrative vertical arrangement between MGM in Hollywood and its parent company in New York, the Loew's organization, which distributed the company's movies to theaters that the company owned. "The government's trustbusters broke up this monopoly, forcing separation of the comfortable, airtight production-distribution-exhibition setup," wrote Ezra Goodman in *The Fifty-Year Decline and Fall of Hollywood.* "Because of the monopolistic setup, moviegoers were getting no opportunity to exercise choice as to the type of picture they wanted to see . . . every week 85 to 90 million people were taking what was dished out to them by the defendants . . . the movie industry had made desperate attempts to quash the anti-trust suit without success . . . had even gone direct to the President in the hope of having the charges called off. . . . It was the beginning of the end for Hollywood."

. . . .

On St. Patrick's Day, 1949, Texas oil tycoon Glenn McCarthy—called "King of the Wildcatters"—opened the Shamrock Hotel in Houston, an event still cited as one of the biggest social events in the city's history. McCarthy was an inspiration for Jett Rink, the sullen, rich oilman in Edna Ferber's *Giant,* played by James Dean in the movie version.

The $21 million, eighteen-story Shamrock Hotel featured a thousand-car garage, a pool big enough for waterskiing, and furnishings and decor in sixty-three shades of green, a nod to the oilman's ancestral Ireland. McCarthy bought a customized Boeing 307 Stratoliner from Howard Hughes to bring hundreds of celebrities to the grand opening, including Errol Flynn, Ginger Rogers, Robert Preston, and Hedda Hopper, from Hollywood. Publicized as "Houston's biggest party," the festivities cost one million dollars and became so raucous that a radio broadcast from the hotel by actress and singer Dorothy Lamour was cut off, and an audio engineer—assuming he was off-air—uttered an expletive heard live nationwide. Lamour fled the microphone in tears.

McCarthy recruited top Hollywood acts to perform at the Shamrock's nightclub, including Harpo and Chico Marx. The wildcatter offered them a choice of $35,000 or an interest in his newest natural-gas field for a two-week stint at his club. "We told McCarthy to keep his cash," said the non-speaking Harpo in his memoir. "We'd take this other deal." After deductions for depletion rights on the field, the Marx Brothers would end up earning pennies at the end of each quarter. "Chico didn't bother to figure the odds," complained Harpo.

McCarthy signed Frank Sinatra on for a weeklong engagement at the Shamrock in late January 1950. No gas-field rights here for Frank. Show him the money, pal.

. . . .

On March 20, 1949, Swedish film star Ingrid Bergman left her husband and daughter to join her lover, director Roberto Rossellini, in Italy. Bergman had been a publically pristine moviegoer favorite since 1939, when she starred in *Intermezzo* with Leslie Howard. She had been nominated for four Oscars in the past five years, and was named Best Actress for *Gaslight.*

Although Ingrid had many lovers during the forties, including director Victor Fleming, Spencer Tracy, Gary Cooper, and photographer Robert Capa, her fans thought of her as she was in *The Bells of St. Mary's* and *Joan of Arc*: a nun, a saint, the embodiment of virtue. But when she left her husband and child, she fell from grace, plummeting from number one at the box office to near oblivion.

Thus was launched the then-biggest scandal in Hollywood history.

. . . .

In the spring of that year, Ava moved nomadically from the apartment across from Sunset Towers to an apartment in Westwood, and then to another on Olympic Boulevard. Finally, in early summer she bought a small three-bedroom pink stucco house in Nichols Canyon, up in the Hollywood Hills. This became her and Frank's love nest.

"To a certain degree, they could keep their relationship secret," said Reenie in her memoir, *Living with Miss G.* "That was important because the whole climate surrounding the movie, radio, recording and the fledgling television industries demanded purity. No scandals, no hopping into bed with chorus girls, no homosexuality, just decency, happy endings, villains getting the chop and Mom's apple pie stretched as far as Louis B. Mayer's eye could see."

. . . .

In May, *Life* magazine ran a photo of Ingrid Bergman and Roberto Rossellini holding hands on the island of Stromboli, accompanied by the heading "Strombolian Idyl." The Motion Picture Association cabled Ingrid that her behavior would "result in complete disaster personally." On August 5, Bergman held a press conference in Rome, saying she had instructed her lawyer to start divorce proceedings. Also, with the conclusion of the picture she was now making with Rossellini, she added, "It is my intention to retire into private life."

Bergman's lawyer was the quasi-legendary Gregson Bautzer, a handsome squire just under forty, who was often featured in Hollywood magazines as an escort of stars around town, including old flame Lana Turner. Initially, Ingrid was reluctant to enlist an "attorney for the stars," but events would prove her choice a wise one. Bautzer and his staff were so thorough in their review of Ingrid's finances that they discovered one of her advisers had shifted eighty thousand dollars into an account in his name in an obscure Los Angeles bank. The adviser disappeared, and later committed suicide in a downtown hotel.

Bergman was vilified in newspaper editorials, and audiences boycotted theaters showing her pictures. Her husband, Petter Lindström, flew to Italy to win her back, to no avail. Ingrid wanted a divorce—and now. She requested half of her holdings, with funds set up for care of their daughter, Pia, but Lindström wanted all of her property and sole custody of the ten-year-old.

There was no progress in negotiations as Lindström played the wronged spouse, until December 1949, when Louella Parsons foghorned the news on the front page of the *Los Angeles Examiner*: INGRID BERGMAN BABY DUE IN 3 MONTHS AT ROME. The couple was going to have a love child, and the actress was still married. "They have been guilty of the most contemptible and outrageous conduct in centuries," said the Right Reverend C. E. Byrne, bishop of the Roman Catholic Archdiocese of Galveston, Texas. The press savored every detail of the ongoing saga.

....

George Evans had a basic recommendation for his clients: Don't embarrass yourself. On-camera, the stars were wonderful. Off-camera, they could be moody, impulsive, hard-living, and self-destructive. Often, they humiliated spouses. Evans's client list included two of Sinatra's pals, Jerry Lewis and Dean Martin. When the comedy duo were seen with women (not their wives), and it made the papers, the publicist went into a rant: "Do you guys realize that your anonymity is gone? That you are now public property? That you cannot do whatever you want anymore?" Evans leaned especially hard on Dean Martin, in a way that could have served as a scolding for Sinatra: "Don't you realize that you, you Italian idiot, are married with three children, *and* you're Catholic? Which is just a tad more serious than it is for the Jew with the one kid? Your people still go to confession!"

Evans and Sinatra were locked in an ongoing battle. Frank thought that his personal life was private, and that Evans—to put it in the vernacular—should mind his own fucking business. For Evans, who had been suppressing story after story about the singer's philandering, Frank's personal life *was* his business. Didn't the man grasp the importance of maintaining an image?

On December 8, 1949, for the opening of Carol Channing's Broadway musical *Gentlemen Prefer Blondes,* Frank and Ava were seen "snuggly, laughing and enjoying each other," reported the columnists. Four days later, at Frank's thirty-fourth birthday party at the Copacabana, Ava was observed on the fringes.

Broadway columnist—and Sinatra biographer—Earl Wilson found George Evans in a grave mood one night at the Copa. "Frank is through," said Evans across the table in the lounge. "The public knows about the trouble with Nancy, and the other dames, and it doesn't like him anymore."

"I can't believe that," said Wilson.

"I've been around the country, looking and listening. They're not going to see his pictures. They're not buying his records. They don't care for Frank Sinatra anymore!"

Evans was trying to disassemble the Ava thing and haul Frank back to Nancy, the kids, and his image. "George Evans didn't know that Ava was one Sinatra girl friend he couldn't shush or put aside," said Earl Wilson.

. . . .

Once she and Frank started getting serious, Ava dumped actor Howard Duff, her lover for nearly two years. Before that, she had had affairs with leading men Fred MacMurray (*Singapore,* 1947) and Robert Taylor (*The Bribe,* 1949), both married. She grew tired of the distrust, the sneaking around. At one point, Ava thought seriously about the possibility of marrying Robert Taylor. But he was more married than she suspected. He was furtive, sneaking in and out of Ava's small apartment, talking about how unhappy he was in his marriage but how hard it was to get a divorce. The lengths he went to in order to keep their romance a total secret were hard to believe. Like many men of the married persuasion, he seemed to enjoy the intrigue as much as the romance. He was a good pilot, and on several occasions he flew Ava out to lonely farmhouses owned by his friends. She soon began to realize this wasn't a romance; it was a fling, and doing things undercover was part of the excitement. Taylor was quite content with his image as a happily married man with a formidable movie-star wife, Barbara Stanwyck.

"I'm sometimes surprised he doesn't wear a black beard when we're off on a trip," Ava told Reenie. "It was far too fugitive and sneaky for Miss G," said Reenie. "She liked him enormously but was female enough to know it couldn't last."

Ava was through dating married men, without the possibility of marriage. And she felt things should be out in the open—and on the divorce track. She started putting pressure on Frank to get with the program. Frank assured her he had asked Nancy for a divorce. One night, after a few rounds, Ava asked him to prove it. They drove to the Holmby Hills residence, where Frank hit the buzzer at the gate. When Nancy responded, he said, "Will you please tell Ava that I've asked you for a divorce?" Nancy could tell they'd been drinking. "Frank, you're out of your mind," she said. "I wouldn't count on it."

As it happened, Missy Stanwyck was Nancy Sinatra's best friend. On Tuesdays, the two shared a pot of tea at Nancy's in Holmby Hills. Now they shared something else in common: Their husbands had both had affairs with Ava Gardner.

. . . .

In his bylined "Frankie Says . . ." column for the December 1949 issue of *Motion Picture* magazine, Frank Sinatra (via George Evans) recalled having been on the road for Christmas shows and events in the past, but this year he said he would be home with Nancy and the kids. Frankie reflected on a Christmas he'd spent ten years earlier, in Cleveland, with Harry James for a theater engagement. About a week before Christmas that year, he caught a cold and ended up in bed for Christmas Eve, when the bellboy brought him Nancy's Christmas package. In it was a pair of heavy leather gloves. "I tried them on but my fingers got stuck and I discovered a rolled-up dollar bill in each finger," recalled Frankie. "Boy, I was rich. Ten whole dollars. Right there and then I decided nothing was going to get me down and that I'd do anything to keep faith with that grand wife of mine."

In real life, Frank may have gone home to Nancy for Christmas in 1949, but as the New Year approached, he found himself rampantly in love with Ava, unable to keep his mind off her. He asked her to go to Houston, where he had to play the Shamrock Hotel in late January, but Evans opposed that idea. As Frank started to slip into a career slump—no movies, record sales dropping, just staying afloat with nightclub work—Ava's latent mothering and dominating instincts were becoming more forceful. She wanted to go public with their relationship; she wanted him to fire George Evans.

············

When George Evans wasn't arguing with Sinatra, he seemed to be arguing *about* Sinatra. On January 26, 1950, one day before Frank was scheduled to open at the Shamrock, the skinny, baldish publicist succumbed to a massive heart attack in New York City after debating with a columnist about Frank and Ava. He was forty-eight.

Frank was en route to Houston when he received the shocking news. He rescheduled the Shamrock engagement and attended Evans's funeral in New York City.

Evans's death, while sad, freed Frank and Ava from any constraints. Now they could be themselves, if they dared, in public.

Ava called Dick Jones, Frank's pianist. She wanted to fly down to Houston with him and cheer Frank up.

"Ava, I don't think that is a wise thing for you to do," Jones said as diplomatically as he could.

"Of course it is, Dick," she said brightly. "We'll just be two old friends wishing him luck."

At the Shamrock Hotel, Frank was delighted to see them. Ava bunked with Frank, and someone gave *Houston Post* columnist Bill Roberts a tip. On February 5, the night before Frank would finally open at the Shamrock, Roberts sent a photographer to the small Italian restaurant where Frank and Ava were having a quiet dinner. Frank exploded, and the next day, Frank and Ava were exposed, their story turning into another "open scandal."

....

When Nancy Barbato Sinatra saw the Houston story, she locked Frank out of the house and called Greg Bautzer, the dashing lawyer who had been representing Ingrid Bergman in the scandal everyone was talking about. Indeed, just a few days before Nancy made her call, Ingrid gave birth in Italy to a son, Robertino.

Bautzer would be expensive, but he was a solid choice for this kind of litigious squalor. In addition to handling Ingrid Bergman, Greg was Howard Hughes's personal lawyer. He knew all of the players in town. "He was tall and husky, with soulful dark eyes, a tanned complexion, and a flashing smile that showed a lot of white teeth," said Lana Turner about Greg Bautzer in her memoir. "He was so smooth, so self-assured, that all the other boys I knew seemed like children."

Bautzer, twenty-six at the time, had deflowered Lana, barely seventeen back in February 1938. "I must confess that I didn't enjoy it at all," reported the motion-picture star. Since then, he had become one of Hollywood's busiest bachelors, dating Ginger Rogers, Joan Crawford, and, yes, Ava Gardner.

⊰ 6 ⊱

America's Original Reality Show

Today anyone's life can be filmed from delivery to death. In 1950, there was no such immortality—unless you were someone in the newsreels, or if you were a movie star. Frank and Ava became both—stars on the screen and in the newsreels of the day. They were precursors of reality TV before there was even TV for the masses. It was *Keeping Up with Frank and Ava.*

In creating the image of Frank as a family man and Nancy as the perfect wife, George Evans had established a backdrop to the drama. Frank was now lamentably the perfect heel, and Nancy the girl next door who failed to keep her man. There was something for everyone. For some, it was the story of Frank pursuing Ava like a man; for others, it was the sorry tale of Frank following Ava around like a lovesick puppy.

As with the Bergman saga, the Catholic Church denounced Frank as an adulterer and Ava as a home wrecker. The Legion of Decency and church leaders advised parishioners to boycott Sinatra's records and Gardner's films.

Even the Mafia was giving Frank no respect.

Guarino "Willie Moore" Moretti, Mafia underboss in New Jersey—reputedly the guy who jammed a gun barrel down Tommy Dorsey's throat as an incentive for letting his boy singer out of a management contract in 1942—continued to take a paternal interest in Frankie. In 1950, the gangster fired off a telegram: "I am very much surprised what I have been reading in the newspapers between you and your darling wife. Remember you have a decent wife and children. You should be very happy. Regards to all. Willie Moore." This from a man who left other men's children without fathers.

············

On February 15, 1950, Frank Sinatra asked Nancy for a divorce. He revealed that he and Ava had been almost inseparable for more than a year. They had gone to Europe twice. He wanted a divorce so that he could surmount frustrations that were affecting his career. Nancy refused.

After the Shamrock gig, Frank was booked into the Copacabana in New York. "Hurricane Ava," as she was now called in the press, attended. They traveled according to the ostensible mores of the time, taking adjoining suites at the Hampshire House, their rooms divided by a large sitting room. Ava and Bappie shared one; Frank roomed alone in the other.

The Copa opening did not go well. Frank had a throat infection and, conversely, suffered from poor judgment in song selection. With Ava sitting near the front, he incredibly started to sing "Nancy (With the Laughing Face)." Laughter. Ava squirmed. "This is my first night," Frank told the audience. "Give me a break."

Ava made her exit and was not at the Hampshire House after the show. Frank was said to be "screaming with jealousy" when he discovered that she had gone to see Artie Shaw, her ex-husband, who was playing at another club, Bop City. No one provoked Frank's ire more than her ex, the guy who once had rejected his bid to join the band.

Frank called Hank Sanicola, his manager and occasional bodyguard, who traveled with him. Before that, Hank played piano in a music shop that sold sheet music, where Frank went to learn popular new tunes. When he started his rise to stardom, he took Hank along. He was a big easygoing Italian who could be intimidating.

In Florida, the head of a large city police department had given Frank a nickel-plated, pearl-handled, snub-nosed handgun that could fit in a suit pocket. Frank was into guns. He carried it that evening.

When Frank reached Artie's hotel room, the bandleader was in pajamas. Shaw was surprised to see Sanicola, wearing a raincoat, hands deep in the pockets. "Come on in and have a drink," said Artie, standing at the door.

Ava was there, starting to feel apprehensive now; she had overplayed her hand. Artie's girlfriend was in sleep attire. Clearly, their evening had been disrupted. Artie was cool. "Take off your coats, boys, and I'll fix you a drink," he said, trying to defuse things.

Frank exchanged glances with Ava, and then he and Hank retreated the way they'd come in. Artie exhaled. "In that case," he said, "let's *us* have another drink." His girlfriend wondered what was going on.

Ava taxied back to the Hampshire House and her side of the suite, where Bappie was sound asleep. The phone rang, and it was Frank. "I can't stand it anymore," the voice said. "I'm going to kill myself." There followed a gunshot.

Bappie slept through the shot, but not Ava's scream. She awoke as Ava rushed across the living room into Frank's bedroom, where he was holding the gun and contemplating the hole he'd blown into the mattress.

Hank Sanicola hadn't heard the shot, either, but he got the call from Frank to come quick. He raced up the back stairs, switched mattresses, and carried the damaged one back to his room. When others arrived, Frank looked wide-eyed and said innocently, "Shot? What shot?"

David O. Selznick, producer of *Gone With the Wind,* happened to be down the hall in the Hampshire House that night. After the disruption, he said indifferently, "I hope the bastard shot himself."

. . . .

In early March, after Ingrid Bergman had given birth to her love child, denunciations emanated from the Vatican. Edwin Johnson, Democratic senator from Colorado, called the actress "a horrible example of womanhood and a powerful influence for evil." He denounced Rossellini as a Nazi collaborator, a black-market operator, and a well-known cocaine addict. *Stromboli*—the movie Bergman made with Rossellini—was boycotted when it opened. "If out of the degradation associated with *Stromboli,* decency and common sense can be established in Hollywood," added Johnson, "Ingrid Bergman will not have destroyed her career for naught. Out of her ashes may come a better Hollywood."

Greg Bautzer tried to reach a settlement with Lindström, whose hard-nosed stand was not acquitting him in the court of public opinion. In exchanges with Ingrid, he sounded like Artie Shaw berating one of his wives. "You shouldn't talk so much," he once scolded Ingrid. "You have a very intelligent face, so let people think you are intelligent, because when you start to chatter it's just a lot of nonsense." In late April, after seven months of litigation, the divorce and property settlement were final. Lindström had custody of Pia. Bergman would have her during half of Pia's school vacations.

The scandal was a milestone in several ways, including the fact that it garnered months of national publicity. Frank could only hope that Nancy would not put him through a similar ordeal.

············

On March 25, Ava and Bappie departed for Spain, where Ava would film *Pandora and the Flying Dutchman* with James Mason. Ava was excited. In the movie, she would play a goddess who disguises herself as an ordinary mortal, Pandora Reynolds, a nightclub singer. It was a chance to sing, with no dub-over, "How Am I to Know?"

Ava was escorted one Sunday to a bullfight in the little town of Tossa del Mar, where she wore red and drank a lot of red wine. The toreador was Mario Cabré, who had acted in a few Spanish films and would be playing Juan Montalvo, Ava's bullfighter lover in *Pandora.*

Cabré bowed to Ava and carried an armful of roses to her in the stands. The next day, more flowers arrived at the hotel for Ava, then a dinner invitation, and her response: "Sure, why not?"

Mario Cabré was Ava's first bullfighter. Within a few years, she would become known for pursuing matadors. There was even a saying: "A *torero* needs more than a cape and fast footwork to escape Ava Gardner." "They're good fun," she said, "but just boys."

As the movie proceeded, Mario proudly announced his love for Ava, and began dispatching his visceral poems about her to the press:

> *How torrid was your blood when you caressed me*
> *And plowed your fingernails under my skin*

The American newspaper writers, who had formed a strong antipathy toward Frank, gleefully reported that the reel affair had become a real affair, and that Ava was involved in a romance with her costar. Frank called. "Oh, for Christ's sake, this is a movie, a setup," said Ava resolutely. "Ava brushed Mario off as nothing more than a publicity prop, and said he had begun to believe the script and play it for real," said a reporter.

But what may have begun as a publicity stunt to promote the film almost broke her romance with Frank as the poetical onslaught continued:

> *The night was one of color*
> *Yet when she came the sky held a rainbow*
> *For Ava was the dawn*

Mario was up nights writing poetry for his "little Hollywood sparrow." He reserved a small hall, decorated it with roses, and showered the town with flyers announcing he was going to read his poems. It was ninety degrees, and getting warmer. Mario wore a new shocking-pink suit of lights with rhinestones and silken stitchery, so tight that two men were needed to pull on the pants. The house was not exactly standing room only, but the press showed up, and a few friends and hard-core fans of bullfighting. A small group of musicians played love songs and tunes from *Carmen*.

Then Mario mounted the speaker's platform and, hands trembling, started reading:

> *Ava, Ava. My own sweet love,*
> *Your lips, your eyes, your hair of black.*
> *Your heart, your soul so like a dove.*

The temperature in the hall rose to ninety-eight degrees. Roses that Mario had hung from the ceiling started dropping their petals. He continued reading:

> *Full blown, a fragrant flower.*
> *Ava, Ava, a summer rose,*
> *Follow me, follow me*
> *To our little bower.*

As the stories developed, even Frank began to think it was more than a press agent's scam. He was doing three shows a night in a long engagement at the Copa. How could he get to Spain and straighten things out?

....

On April 26, Nancy Sinatra filed for separate maintenance, requiring Frank to pay alimony while they lived apart. "Mrs. Sinatra has no plans for divorce," Greg Bautzer told the *Los Angeles Times*. "The separate maintenance suit is just her way of making Sinatra save his money. She'll put it away as a nest egg. Then, when nobody else wants him, she'll take him back, and they'll have something to live on."

When nobody else *wants* him? "She's miserable about all his gallivanting," said Bautzer, "but she's still very much in love with him."

The court awarded Nancy a month's temporary alimony. Community property included an office building in Los Angeles, homes in Holmby Hills and Palm Springs, and the Hoboken home Frank had purchased for his parents.

．．．．．．．．．．．

On Wednesday, April 26, 1950, Frank opened his mouth to sing "Bali Ha'i" during the third show at the Copa at 2:30 A.M. "I went for a note, and nothing came out . . . absolutely nothing," he said. "Just dust." Frank looked at a startled Skitch Henderson, who was playing piano; then he looked at the audience, about seventy people, whispered "Good night," and walked off the floor. The next day, Frank underwent an exam and got a note from Dr. Irving Goldman, who recommended a two-week "voice vacation."

．．．．．．．．．．．

Apart from making movies, Louis B. Mayer's true passion was horses. He bred racehorses and started each day riding with publicity head Howard Strickling before going to the studio. One morning, a horse threw him, and he broke several bones, ending up in a knees-to-chest cast.

"He didn't fall off a horse," said Frank after he heard about the accident in the MGM commissary. "He fell off Ginny Simms," the singer and actress L.B. was dating on the side.

Mayer heard about the joke, of course, and did not laugh. "L.B. didn't like Frank because he was banging starlets, chorus girls, Gloria DeHaven, whoever was around," said Mayer biographer Scott Eyman. "Sinatra was obstreperous, and, when the camera wasn't running, he was like a teenage boy who couldn't control his urges. And, when his movies weren't doing well, he was expendable."

On April 28, Louis B. Mayer called Frank in for a chat.

"So? I hear you been making jokes about my lady friend," said Mayer.

"Yeah, oh, I wish I could take that back," said Sinatra. "I'm so sorry. I wish I'd never said anything so stupid."

"That's not a very nice thing to do," said Mayer stonily. "I want you to leave here, and I don't ever want you to come back again."

．．．．．．．．．．．

Frank knew the perfect spot for his voice vacation: a little town in Spain called Tossa del Mar. On May 12, he flew by regular carrier to London, and then—saying he was too impatient to wait for the regular flight—took a chartered plane to Spain. He also said he was giving Ava a ten-thousand-dollar necklace, "a full description of which circulated in the press," said publicist David Hanna.

With Frank on his way, Ava called her maid confidante in California. "Reenie, what the hell am I going to do?" she asked.

"You say, 'Mario who? Never heard of him,'" suggested Reenie. "And when he says, 'You know, the one who's in the film with you,' you say, 'Oh, him.' And excuse yourself as if it's martini time."

"At Barcelona, Frank represented himself as an avenging suitor who had come to beat the daylights out of Cabré," said Hanna. "The papers said he challenged Cabré to a duel."

Mario prudently found bullfighting engagements far removed from Tossa del Mar as Ava took Frank far from the movie set to a secluded area, where they enjoyed a three-day romantic interlude. Afterward, Frank told columnist Earl Wilson that Mario Cabré was nothing to Ava. "He is nothing to her, nothing, NOTHING! Don't you understand? The Spanish press is trying to make a hero out of this guy because it would be a feather in their cap if they could show that this girl was interested in him. This girl has had nothing to do with this boy.

"And there's something else I'd like to get across," said Frank. "Ava and I have kept this as clean as anybody could. We were chaperoned all the time. ALL THE TIME! Just like at a high school dance."

....

In June, Frank and Nancy agreed to transfer ownership of the Hoboken house to Frank's parents, Dolly and Marty. "Better let him go," Dolly advised Nancy. "Better for you, better for the children. You can't keep a man if he doesn't want to be there."

Nancy's relationship with her tempestuous mother-in-law would never be the same. Good-bye, Dolly.

....

The *Pandora* cast moved to London that summer to shoot interiors. Frank gave Ava a corgi, which they named Rags, after Frank's pal, the comedian Rags Ragland, and on July 12, in his first British stage appearance, Frank wowed them at the London Palladium. He described himself as "a very scared young Italian lad" in one of his unassuming asides. "He stands at the mike in a midnight blue dinner jacket and outsized bow tie," said London *Times* critic Pat Brand. "Sinatra does not milk the audience . . . But the vamping is there all the same: in the body movement, the clinch of the fist, the narrowing of the eyes. And when it becomes too much for the fans to stand, and they start to go over the edge, he gently pushes them back to momentary sanity with an admonishing, 'Steady, now.' Above all, he sings in a voice somewhat deeper than his records have led us to expect in a manner that makes you believe every word of the lyric."

Frank had tea with Princess Margaret the next day. Ava was not invited.

....

On July 27, at the Spanish Institute in London, Mario Cabré wore his heart on his toreador's sleeve for the publication (or printing, anyway) of his *Dietario poético a Ava Gardner,* also known as the "Ava Poems." There were sixty-six poems in all, and Mario had a capacity audience, but Ava was conspicuously absent. To a question of whether his love for Ava had ended, he offered a fittingly poetic reply: "One cannot finish something that is eternal."

Mario would continue to appear in films in Spain, and during the 1960s, he would host the popular Spanish TV show *Queen for a Day.*

....

Ava ducked the topic of Mario for a while, but Frank persisted, and gradually made inroads as he returned to the rumors about Mario. "Gee, honey, it's long ago now. Who cares? We all make little mistakes when we've had a few drinks."

Ava confessed. Frank was enraged.

"You should have kept that revelation in that Pandora's box of yours," said Reenie. "Every woman needs one."

"Dead right," said Ava sadly. "You know, he never forgave me—ever!"

. . . .

Greg Bautzer could read the signs. It was similar to the Bergman battle, when Ingrid's husband became the bad guy for being an obstacle to true love. Now Nancy Sinatra was starting to get her comeuppance in the press. One story characterized her as a spoilsport for trying to hold the family together. Another compared Frank and Ava to Romeo and Juliet.

"Many women of today would ask what she would want him back for, after everything she'd been through," said Sinatra biographer Donald Clarke. "Some of their friends also said that she wouldn't have lost him in the first place if she had developed with him, and that he went out alone a lot because she didn't like parties, but it seems hard to blame a mother and homemaker for not being able to stay out all night. The truth is simply that Nancy was a nice Italian girl who fell in love with the wrong man."

Years later, Wilfrid Sheed would wonder if there wasn't perhaps a subliminal upside to the whole affair. Sheed called Ingrid and Frank "perhaps the two most unlikely war criminals of all time" in Hollywood lore: "Ingrid Bergman for sinning against her role in *Casablanca* and running off with a foreign (ugh) film director, and Frank Sinatra for betraying his own publicity and doing what practically every man in America at least wanted to do—cheating on his wife and chasing after Ava Gardner."

On September 29, Nancy obtained permanent separate maintenance on the charge of mental cruelty.

. . . .

At MGM that summer, plans were under way for another film version of *Show Boat,* based on the Jerome Kern and Oscar Hammerstein stage production. Two previous screen versions had lost money. Musical producer Arthur Freed and director George Sidney wanted Judy Garland as the third lead in the film, the biracial Julie, who is driven off the boat because of her mixed blood. Considered "one of the choicest of all musical roles," it included the popular classic songs, "Bill" and "Can't Help Lovin' Dat Man." Judy's weight had ballooned, however, and she was deemed uncastable.

Lena Horne thought the part was hers, and for good reason. In *Till the Clouds Roll By,* the paean to composer Jerome Kern, released in December 1946, there is a capsule version of the first act of *Show Boat,* and Lena sang a heartrending version of "Can't Help Lovin' Dat Man."

"When Lena Horne came on the screen, one could have heard a pin drop," said Howard Strickling, never one to miss a cliché. "She was ravishing. . . . Everyone was overwhelmed by this beautiful star." It was like an on-camera audition for the role of Julie in the remake.

In the early 1940s, Lena had gained popularity as a girl singer with the Artie Shaw Band, and as the torch crooner who sang "The Man I Love" at the Savoy Plaza. In 1943, she and Ava became friends as starlet "strays" on the set of *Swing Fever,* a silly comedy musical that showcased bandleaders Harry James and Tommy Dorsey. They shared many southern traits, and in the late 1940s Lena and musician Lennie Hayton—one of the earliest biracial couples in Hollywood—bought a home at 2136 Nichols Canyon, just down the road from Ava and Bappie's pink stucco house.

On Sundays, Lennie would try a new drink from a book called *The Gentleman's Drinking Companion,* and the gals and friends (including Betty Garrett, also close by) would imbibe until the late hours, laughing and sharing backstage stories about life in Culver City and the men they'd had in common, including Artie Shaw. "And his mental domination, which drove both of us crazy," said Lena, who had an affair with Artie in 1941. "We laughed because he liked his women to read a lot of books." Hayton called them "MGM's bad girls."

George Sidney tested an array of actresses for the role of Julie—Dinah

Shore, Lee Wiley, Ginny Simms, Julie London, and Julie Wilson—but he did not test Lena Horne, explaining that an obviously black actress could not play Julie, who passed for white and was married to a white man, which was against the law in turn-of-the-century Mississippi. Such miscasting would distort that poignant moment in the story, the discovery of Julie's blackness. Lena Horne was perplexed.

Finally, George Sidney tested Ava Gardner—and cast her as Julie. Lena Horne was devastated.

. . . .

On February 14, 1951, Nancy Sinatra, weary of the public degradation, served Frank with separation papers on Valentine's Day, playing directly to the press—for Frank, a sad little jab to the heart.

. . . .

On March 27, 1951, Frank Sinatra entered the Columbia studios in New York to record "I'm a Fool to Want You" with Axel Stordahl and orchestra. The song was originally written for a radio drama. Sinatra changed a few words, and the writers (Jack Wolf and Joel Herron) gave him a shared credit on a song that he not only helped compose; he was living it.

Sinatra connoisseurs generally agree that Frank put his grief over Ava Gardner into the recording, which many consider the most emotion-filled performance of his career. He did the song in one take. It was said he left the studio teary-eyed. In fact, he went on to record "Love Me" at the same session—another plaintive cry for Ava to hear.

The song was not a commercial success. It sold a feeble 35,000 copies, perhaps because of the B side, "Mama Will Bark," the infamous novelty duet with Dagmar, a celebrity famous for showing more cleavage than singing skills on television. According to the lyric, the dog's name is Mama, and she will bark if the boy tries to get his hands on the girl's prominent features.

Sinatra drew the line at barking like a dog, and A&R chief Mitch Miller had to hire someone else to do that. Frank's career was in precipitous decline, marked by a lack of hit singles from 1948 through 1952. After "Mama Will Bark," the joke was that his singing career was going to the dogs.

Long after Frank's departure from Columbia, Mitch Miller saw Sinatra in Las Vegas. "Let bygones be bygones," he said genially, extending his hand. "Fuck you," said Frank ungenially. "Keep walking."

. . . .

On April 25, Nancy filed for legal separation in Santa Monica court.

. . . .

After departing MGM ahead of schedule, Frank made *Double Dynamite* at RKO, with Groucho Marx and Jane Russell. A flop. In early June of 1951, filming got under way for *Meet Danny Wilson,* from Universal. The story line was close to the bone—Frank played an unpleasant nightclub singer who rose to the top with mob backing and took nonsense from no one.

Some critics saw a protodramatic actor emerging in the movie. Frank's costar Shelley Winters said, "The only good part of the picture was Sinatra's wonderful singing." Frank and Shelley feuded throughout the making of the movie. "This forgettable picture began shooting in chaos and ended in disaster," said Shelley in her memoir. She blamed most of the problems on off-camera stress. "Frank Sinatra was in the process of divorcing Nancy to marry Ava Gardner. . . . His children were quite young, and there were always psychiatrists and priests and his kids visiting him on the set or in the commissary." There were tales of Frank's temper tantrums and his kindness. "I was really scared of him," said Shelley. She felt she was making a film "with Dr. Jekyll and Mr. Hyde."

The feud led to a screaming match at about three o'clock in the morning, and Shelley slugged Frank. "For a second I thought Frank's makeup man/bodyguard—who I suspected carried a gun—was going to shoot me. Contrary to other Italians I have known since, he didn't hit me back—I guess I was lucky—he just slammed into his limousine and roared away. Maybe he went home and hit Ava Gardner."

They returned to shoot the final scene, and everything went beautifully until Sinatra's last line, which was "I'll have a cup of coffee and leave you two lovebirds alone," as the picture faded out on Frank's sad but funny grin. During the shoot, however, Sinatra said, "I'll go have a cup of Jack Daniel's, or I'm gonna pull that blonde broad's hair out by its black roots."

Shelley threw a bedpan and the fight was on again, worse than the previous night's. The picture was shut down and Shelley stayed home with the phone off. Marilyn Monroe, her then roommate, came home from Twentieth Century–Fox with an urgent message from Nancy Sinatra: Please call her.

In tears, Nancy said she was awaiting a payment from Frank, and now everything was suspended. "Shelley, the bank might foreclose the mortgage on the house," she said. "My children are going to be out in the street. Please finish the picture, or they won't give me the twenty-five thousand dollars." Next morning on the set, Shelley told Frank, "You can say any damn thing you want. But you just might want to make another picture again sometime, and the audience is going to think you're tacky and tasteless."

. . . .

On July 17, 1951, Frank escorted Ava to the premiere of *Show Boat*. Most of the movie was filmed on the MGM back lot, where the steam paddle wheeler was constructed to scale, and the Mississippi River was a lake built for the old Johnny Weissmuller *Tarzan* movies.

George Jacobs, Sinatra's longtime black valet, said that Ava, "a frustrated singer," totally identified with her role in *Show Boat,* though she never forgave MGM for dubbing her songs. Jacobs developed a bond with Ava, "which was easy to do," he said, "considering she was the earthiest, and most down-to-earth movie star you could ever imagine. She always told me she was part black, that 'poor white trash,' the stock she came from in North Carolina, always had black blood in them."

Ava had an untrained but attractive alto singing voice. Annette Warren's dubbed-in vocal tracks—which sounded nothing like Ava— were used in the film for "Can't Help Lovin' Dat Man," and "Bill." "I wanted to sing those songs," Ava told Rex Reed years later. "Christ, songs like 'Bill' shouldn't sound like an opera. They substituted her voice for mine, and now in the movie my Southern twang stops talking and her soprano starts singing—hell, what a mess. They wasted God knows how many thousands of dollars and ended up with crap."

Coached by Frank, who enlisted his arranger Axel Stordahl, Ava insisted on being tested for the singing role. She was so nervous in the presence of the microphone that the studio lights were dimmed, and she performed both songs in darkness—stunning half-spoken half-sung renditions that brought applause from the crew. Two weeks later, when she arrived on the set, she was told that the studio couldn't take the risk of using an untrained singer in so famous a part. Ava told Rex Reed, "So, what did they say? 'Ava, baby, you can't sing, you'll hit the wrong keys, you're up against real pros in this film, so don't make a fool of yourself.'

"*Pros*! Howard Keel? And Kathryn Grayson, who had the biggest boobs in Hollywood? I mean, I like Graysie, she's a sweet girl, but with her they didn't even need 3-D!"

Ava, whose career was peaking, walked out for three days and returned only after coaxing by Sinatra and pleading from Louis B. Mayer. Because of sound-recording regulations, however, Ava's tracks had to be used on the *Show Boat* soundtrack album, and she delighted in receiving royalties for many years afterward. "Gardner's versions sound anything but operatic," said Bruce Eder, who annotated the soundtrack recording. "Acted as much as sung, by the only cast member in the film who was acting full out, they have a warm, personal feel that makes them among the most affecting parts of this score." When Ted Turner purchased the MGM film library, he had Ava's tracks reinstated in the movie version.

....

Meet Danny Wilson wrapped on July 30. In previews, it was a bomb. Frank, whose customary fee was $150,000 per film, next signed a Universal-International three-picture deal at $25,000 a film. Even at that bargain price, his future with the studio was uncertain.

. . . .

Frank feared they were going to break up. "He was depressed—depressed about me, depressed about the fact that no one seemed to want him during his visit to New York," said Ava. "He brooded all the way back from New York to Chicago. He should have continued on to L.A., but he got off in Chicago and rang me up. God, was he in a state. 'Ava,' he cried, 'I can't stand this any longer. I'm going to throw myself off the train before I reach Los Angeles.'"

In Palm Springs one evening, Ava came out of the bathroom into the bedroom and Frank was sitting on the edge of the bed with a revolver pointed at his temple. She grabbed for his hand, screaming, "You phony!" They fell on the floor, and the gun went bouncing and discharged a bullet that ricocheted, making a two-inch hole in a solid wooden door. Jimmy Van Heusen, who was staying over that night, came running in, stark naked. He looked around, smiled, and said, "Just wanted to know what the shooting match was all about." He closed the door and left. "I knew I was wrong," said Ava. "There was nothing phony about that gun."

The *Los Angeles Herald Examiner* reported that Sinatra had taken an overdose of sleeping pills after a fight with Ava at Cal-Neva Lodge at Lake Tahoe. Hank Sanicola called Ava and said the doctor was with Frank but wasn't sure he could do anything. Ava came rushing back, and found Frank waking up on cue. "Oh, God, I thought you were gone," he said in a sad little voice. "I could have killed him," said Ava. The circumstances were similar to the Hampshire House "acting out" episode. "He's the only one who's had any sleep. You can be sure he counted exactly how many sleeping pills he took. There he is, rested and fine. . . . I could have kicked the crap out of him."

Beneath his tough exterior, Frank could be an emotional, even fragile, man. It was remarkable that he did not do harm to himself and to others. The question isn't whether or not Frank tried to commit suicide but, rather, is someone who *fakes* suicides mentally healthy? Or is he, in fact, suicidal? Either way, from Ava's point of view, this was not the sort of behavior that enriched a relationship.

Now approaching his late thirties, Frank Sinatra had a history at work and home that included many infidelities, depression, violent episodes, and several alleged suicide attempts. "Nobody else cares whether he blows his brains out or takes an overdose," said Ava. "I care. He knows that it would blow me apart and that I will always protect him. Hell, it's destroying me too."

Ava maintained a droll sense of humor, suggesting that with Frank you needed a scorecard to keep track of his suicide attempts. It was reminiscent, perhaps, of the time playwright George S. Kaufman ran into Dorothy Parker after one of her well-publicized suicide attempts, looked at her bandaged wrists, and said, "You'd better be careful, Dottie. Next time you might hurt yourself."

. . . .

On September 3, 1951, Ava Gardner appeared on the cover of *Time*. In a story titled "The Farmer's Daughter," the newsmagazine reported that Ava didn't brag about her acting but considered herself a singer. The editors said that Ava had that bigger-than-life quality, on the big screen, where an image is projected at thirty-two times life size, and that she just might be the one new star who could bring glamour back to Hollywood. "The consensus is that Ava Gardner may well turn out to be the best thing for Hollywood since the late Jean Harlow."

For Ava, it was a striking comparison, for Harlow—the "blonde bombshell"—was the memorable costar in *Red Dust,* the Clark Gable movie she and her mama had seen when Ava was a youngster. It was a worrisome analogy at MGM, however, where Harlow was remembered as the most dynamic sex symbol of her era and one of the 1930s brightest stars, whose sudden death at twenty-six shocked the movie world. Howard Strickling, the longtime publicity director, told publicist David Hanna that he was concerned about Ava's dangerous lifestyle, and that Ava and Jean

Harlow possessed the same "devil-may-care, flamboyant personalities that often led them to do things they regretted later." This was hardly news to Hanna, who traveled with Ava extensively. "Any notion that she was simply another stupid Hollywood beauty had been dispelled," he said. "Ava definitely counted in my book as a bright, witty and intelligent person."

Ava deplored the fact that she had not been formally educated. But she underestimated herself, and overestimated others, especially her husbands, said Hanna. "Frank Sinatra can claim a superficial knowledge of many things, ranging from politics to books, from art to racial problems. When he tackles one in conversation he can be positively impressive, dogmatically sure of himself. I soon came to the conclusion that Ava, unlike myself, who had been reared in a theatrical family, had never learned the first important lesson in maintaining a relationship with an actor—never confuse his ability to read lines well with erudition."

....

On October 15, Nancy Sinatra filed for a California divorce. According to the settlement, Frank agreed to pay Nancy one-third of his gross income up to $150,000 and one-tenth of the gross above that figure. Nancy got the Holmby Hills house, stock in Frank's music-publishing company, their 1950 gray Cadillac, and custody of the children. Frank got the Palm Springs house and a 1949 Cadillac convertible.

The wedding was on: early November, location known only to the wedding party, somewhere in Philadelphia, of all places.

The night before their wedding, Ava received a letter from a woman who claimed she had been having an affair with Frank. The letter included Frank's favorite sexual positions, the times and places of their trysts, and a vivid description of his genitals. "It was filthy, and it gave details that I found convincing," said Ava. She told Bappie that all she could do was vomit. The wedding was off.

Ava removed the six-karat emerald engagement ring that Frank had given her and threw it out the window from the fourteenth floor of the Hampshire House, and Frank spent the night pleading with her not to believe the letter, which, he argued, Howard Hughes had probably paid some whore to write. After hours of searching by flashlight, Tony Consiglio found the ring and hurried back to the suite. "Great," said Frank, very cool, as though this sort of thing happened all the time. By now, Ava had calmed down. The wedding was back on.

The next morning, the wedding party drove to Philadelphia, believing they could get a judge to waive the three-day cooling-off period so they could marry immediately at the home of a close friend of Manie Sacks. When the judge refused, the nearly-weds returned to New York for a weekend of jitters, quarrels, drinking, and his-and-her threats to kill themselves. The bride-to-be would not let the groom-to-be into her room. The wedding, once again, was off. "What was to have been a celebration is a shambles," said Frank.

Things cooled down. On Wednesday, November 7, the wedding was on again. When Frank heard that reporters knew of the plan, he asked Manie Sacks to change the location. Not a problem.

It was rainy; it was dusk at 5:30, when they arrived at the new site in West Germantown, Pennsylvania, where reporters and photographers were clustered outside the house. "How did these creeps know we were here?" snarled Frank. He barged into the house, slamming the door. Encountering a written request inside from photographers to pose for pictures, he opened the door and shouted out, "OK, who sent the note? Which one? You're not going to get any pictures. You'll get shots from the commercial photographer when he gets around to it." One photographer said he'd like to take his own. "I'll bet you $500 you don't get a picture," said Frank, "and if you do I'll knock you on your ass."

Inside, Frank changed in one of the children's bedrooms. Ava washed her hair and fluffed it up. "No curlers, no fuss. My mother couldn't get over that," said Adrienne Sacks years later.

Guests included Frank's parents, Bappie, and the Sacks family clan.

Axel Stordahl was best man; his wife, June Hutton, matron of honor. Dick Jones played the Mendelssohn "Wedding March" and then "Here Comes the Bride."

The bride wore an eggshell-tinted Howard Greer cocktail-length dress of mauve-toned marquisette, stiffened like brocade, with a strapless top of pink taffeta. She added a double strand of large pearls and small pearl and diamond earrings.

As Ava started down the stairs, she leaned heavily on Manie's arm. He missed his footing and slid a few steps as Ava caught and steadied him. Frank, who wore a white carnation in the buttonhole of his tailored dark suit, flashed her a smile. Ava felt tears building.

Police court judge Joseph Sloane married them, following an exchange of wedding bands, narrow platinum circlets without ornament.

The newlyweds kissed several times. Frank grinned. Ava rushed into the arms of Martin and Dolly Sinatra. The women cried.

"Well, we finally made it," said Frank, as if they were a couple of long-distance runners crossing the finish line. The married couple kissed, cut a four-tiered white wedding cake, and everyone drank champagne, including the Sacks's family dog, Noel. The party lasted until 9:00 P.M.

Ava changed into her going-away outfit: a Christian Dior creation in dark brown and a sapphire mink stole (Frank's wedding present). She had given him a gold locket with Saint Christopher and Saint Francis medals, one on either side, and a picture of her inside.

Before the couple departed, a female guest and Manie, who resembled Frank just a bit, left in the limo to divert the press. Frank and Ava sneaked out the back door and drove in heavy rain to a twin-engine Beechcraft waiting at Wings Field in Blue Bell. Then Ava discovered that she had taken the wrong suitcase (with the outfit she wore when she arrived) instead of her honeymoon trousseau. Shrugging, she said, "Let's fly to Miami without it."

At dawn, they arrived in Miami and were driven to the Green Heron Hotel. The next morning, Ava sent out for groceries and cooked the wedding breakfast in their suite—Frank's usual, scrambled eggs in olive oil. That afternoon, a photographer grabbed a lonely shot of the couple, holding hands as they barefooted it along a cold, windy beach, dressed in an odd mix of clothes. Ava wore one of Frank's jackets. The trousseau bag still had not arrived.

The following day the newlyweds flew on to Havana for a honeymoon that, according to one newspaper report, was paid for by Ava.

∾ 7 ∾

A Star Is Reborn

If the courtship of Frank and Ava was a reality show, the marriage was like a bad war movie, one you think will never end. When the honeymooners returned from Havana, Ava had to restrain Frank as he threatened to slug a reporter at the airport in New York. After a stopover in Hoboken for dinner with Dolly and Marty, the newlyweds flew to L.A. on November 15. The following week, a late-night argument in Palm Springs evolved into a heated battle. Ava drove off into the desert.

On December 7, they flew to London for a Royal Command charity show. The duke of Edinburgh threw a cocktail party for the stars—Rhonda Fleming, Dorothy Kirsten, Jimmy Van Heusen, Jimmy McHugh, Tony Curtis, and Janet Leigh—and Ava danced a samba with him. "We were very nervous," recalled Janet Leigh. "We had to remember to bow to the royal box before starting our act." Ava had promised to sing a duet with Frank at the benefit, but she changed her mind. Frank didn't sing his best, and during one number he stopped and scolded the band, to the embarrassment of all. Jimmy Van Heusen, on piano, was Frank's lone accompaniment during the show. The evening was a disaster.

The next day, everyone was off to Wiesbaden, Germany, for another charity performance—except for Frank and Ava. They "were having a honeymoon spat," said Leigh. Moreover, their hotel suite had been robbed; the stolen items included a diamond and emerald necklace that Frank had given Ava for Christmas, one of her favorites, and one that he had probably put on Ava's tab, as she was the family wage earner.

The marriage became a series of bids and bluffs; it was like a game of liar's poker. They fought over every little thing. She grew tired of his outbursts against the press, his threats to photographers. They started bringing up old alliances—Mickey, Artie, Marilyn, Lana. They were apart often. There were temptations. He still harbored some guilt about Nancy and the kids. "If you have to go to war with a country, maybe you stand a chance of winning," Frank told Tony Consiglio. "When you're at war with a woman, you don't have any chance. The best you can hope for is an occasional truce."

"It was all about jealousy," said author Stephen Birmingham. "Sinatra liked to be recognized, and if a pretty girl came up and spoke to him, Ava would get furious. And Ava's eyes liked to travel around the room; she'd fix on this one and that one, and the next thing you'd know the person would be over at the table and Frank would get furious. So they were always jealous of each other, just like teenagers."

Artist Paul Clemens and his wife weekended with Frank and Ava at the Springs. "It was fun, but there was always tension," he said. On their way to a table at the Racquet Club, Frank paused to say hello to the owner, actor Charlie Farrell. "I'll be right along," said Frank. "There were people milling around, and among them were attractive girls who were pleased to meet Frank," said Clemens. The threesome had waited at their table for five minutes, when Ava announced, "I'm leaving." Clemens said he would drive her home "not merely to see that she got home, so that we knew where she was, but also to secure our transportation, because we had all come there in one car." He added, "When Ava says, 'I'm leaving,' that's an open-ended itinerary because she's a woman of means and temperament." One evening, after an argument with Frank in an L.A. restaurant, she made her exit. Two days later, she called him from Italy.

Now that Frank was now married to Ava, he expected all of the rights of any other Italian husband—he was in charge. Ava had many of the qualities Frank idealized in a wife. Around her, he would talk with others, tell stories, was comfortable sharing the spotlight, but only up to a point. Frank's charm was nearly irresistible, but when he couldn't have things his way, charm was out, and Italian machismo prevailed. No way was Ava going to boss him the way Dolly bossed his father around.

But Ava was a beautiful woman with a fiercely independent nature. Elia Kazan recalled a conversation with a scene designer named Boris, who said that when he met Marilyn Monroe for the first time, he understood why Arthur Miller wanted her. "But," Boris added, with a heavy Jewish intonation and challenging lilt, "that's a *wife*?"

It was a dramatic relationship, full of the deepest kind of love and every extreme emotion imaginable. It was a painful, ever-changing, messy ride. "Frank talked to me a lot about Ava," said Tony Consiglio. "He believed that their marriage failed mainly because she wanted to keep her career going." Who could blame her? To rework an old Henny Youngman line: That was no woman . . . that was my love goddess.

Ava did things *her* way. "If Frank said she had to stay in New York, Ava would fly to Spain and make certain that photographers took pictures of her with handsome and young bullfighters and actors," said Tony. "When Frank saw the photographs, he didn't care if he had a recording session or a show to do. On a moment's notice he was gone, flying to Spain to confront her. Sometimes Frank would go to her even if it meant missing concerts and not taking care of business, which was something Frank had never done before and never did again after Ava. They wore each other out emotionally."

The affair had become a courtship, but it always had the allure of excitement that accompanies illicit sex. Frank and Ava both loved the sex, and there were long stretches between rounds because of their dueling schedules. But marriage and frequent encounters can lead to tedium in the bedroom. It wasn't long before what had seemed so exciting at first started to create friction. "He doesn't take all that fire to bed with him," Ava told Artie Shaw, who remained an occasional confessor (another part of the problem). "And you, of all people, know I like it rough. With Frank, it's impossible. It's like being in bed with a woman. He's so gentle. It's as if he thinks I'll break, as if I'm a piece of Dresden china that he's gonna crack."

"Marriage and sexual love are not the same," said Elia Kazan. "The requirements are mixed. Lovers often release the inhibited part of a person's life. Marriage is an opposite need. What you look for in a marriage partner is that he or she be a stable person, a homemaker, a mother or father candidate, that above all."

Although Frank liked to play the loving parent, and (now) the telephone dad, never without a roll of dimes, and Ava would talk to columnists about settling down and having kids and a man she could really love for life, this was what they did for a living: playing to the cameras. Ava and Frank were career-driven stars, in a highly competitive workplace, whose job was to keep a good thing going. The fifties were not much different from what we have today. Celebrity magazines pretend that the stars are "just like us," with photos of them eating pizza or pushing kids around in the park. The unadorned truth is that show-business people *are* different from you and me. Yes, they have more money (or credit, anyway), but they also have managers and imaginations for getting their way as they marry and divorce and lead calculated public lives that are part of career strategies. But their lives are rarely whole and intact, for the entertainment business is a world of chaos, comings and goings, deals bartered and broken, relationships often uncertain or in need of repair. The mantra for survival: Trust no one.

....

A few weeks after the wedding, MGM loaned Ava out to Twentieth Century–Fox to star in *The Snows of Kilimanjaro,* produced by Darryl F. Zanuck. Ava's costar was Gregory Peck in Hemingway's story about a big-game hunter in the 1920s who loves, loses, and finds again the woman he loves, just before he dies.

"Frank was not thrilled to see his wife return to work," said Ava biographer Roland Flamini. "His Italian heritage demanded a family-oriented spouse." Ava liked to cook, when she felt like cooking; and she was in-different about household tasks—that was why God created maids. "When his friends came to visit, Frank sensed the unspoken comparison with Nancy's well-ordered household," said Flamini. "And now Ava was going back to work, just when Frank needed her to dispense reassurance and encouragement in his current mood of doubt and self-pity."

Because of the Hemingway imprint and the story's setting, *Kilimanjaro* had the potential of making Ava an international star. Cynthia, the hero-ine, was someone she could relate to—and the movie, despite its African backdrop, would be shot on the Fox lot in Century City. No extended trips to unromantic places. "It's the perfect part for me," said Ava. Unfortu-nately, Frank would be doing shows at the Paramount in New York (and promoting his *Meet Danny Wilson*) in March—and he wanted her at his side. "The perfect part for you is being my wife," said Frank.

Ava and director Henry King trimmed her shooting schedule so that she would complete her scenes and be in New York before Frank's open-ing night. But there was tension—exacerbated by Frank's daily calls to Ava on the set—and the shooting fell behind schedule. "That motherfucker is going to give me hell when I tell him," she said. "And I'm just going to sit there and take it."

In March, Frank appeared onstage when *Meet Danny Wilson* opened at the Paramount in New York. Ten years earlier, the bobby-soxers had fainted at the sound of his voice, but now George Evans was gone, and Sinatra was just another name. The picture was panned, and you had to read the reviews closely to discover that Frank was appearing live.

One afternoon, Johnnie Ray, a popular singer of the day, showed up backstage at the Paramount with his manager to say hello to Frank and Ava. The conversation was polite, but when Frank left for a few minutes, Ava went over to Johnnie and sat on his lap. "Ava was always a hot num-ber and always used other men to make Frank jealous," said Tony Con-siglio. "She started kissing Johnnie, and in spite of the rumors that he was gay, Johnnie joined in. They were kissing each other while Ava wig-gled her beautiful ass into Johnnie. Naturally, this is when Frank came back into the dressing room. He grabbed Ava off Johnnie's lap and dragged her out of the dressing room."

As Tony closed the door, Frank slammed Ava against the wall and pointed his finger in her face. "If only they could have stopped fighting and screwing around," said Tony. "Ava taunting Frank with matadors and nothing people like Johnnie Ray. And Frank was busy himself with nobodies. But they both needed constant attention and affection."

....

It was all too bad to be true.

On March 6, 1952, Universal canceled its deal with Frank Sinatra for three pictures. *Meet Danny Wilson* had failed, and *Nothing But the Blues*—a movie in progress—was being retrofitted for Donald O'Connor.

Later that month, CBS announced the network was dropping Frank's TV program, ostensibly for its poor ratings versus Milton Berle and a newcomer on the DuMont channel: Bishop Fulton Sheen's *Life Is Worth Living*. Frank helped the decision along by refusing to rehearse and provoking problems on the set.

The "Your Hit Parade" radio program replaced Frank with opera star Lawrence Tibbett.

Frank's booking agency, MCA, dropped him, and announced that he owed them forty thousand dollars in commissions.

Frank owed the IRS over $100,000 in taxes.

....

"When it became increasingly clear that he and Ava could not coexist under one roof without killing each other," said George Jacobs, Frank moved to a duplex garden apartment on Wilshire and Glen. "He's a dead man," said agent Irving "Swifty" Lazar, Frank's next-door apartment neighbor. "Once you lose it in Hollywood, you don't come back. Even Jesus couldn't get resurrected in this town."

Frank tried being friendlier, more amenable to reporters and photographers, but the press had turned. Reporters reminded him of his oft-repeated "I don't have to talk to anyone. It wasn't the press who made me famous. It was my singing and the American public." When someone told Swifty Lazar about the new, improved Frank, who smiled back at greeters, the agent explained, "Everybody's nice when they're down and desperate. Losers have the *time* to be nice."

....

Frank's primary occupation now was saloon singer. "The poor guy was literally without a job," said Ava. "He said all he could do was play saloons and crappy nightclubs. He was in a terrible state. His ego and self-esteem was at its lowest ever. And mine was practically at its peak. So it was hell for him and a terrible thing to go through because I had to work. He was such a proud man, such a giving man—to have a woman pay all his bills was a bitch." He signed with William Morris, the agency with the biggest nightclub roster in the business—Milton Berle, Jimmy Durante, Danny Thomas, and Joe E. Lewis, among others, many with roots that went back to the adventurous speakeasy days. Abe Lastfogel, who ran the agency, was a very short man, whose feet dangled when he sat in most chairs, and famous for honesty, cunning, and for being the world's fastest golfer—at the Hillcrest Club in L.A., nine holes in seventy minutes. Abe's right-hand guy was George Wood, who joined the Morris office in 1941 and knew everyone after years of booking talent into the speaks during Prohibition. Wood became Abe's key operator, "specializing in difficult clients and tricky situations," said journalist Frank Rose in his book *The Agency*. "Being pals with Frank Costello made him a natural for the job."

Frank Costello, a rumrunner from the old days, took over for Charles "Lucky" Luciano as boss of New York's top Mafia family when Lucky was deported to Italy. Costello also ran the Copacabana, and had his man "Jimmy Blue Eyes" Alo overseeing construction of the Sands in Vegas, which would open in late 1952 and be managed by Jack Entratter, former bouncer and manager at the Copacabana. On Friday nights, after dinner, Costello and Frank Sinatra would often catch the fights at Madison Square Garden, where Costello had center ringside seats.

Wood was a legendary bachelor, a sharp dresser who loved gambling, women, and having a good time. His apartment at 40 Central Park South had dramatic views of the park and, when Meyer Lansky was having marital problems, the Mafia chieftain became Wood's apartment mate. Wood's job gave him access to the top models and ambitious actresses of the day. For sport, he liked to let his secretary listen in on the intercom when he entertained a starlet on the office sofa.

....

The movie rights that everyone was talking about were for James Jones's *From Here to Eternity.* Published in 1951, the novel followed a group of soldiers at an army post in Hawaii a few months before the Japanese attack on Pearl Harbor. It won the National Book Award and would sell millions over the decade. Columbia Pictures paid $82,000 for movie rights, a large figure for the time, and president Harry Cohn announced that the director was Fred Zinnemann, who would go on to win an Oscar for *High Noon* the following year. Casting was now under way.

Frank Sinatra had read the book and knew it well. He told Abe Lastfogel that he would do anything to get the part of Pvt. Angelo Maggio, even do it for nothing. Abe said he would talk to Fred Zinnemann, who was also a Morris client. In the meantime, Frank should talk with Cohn himself. How could it hurt?

"Anybody who had worked in Hollywood for as long as an hour and a half had heard stories about what an ornery bastard Harry Cohn could be," said Stanley Kramer, who joined Columbia in 1951. He ran Columbia like an Orwellian private police state. He liked to thump a riding crop on his desk for emphasis. It was said he had listening devices on all soundstages and could tune in to any conversation on the set, then boom in over a loudspeaker if he heard anything that displeased him.

"He was tough, feared, ruthless and courageous, unbearably crude, profane, quirky, a hammer-headed power machine who held total financial and physical control over his self-made empire," said Jesse L. Lasky, Jr. "He chewed cigars and relatives. Yet others insisted that a nod or handshake from him was worth more than a contract. Certainly, Cohn's vision was sound. His taste was somehow universal. His success was enormous."

. . . .

Hinting that he had something of major importance to tell him, Frank persuaded Harry Cohn to take a meeting. When Frank arrived at Cohn's office, he had to wait two hours before Harry was available, a standard test the mogul liked to use for difficult visitors.

"Harry, I want to play Maggio," said Frank.

"Look, Frank, that's a stage actor's part." For Cohn, it was nothing personal; it was Frank's crooner image, and he was not good box office. "You're nothing but a fucking hoofer."

"Harry, you've known me for a long time. This part was written about a guy like me. I'm an actor. Give me the chance to act."

Sinatra knew from Vegas sources that Cohn was a gambler, known for carrying big bills in an inside jacket pocket. Frank laid out his cards. "I've been getting $150,000 a picture," Frank said, now bluffing. "Well, you can get Maggio for my expenses."

"You want it that much, Frank?"

"I told you, it was written for me."

"Well, we'll see, Frank," said Cohn. "It's a wild idea."

. . . .

Sinatra called Buddy Adler. When he asked the producer for the role, Buddy was incredulous. "It's an acting part, Frankie," he said, trying vainly to keep a straight face.

"It's *me*," said Frank.

"I'll have to think about it," he told Frank. Adler said screen tests were under way; he was testing five others for the role.

. . . .

Fred Zinnemann wanted Eli Wallach, an esteemed Broadway actor, to play Maggio. For Wallach, this would be his first movie role.

Zinnemann said that if he gave the part to Sinatra, people would think it was a joke.

"When I heard that Eli Wallach was testing for the part, I thought I was dead," said Frank. "He was such a good performer."

....

For most of the year, Frank Sinatra was like a Dale Carnegie honor student. He publicized his determination to win the part, saying that money was no object. He was willing to accept any salary, even none at all.

Harry Cohn recalled something similar back in the late thirties when David O. Selznick and publicist Russell Birdwell conducted the famous nationwide search for an actress to play Scarlett O'Hara in *Gone With the Wind*. These campaigns were usually bogus, but they generated nice advance publicity for a movie. How could it hurt?

....

Artist Paul Clemens was using amateur artist Joan Cohn's studio, a converted coach house on the property of Joan and Harry Cohn. Clemens, who had separated from his wife, was sketching Ava Gardner, also a friend of Joan.

Ava decided to see Joan Cohn and ask a favor. "She was very sweet and arranged for me to see Harry myself," she said. According to Paul Clemens, the meeting occurred over dinner one evening at the Cohn estate. Harry tried to sell Ava on a project. "He had a bunch of second-unit footage on something called *Joseph and His Brethren*, which was shot in Egypt," said Clemens.

Ava was evasive about *Joseph and His Brethren*, but when the conversation turned to *From Here to Eternity*, she said, "You know who's right for that part of Maggio, don't you? That sonofabitch of a husband of mine. He's perfect for it."

"My God, you're right!" said Joan Cohn.

"Oh, Christ, he's no actor, he's a singer," said Harry.

"Same thing people said about me, 'She can't act, she's only pretty,'" said Ava. "Just do me a favor and test him. He's willing to test. And he literally will work for whatever you want to give him."

That seemed to be the subtext to Frank's under- and aboveground campaign in a town where money didn't merely talk; it shouted.

....

In early September, Ava attended the New York premier of *The Snows of Kilimanjaro* without Frank, who was appearing at the Riviera Club in Fort Lee, New Jersey. Later, Ava arrived for the late show and was unhappy to see Marilyn Maxwell in the audience, and Frank appeared to be playing to his old flame. After the show, they got into a heated exchange. She accused him of "putting on a special show for Marilyn. . . . Some of your cute little gestures were intended especially for her."

They battled all the way back to the Hampshire House, where Ava made an unwise exit. "That night, I was lucky I wasn't killed," she later recalled. She ran into Central Park, walked around for an hour, and then decided to take the subway—anywhere. She stayed on a train for an hour to the end of the line. "I had no idea what neighborhood I was in when I got out, and I didn't have a fucking penny," she said. "And it was a long way from the Hampshire House."

She walked the streets and became frightened. She signaled a cab. The driver thought she was a prostitute. "Whoever you are going to, I hope you scrunch it, calling a girl out this time of night," he said. They arrived at the Hampshire House as the sun was coming up, and the doorman said, "Good morning, Mrs. Sinatra." When the doorman paid him, the cabdriver, aghast, realized who his passenger was and tried to apologize. "Don't worry about mistaking me for a whore," said Ava. "You saved my life."

Back in the suite, a relieved Frank made breakfast. "He scrambled eggs better than anybody, cooked them with olive oil, stirred them in a very hot pan, slapped them between soft white bread," said Ava. "He made me an egg sandwich and we never discussed it. He was pleased to see that I was okay and I was pleased to be home."

....

As his recording contract with Columbia terminated, Frank Sinatra owed the label $100,000, which may have been money he borrowed to pay his back taxes. On September 17, 1952, Frank's last recording session at Columbia was a single tune, "Why Try to Change Me Now?" There would be many changes ahead.

....

In October, Frank and Ava met with Hedda Hopper at Frascati's restaurant in Beverly Hills. The columnist reported that she had "never seen a more loving couple. They were extremely considerate and attentive to one another." Ava was preparing to do *Mogambo* in Africa, and "Frank will stay as closely as possible to her. He told us that there were 50 theaters in Africa in which he could play. When the company goes to England, it'll be easy for Frank to be on hand as he has a standing offer from the Palladium. He also wants to tour the provinces. He may do a picture there, being wanted for a film in which he'd play a private eye."

Later that month, Lana Turner asked Frank if she could use the Palm Springs house for a weekend. She'd had a big fight with her boyfriend. Frank said fine. When Ava heard about the arrangement, she and Frank had a heated discussion, followed by a scorching fight. This time, Frank took off in their car, screaming, "I'm going to Palm Springs to fuck Lana Turner."

Ava called Bappie. "Pick me up, we're going to Palm Springs," she said. Ava drove like it was a getaway car. "But I was going to catch Frank with Lana." At the house, the curtains were drawn. Ava went to the back door and rang the doorbell. Ben Cole, who was Ava's and Lana's business manager, opened the door, and there were Lana and Frank, sitting at the little bar, having a drink with Ben.

Feeling like a fool, Ava joined the party. Then she looked at Frank and said, "I thought you'd come down here to fuck Lana."

That did it. Lana affected her own MGM-style exit and drove off with

Ben. Frank was furious. He said he was going to find Lana and fuck her, and the battle raged. This was the end. Ava decided to take her stuff from the house. "Frank grabbed it and threw everything into the driveway," she said. "Then he called the cops on me. Can you believe that!?"

Lana returned to retrieve some things and found a police car parked in front of the house, with Frank screaming, "Get her out of here! Get her out!"

"The cops came, saw we were having a drunken battle, and tried to get us to calm down," said Ava. "Then Bappie and I drove back home."

The battle of the stars made the papers. "I was off duty and there's nothing on the record about a disturbance," Palm Springs police chief August Kettmann told the press. When asked if Sinatra allegedly ordered his beautiful film actress wife out of their home, Kettmann said, "Well, if John Smith and his wife had a fight at their house I wouldn't feel privileged to tell you of any discussion that went on in their bedroom between Mr. and Mrs. Smith and our officers. I know nothing about it."

Ava told friends, "We've had these little tiffs before."

. . . .

On October 28, Frank and Ava appeared arm in arm at a political rally for presidential candidate Adlai Stevenson at the Palladium Ballroom in Hollywood. POLITICS HEALS AVA GARDNER, SINATRA RIFT was the headline next day. Ava introduced Frank to the crowd as a "wonderful, wonderful guy. I'm a great fan of him myself." "It was just one of those family squabbles," said Hank Sanicola, Frank's manager. "You know, it's their own business. But they've made up."

On November 7, Frank and Ava celebrated their first wedding anniversary on a Boeing Stratocruiser en route to Kenya, where Ava would be starring in *Mogambo* with Clark Gable and Grace Kelly. Frank gave Ava a diamond ring (for which she got the bill). "It was quite an occasion for me," she said. "I had been married twice, but never for a whole year."

. . . .

In Africa, Frank brooded. Ava hated his damn suffering. Was there no end to it? He kept sending cables, signed "Maggio," to Cohn and Adler. She followed up with another call to Cohn. "You've got to test Frank for that part," she said. "If he doesn't get it, he'll kill himself."

Frank flew back to New York for a club date, then returned to Kenya, where he received a cable from Buddy Adler saying he could do a screen test, no mention of expenses. Ava paid for the ticket. On November 14, 1952, Adler was astonished to see Frank in his office thirty-six hours after sending the telegram. He handed him a copy of the script. "I don't need it," said Frank. He knew the lines cold.

A few days later, Harry Cohn called his wife, Joan, and asked her to come see the screen tests for Eli Wallach and Frank Sinatra. "He sat me down . . . in a projection room and he ran the two screen tests," she said. "Not once, not twice, but three times. One, then the other, one, and then the other. I sat there and watched them three times."

"Well you've got a nice Jewish boy and you've got a nice Italian boy, Harry," said his wife. "What's your problem?"

Screenwriter Daniel Taradash thought that Wallach was too muscular, too self-sufficient for the vulnerable Maggio, but Wallach's screen test was excellent, and all of the production minds agreed that the actor should be signed.

When Wallach learned the film conflicted with a commitment he had made with Elia Kazan to appear in *Camino Real,* a Tennessee Williams play on Broadway, he declined the role of Maggio.

Harry called Frank in Montreal, where the singer had a nightclub date. He was now Maggio.

"Sinatra won it by default," said Cohn biographer Bob Thomas.

. . . .

After Frank took the production plane from Kenya to Nairobi and headed back to Hollywood, Ava fell into the arms of Frank "Bunny" Allen, the professional hunter who advised on wild animal scenes on the *Mogambo* shoot. "Ava couldn't be alone," location manager Eva Monley told Ava's biographer Lee Server. "That was the big thing with her. Something to do with her childhood or something, but she didn't like to be alone. That was, I think, why she had so many affairs.

"She'd bring someone back to her tent, say, 'Hey, come on, have a drink with me, I'm bored all by myself,'" said Monley, who worked on three Ava movies and, years later, befriended her in London. "She liked to have lots of men around her. She just enjoyed them. She got rid of one, and she'd go find another one. She had a great time with Frank and then he was gone, and she found a prop man and he was rather good. I only know because I was in charge of the tents and I'd come by and she'd say, 'Monley, come over here, I've got to tell you something . . . I was with this man . . .' It was crazy, the whole thing. But she enjoyed herself. She just lived life from day to day."

In late November, Ava learned that she was pregnant. It came as a shock to a woman who had been told that she would probably never have children. "I had what they called a tipped and infantile uterus," she told journalist Lawrence Grobel years later. "I could have had an operation but I never did. And I never took any precaution, no birth control."

For a multitude of reasons, she decided on an abortion before Sinatra returned. Director John Ford, a devout Catholic, tried to talk Ava out of it, but a plan was soon under way. MGM issued a press release saying that the star had flown to London for treatment of a tropical infection, nothing serious, and she would return to the movie location in a couple of days. Even Sinatra believed the ruse. "The time wasn't right," said Ava. "It wasn't easy—they made me see a shrink first."

Frank learned the truth when he returned to Kenya for Christmas with Ava—and she became pregnant again. She decided to have another abortion. "Frank didn't know the first time, and found out right after the second," she said. "But he knew it wasn't meant to be, not with the lives we were living."

They were in a volatile relationship, and Ava was just coming into her own. The studio would be angry. Love goddesses didn't have babies, said L. B. Mayer. In addition to professional concerns, with Bunny Allen in the scenario, there might also be paternity issues.

"I'm very definitely pro-abortion," Ava told Lawrence Grobel. "In those days, it was a tremendous step because it was illegal; you were putting your health and your life in danger. I just never had this great yearning that I've got to have a child."

....

For Harry Cohn, casting Sinatra was a win/win decision. It was a bargain, of course. In addition, the screen test revealed that inside this crooner was an extraordinary actor trying to get out. There was also the publicity value of surprise casting—Deborah Kerr, whose career had largely been playing aloof British ladies at MGM, was cast as Karen Holmes, the officer's wife, who slept with enlisted men (it took three weeks of coaching to tame Kerr's British accent), and now Sinatra, a singer in his first real dramatic role.

There has always thrived a conspiracy theory about how Frank Sinatra won the role of Maggio, reinforced in 1969 when *The Godfather* was published. Mario Puzo's novel (and the movie to follow) included a popular singer who got his big break through Mafia intimidations, complete with a severed horse head in a reluctant producer's bed. This whole Eli Wallach tale—might it have been just a cover story for Harry Cohn so that he could pretend to agonize over a decision, when Frank had made him an offer he couldn't refuse? Delicious.

Ava often talked about how charming Frank could be. But he also had difficulty restraining a violent temper. Frank craved moving easefully among the social and political elite, but he surrounded himself with thugs and associated with underworld hoods. Sam Giancana, the head of the Chicago family, and Johnny Rosselli, the Mafia's man in Hollywood, were visitors at Twin Palms in the Springs. Rosselli was often seen at the best tables at Romanoff's and Perino's, with starlets as well as with Harry Cohn.

Rosselli and Cohn frequented the Santa Anita racetrack together, and wore identical "blood brother" ruby rings, made by Rosselli's jeweler.

Years later, when George Jacobs asked Sinatra if Giancana had leaned on Rosselli to lean on Cohn for the part of Maggio, Frank gave his valet a big grin. "Hey, I got that part through my own fucking *talent*," he said with a wink.

....

During the *Mogambo* shoot, Ava and Grace Kelly became close, particularly in the painful weeks surrounding Ava's first abortion. Grace delighted in Ava's ribald sense of humor and bawdiness. The movie location had many tall Watusi warriors who had been hired as extras, wearing their breechclouts. The actresses were walking alone one day, and Ava said to Grace, "I wonder if their cocks are as big as people say? Have you ever seen a black cock?"

"Stop that, don't talk like that," said Grace, the girl from Main Line Philadelphia.

With that, Ava pulled up the breechclout of one of the Watusis, whose large member flopped out. The warrior gave a big grin. Ava turned to Grace. "Frank's is bigger than that," she said.

....

After the holidays, Frank returned to the States for nightclub work, and to prepare for the filming of *From Here to Eternity* in Hawaii. Ava went to London to do *Mogambo* interiors. She took a flat and came to know the city that would eventually be her home. On vacation, she visited friends in Madrid, where she met another bullfighter at a party. "The first time I met Luis Miguel Dominguín," said Ava, "it was the same old story all over again: I knew without a doubt that he was for me."

Luis Miguel Dominguín, Spain's top matador, was a lithe, handsome man who came from a wealthy family of bullfighters. He was tall and graceful, with piercing, watchful dark eyes, which he liked to move without turning his head. He was twenty-six—four years younger than Ava—and had not fought for over a year, following a severe stomach wound, but was thinking of returning to the bullfight wars.

Luis Miguel Dominguín smiled and bowed. "No English," he said. Ava smiled back. "No Español." Language would not be a problem. And there'd be no stupid poems this time.

. . . .

The Hawaii filming of *From Here to Eternity* began in April 1953. The picture was wrapped up in forty-one days. Frank, Montgomery Clift, and Burt Lancaster spent a lot of time together drinking and crying on each other's shoulders. For Frank, loving well was the best revenge for a career on the rocks. He had a martini bar in his room. "We'd sit and chat about the day's work and he would try his nightly call to Ava, who was in Spain," said Lancaster. "In those days in Spain, if you lived *next door* to your friends, you couldn't get them on the telephone, let alone trying to get them on the phone from Hawaii. He never got through. Not one night."

"Sinatra was an actor with far greater range than most people noticed," said Stanley Kramer. "His fame as a singer and entertainer was so great that many assumed he could do nothing else. Not so."

On the last day of filming, with Harry Cohn visiting the set, Sinatra disagreed so vehemently with others on how a scene should be done that Cohn sent him away before he'd even seen the final rushes. The old attitude—an angry form of confidence—was reasserting itself. But Frank sensed he had a hit, and he returned to the mainland, where he would wake up and find himself famous all over again.

When the movie opened on August 5, 1953, in New York, it did record business at the Capitol Theatre on Broadway. Frank received rave reviews. Richard Watts in the *New York Post*: "Instead of exploiting a personality, he proves he is an actor by playing the luckless Maggio with a kind of doomed gaiety that is both real and immensely touching."

When Frank's daughter Nancy was writing her memoir, Burt Lancaster told her, "Your father's fervor, his anger, his bitterness had something to do with the character of 'Maggio,' but also with what he had gone through in the last number of years: a sense of defeat, and the whole world crashing in on him, his marriage to Ava going to pieces—all of these things caused this ferment in him, and they all came out in that performance. You knew that this was a raging little man who was, at the same time, a *good* human being."

"The movie also shifted the way he was viewed by large numbers of men," said journalist Pete Hamill. "Many seemed to merge Sinatra with Maggio, and when the thin, brave character of the movie is beaten to death by the character played by Ernest Borgnine, it was a kind of symbolic expiation. Sinatra had shown an aspect of his character that many had never witnessed before in a Sinatra movie or heard singing from jukeboxes. Sinatra/Maggio had lost. But in death, he had won."

. . . .

Advance word on his performance in *Eternity* "confirmed to Frank that he had scored a great comeback," said Earl Wilson. "His crowd of hangers-on irritated Ava, who could remember when many of them were ignoring him and she was picking up the tabs. It was back-slapping time, and Ava saw her old man, as she called him, getting to be impossible to live with because of his ego." And his entourage.

When Frank and Ava were checking in at the Ritz in New York later that year, the elevator man said, "Oh, Mr. Sinatra, last time you were here it was with Miss Kerr." Uh-oh, thought Ava, the costars have been here together. "Frank could have killed the man," she said. "And of course he lied outright to me. Once you lose your faith in what the man you love is telling you, there is nothing left to save."

. . . .

That summer, Ava started filming *Knights of the Round Table* in London with old beau Robert Taylor. She took leave to accompany Frank on a European series of concerts. In early 1953, the IRS had filed a lien for $109,997 against him. Now Frank, riding high again, was just trying to make an honest million. They both needed some time together to heal a few wounds. There had been more than a few infidelities.

Frank's tour was greeted with great indifference.

In Rome, Milan, and Scandinavia, the theaters were half-empty. At the Empire Theatre, the largest two-tier auditorium in England, with a seating capacity of 2,350, the balcony was closed; Frank pulled about four hundred people. In Naples, halfway through Frank's first song, fans started yelling, "Ava! Ava! Ava!" Unbeknownst to Frank, the theater manager had announced that Ava would join him on stage—totally bogus—and he raised the ticket price accordingly. Ava remained back at the hotel. The audience booed and whistled. Frank walked off the stage. After a delay, Frank finished the show. But Frank's comeback had not yet reached Europe, where he found himself playing to half-empty halls and jeering fans who considered him Mr. Ava Gardner.

They returned to London, where Frank departed, insisting he had to rehearse for a date at Bill Miller's Riviera in New Jersey. Rehearse? Since when did Frank fly across oceans to rehearse a nightclub act?

Ava lingered in London, visited friends in Madrid—where she encountered Luis Miguel Domínguín again—and then she flew to New York, where Frank failed to show when she arrived. She went to the Hampshire House, refused his calls, and ignored his opening at Miller's Riviera. At this point, Dolly Sinatra arranged an intervention, inviting both parties to a nice Italian meal in Hoboken. They made up.

Frank returned to the Riviera, where he sang every song to Ava at the late show. But then, after a few drinks, as the conversation turned toward indiscretions of the past, Ava could see that the old black arrogance was back (if it had ever left). "Don't cut the corners too close on me, Baby," said Frank. "That's the way it's gonna be from now on."

. . . .

In October, Frank opened at the Sands, where Jack Entratter—the former manager at the Copa—treated him royally, escorting him to the Presidential Suite, with three bedrooms and a pool. The Vegas crowd loved Frank. He packed the casino with high rollers. This was no Naples; there was no crowd calling "Ava! Ava! Ava!" Louella Parsons, covering Frank's opening, asked him what was going on. "No, Ava doesn't love me anymore," he said. "If she did, she'd be here where she belongs—with me. Instead she's in Palm Springs having a wonderful time."

On October 8, Ava went to the *Mogambo* premiere in Los Angeles, then returned to Palm Springs, where she had rented a small place of her own. "I sat there and just suffered for a couple of weeks," she said, "until I was strong enough to face it."

Frank called from the Presidential Suite one day, announcing that he was in bed with another woman. "And he made it plain that if he was going to be constantly accused of infidelity when he was innocent, there had to come a time when he'd decide he might as well be guilty," said Ava. "But for me, it was a chilling moment. I was deeply hurt. I knew then that we had reached a crossroads. Not because we had fallen out of love, but because our love had so battered and bruised us that we couldn't stand it anymore."

Ava called Howard Strickling at MGM. On October 23, the studio issued a "joint announcement," saying that Frank and Ava were separating. "Ava Gardner and Frank Sinatra stated today that having reluctantly exhausted every effort to reconcile their differences, they could find no mutual basis on which to continue their marriage. Both expressed deep regret and great respect for each other. Their separation is final and Miss Gardner will seek a divorce."

. . . .

"The breakup after less than two years of marriage was due to the facts that Ava was on the verge of a nervous breakdown, that Frank was suffering the strain of career worries, and that he was domineering and Ava wouldn't accept his bossy treatment," said Earl Wilson.

For Frank, after the MGM announcement, it gradually began to sink in that this was not just another one of their battles. He had deep regrets for what he had wrought. In the words of Ava biographer Lee Server, Frank "had gradually and painfully begun to understand that this was not like the feuds and separations of the past. The confidence that had fueled his taunting assault from Las Vegas went away. He took stock, humbled himself, and called with protestations, apologies. Ava made herself unavailable, or talked to him briefly, bluntly. She had been angry, stubborn, and cruel even, many times in the past, but now, he found, there was a cold intractability that had never been there before. A fear of actually losing her began to invade him like a terrible spreading fever."

On November 16, it was announced that Ava would star in *The Barefoot Contessa* with Humphrey Bogart. Principal shooting would begin in Rome in January.

Ava had to save herself. Her career was the net below the wire now. As for relationships, Ava had no trouble attracting men. In most ways, it was a lot easier than her very complicated marriage to Sinatra. She had to make it on her own now. It wasn't a matter of career over personal considerations. It was survival.

Sinatra was devastated. He turned morose; friends worried about him. He was staying with Jimmy Van Heusen in New York on November 18 when the songwriter returned to the apartment at 2:00 A.M. and found Frank sprawled on the floor with his left wrist slashed. Jimmy rushed him to Mount Sinai Hospital, where Frank spent two days recovering, then, saying that there had been an accident with some broken glass, he returned to work. Was it a cry for help, or another theatrical Sicilian tantrum? This time, Ava was nowhere to be found.

To protect their investment, the William Morris office assigned George Wood to baby-sit Sinatra. "When Frank ate, I ate," said the agent. "When he slept, I slept, when he felt like walking, I walked with him. When he took a haircut, I took a haircut."

On the *Colgate Comedy Hour with Eddie Cantor* later that week, Sinatra put his arm around Eddie Fisher's shoulders, and the singer noticed thin cuts on Frank's left wrist. "Cuts he made when supposedly he'd tried to commit suicide over Ava Gardner," said Fisher, "the one woman in his life he couldn't control."

. . . .

In late November, Ava left for Rome nearly two months before she was needed to film *The Barefoot Contessa*. For Ava, this was not just another trip to a movie location. It was the first step on a permanent getaway. In Rome, she would be working with Humphrey Bogart as her leading man in the film. But, within a few weeks, Frank would learn that Ava's leading man after hours was Luis Miguel Dominguín.

⊰ 8 ⊱

The Barefoot Diva

Humphrey Bogart's closest friend in Hollywood was Frank Sinatra. It was a friendship begun in the forties, when Sinatra was breaking into movies and Bogie's star was rising under the guidance of Mark Hellinger. Although Bogie was fifteen years older than Frank, the parallels were remarkable. They were neighbors in the upscale Holmby Hills section of L.A., about the same size, small in stature, losing their hair, and very like-minded. They felt, even as public figures, they didn't have to explain their behavior to anyone, least of all the press. "The only thing you owe the public is a good performance," Bogart said, famously. They both enjoyed a drink. Bogie's favorite maxim: "The whole world is three drinks behind and it's high time it caught up." When Bogie's first and only son was born, Frank hosted the paternity party at Romanoff's. "Bogie was furious that I was giving Frank a hard time," said Ava. "He loved Frank like a brother."

At Christmas, Frank flew to Spain to try to win Ava back, to no avail. Ava was having a passionate affair with Luis Miguel Dominguín. "Ava had a thing for matadors," said Robert Evans. "They weren't movie stars, they were gods who played with death." Frank returned to Hollywood quietly, managing to elude the press, and started hanging out at the Bogarts'. "I don't know what it is about this joint; it seems to be a kind of home for him," said Bogie. "We seem to be parent symbols or something. Or maybe it's just that he likes a place where we can relax completely."

"It was not a great career time for Frank," said Lauren Bacall. "He was lonely and still in love with Ava Gardner—I do believe it was the first and only time that someone else had done the leaving. . . . He was a restless man, totally incapable of being alone."

Bogie loved to tease. "You don't think he comes to see *me*, do you?" he said to Bacall.

. . . .

The Bogart residence, purchased from Hedy Lamarr, was a long two-story white brick structure, hidden from the street by heavy foliage. There was a well-tended lawn, a swimming pool and patio, a tennis court. Most of the living was done in the library, a paneled room with bookcases, a bar, comfortable chairs, and a screen that could be let down for the showing of movies. One of Bogie's favorites was *A Star Is Born,* starring Janet Gaynor and Fredric March, which he liked to show during the Christmas season (his birthday was Christmas Day). Director Richard Brooks, a friend and frequent visitor, recalled being with Bogie and Frank as they watched the movie together with tears streaming down their faces at the fate of Norman Maine, a matinee idol down on his luck. After an emcee introduces Norman's wife, Vicki Lester, by her professional name, she reminds an adoring audience of her indebtedness to her deceased husband. "Hello, everybody," she says, "this is Mrs. Norman Maine."

"I remember Frank and Bogie, both of them, weeping, and wondering, why are they crying? I'm moved, very moved by the picture, but why are they crying? And they cry every time they see the movie," said Brooks. "Why? Something has touched their own personal experience. They're identifying with these two people. Very deeply. Which has to do with their own vulnerability. So when I look at Frank Sinatra and he's standing there like he's got on a bulletproof vest, untouchable, remote, I don't *see* him that way. He's a very vulnerable man. He can be hurt easily."

For Frank, the saga of Norman Maine, who committed suicide, must have been especially meaningful. Like Norman, Frank was married to a big star—he was Mr. Ava Gardner to his critics—and the scars on his left wrist were not completely healed. The irony of Frank's situation was further intensified by a role he had failed to land the previous summer— Norman Maine, in the remake of *A Star Is Born,* starring Judy Garland. Filming had begun on October 12.

Sid Luft, producer and husband of Garland, had met with Frank before he left to do *From Here to Eternity.* "He was a great friend of ours, an old and close friend of Judy's," said Luft. "Frank wanted to do it. I thought he and Judy would be great together." Luft met with director George Cukor, screenwriter Moss Hart, and studio head Jack Warner. "I brought up Frank's name, but at the time he was considered poison. His records weren't selling. As a matter of fact, I went down to see him when he was at the Cocoanut Grove—must have been about thirty people in the crowd, that's all. And he was having problems with Ava. . . . Frank was going over to Africa to settle up with her; when he came back he wanted to do *A Star Is Born.* But the name Sinatra was taboo . . . nobody liked it except Judy and myself."

. . . .

Along with his reputation as a hard drinking, no-nonsense personality who gave indelible performances in such films as *The Maltese Falcon, Casablanca,* and *The African Queen,* Humphrey Bogart was also famous for his outwardly ideal marriage to Lauren Bacall, his fourth wife, who gave him two children. Bogie was twenty-five years older than Bacall. When director Howard Hawks introduced them to each other on the set of the 1944 film *To Have and Have Not,* it was the beginning of a beautiful friendship. "I saw your test," Bogie said to the nineteen-year-old virgin, who was making her first movie. "We'll have a lot of fun together."

Their romance was one of the most celebrated Hollywood idylls of the time. It came on the heels of heavy drinking and bitter quarrels between Bogie and his previous wife, actress Mayo Methot, whom he called

"Sluggy." (On their fifth wedding anniversary, Bogie sent her a hand-carved rolling pin.) Bacall and Bogart married in the Ohio home of author Louis Bromfield, one of Bogie's closest friends, on May 21, 1945. Bacall—born Betty Perske in the Bronx, New York—was trim, and she matched Bogart's five-foot-eight-inch height. She had "wide-apart eyes that seemed always to be looking at you from a pillow," wrote Bogie's pal Nathaniel Benchley. When her father vanished, her mother restored her family name of Bacal (later adding an *l*), and a press agent thought Lauren was more intriguing than Betty.

Bogie drank only scotch or martinis. Bacall drank Jack Daniel's a few years before Frank would switch to it with vigor.

....

In early January 1954, Bogie arrived in Rome, where Ava greeted him warmly. They were meeting for the first time. "My, you look fit and as trim as Sinatra," she said.

"Nobody's as trim as Sinatra," said Bogie, the consummate teaser. "And how come he's not here?"

"Aren't you being just a bit nosy?" asked Ava, arching an eyebrow.

"I'll never figure you broads out," said Bogie. "Half the world's female population would throw themselves at Frank's feet, and here you are flouncing around with guys who wear capes and little ballerina slippers." The battle was on.

....

The Barefoot Contessa was written by director Joseph L. Mankiewicz, who had written and directed the highly successful 1950 film *All About Eve*, a cynical idyll about backstage lives in the New York theater. That movie had received six Academy Awards. *Contessa* was intended to be a scenario à clef about backstage lives in Hollywood, with thinly disguised caricatures of Howard Hughes; his press agent, Johnny Meyer; and screen goddess Rita Hayworth. Ava was cast as Maria Vargas, a flamenco dancer who becomes a superglamorous star after being discovered by Harry Dawes, played by Bogie, a washed-up director newly on the wagon.

This was to be a formative movie for Ava—dubbed "the world's most beautiful animal" for the occasion by the publicity department.

At their first meeting, Ava admitted to Mankiewicz that she had not read the script, only an outline. "When this thing came up with Frank, I was frantic," she said. "I just had to get out of Hollywood now—right now—or I'd blow my top." Mank liked what Ava brought to the role, a Spanish peasant girl who could command men with a glance. While Ava might claim that she was insecure as an actress, she never *looked* insecure on the screen. She had what director George Cukor called "sexual elegance."

． ． ． ． ． ． ． ． ． ． ． ．

After checking into a hotel, Ava called David Hanna, the movie's publicist, at three in the morning. "I want to look at apartments," she said. "I hate hotels. I want to move right away."

Hanna said that apartments couldn't be visited so early in the morning, and that she would have to wait until later. Ava screamed, "But I want to move right now!"

She may have left Frank behind, but Ava carried the Sinatra effect with her. "Early on, Ava was fun, wide open," said Bob Thomas, AP's veteran Hollywood reporter. "Then along came Frank, who was alert to handling reporters. Ava learned how to be difficult from the master." In addition to being hostile toward the press, Ava was much more demanding now, all diva all the time, softened with a "darling" here and there.

Bogie said the MGM girls were so pampered, so catered to, that they were totally spoiled and self-indulgent. Ava had been a movie star since her late teens. Was she spoiled? Of course. "As the Queen of England is spoiled," explained actress Evelyn Keyes on how divas function. "Would the Queen know how to live like 'ordinary folk' after living in a palace all her life?" There are times, indeed, when you must act like the diva your audience *wants* you to be. To have diva allure, divas often make demands just to be demanding.

Ava had an entourage now, something else she had learned from Sinatra and his traveling audience. Trailing behind Ava was Bappie, a wardrobe person, a couple of makeup people, and a few gofers, who carried a record player and stacks of flamenco and Sinatra records for milady's dressing room.

David Hanna, in his *Ava: A Portrait of a Star,* said that a production assistant would help her first thing in the morning. "Have him here at nine," said Ava. She then called Mankiewicz, insisting that if she couldn't move out of the hotel right then, she would go back to Hollywood. A large apartment, complete with untuned piano in the living room, was quickly found. Her entourage soon expanded to include a driver, her personal maid, a chef, and kitchen maid.

....

Lauren Bacall was back in California with the kids and would be arriving in a couple of weeks. Principal photography would begin on January 11. The shooting would take at least three months. Ava still hadn't read the screenplay.

Bogie was traveling with Verita Thompson, his personal assistant and mistress of twelve years. He had met Verita at the wrap party for *Casablanca* back in 1942, when she was a struggling starlet and a wig maker. Bogie called her "Pete," after her marriage name at the time: Peterson. She had a valid reason to be around Bogart—he wore a toupee and she was a wig maker—and he eventually put her on his permanent staff so that her continued presence could be accounted for.

To inquiring reporters, Bogie would explain, "That's Pete, my executive secretary and mistress." Most interviewers either took his answer as a joke or went on to more important and less personal questions, or they were so startled by it that they hurriedly changed the subject. In any case, that answer wouldn't be printed or even pursued by the press in the fifties.

Verita dined regularly at the Bogart home, helping with tasks, giving young Steve haircuts. Bogie said it would raise suspicions if she didn't act as an employee normally would. "And so I became more familiar with Betty and the two children than I wanted to under the circumstances," she said.

Lauren questioned Bogie about Verita, but she didn't probe deeply. They both knew that, in an era when infidelity could ruin a career, the studios and the stars collaborated to keep such stories away from the press or public scrutiny. Look at the trouble Ingrid Bergman, his old costar in *Casablanca,* had gotten herself into. And now Frank and Ava.

"Bogie told Lauren he had to have someone work with him, and the fact that I could do his hair, too—which was vital to his public appearances—was to his advantage," said Verita. "Anyway, for whatever reason, Betty was always a little condescending toward me. Perhaps it was owing to my own attitude toward her. I had always considered her an opportunistic interloper, and when I got to know her better, I amended my opinion. I considered her a *pretentious,* opportunistic interloper."

. . . .

Bogie considered himself an actor, not a movie star. Like Frank, he hated signing pictures—"movie star stuff," he called it. He never had an acting lesson. "I thank God I'm not one of those new breed—the method actors who have to live the part," he said. He had a photographic mind, could learn pages of dialogue with one reading. He never took a script home to study. He showed up on time, asked for a run-through before a scene was shot, and knew not only his lines but also those of everyone else.

He had enormous powers of concentration, which he attributed to his early stage experience in New York, where he learned on the job. There he loved the sounds of the city, staying out of cabs. "New York is a place for walking," he said, "not like Hollywood, where you can walk your ass off and get nowhere—that's because Hollywood *is* nowhere."

He called Ava's entourage "her tribe." During one encounter, he looked at the cluster around Ava and said, "Let me get a running start toward the set. I don't want to get trampled by your entourage. And if I waited until it passed, I wouldn't get to the set until Thursday."

"I'll give you a ten-second head start," said Ava. "Then you're on your own." Divas quickly learn repartee.

. . . .

In late January, Lauren Bacall arrived, carrying a large coconut cake for Ava, from Frank—a delayed birthday tradition, and a peace offering. The cake was delivered the morning of Bacall's departure from New York in a large white box, which Bacall had to hand-carry from New York through London for an overnight and then on to Rome, where Bogie was waiting at the airport. The next day, Bogie told Ava about the cake, but she did nothing.

Two days later, Lauren decided to take it to her before it went stale. "I didn't know her and felt very awkward," said Bacall. Verita went along to Ava's dressing room, where her entourage now included Dominguín, who had flown in from Madrid. "I brought this cake for you—Frank sent it to me in New York, he thought you'd like it," said Bacall. Ava said nothing. She pointed to a table, where Lauren placed the cake. "Ava pushed it aside and didn't even open the box," said Verita. "The action was so uncharacteristic of Ava that we figured it signaled the end of her relationship with Frank."

. . . .

Born in Madrid in 1926, Luis Miguel González Lucas adopted his father's bullfighting nickname, Dominguín, and became a leading toreador, who would achieve even greater renown when he and his brother-in-law, Antonio Ordóñez, fought in a series of bullfights in 1959, chronicled by Ernest Hemingway in *The Dangerous Summer*. His family had large landholdings, and he had established a fine business as a breeder of bulls. Luis drove a custom Cadillac, and he had his pick of women; he did not need to be seen with Ava to achieve fame. "He's not looking for publicity like so

many of the men over here," said Ava. "He's willing to stay in the background and that's not easy for a man."

Dominguín was trying to learn English while recovering from a wound
and tending to Ava. "If I was part of Luis Miguel's convalescence," said
Ava, "he was part of mine after the goring Frank and I had given each
other."

············

Although Ava would laugh at Bogie's jokes, and outwardly they remained
cordial, there was an undercurrent of hostility between the two stars.
Bogie thought little of Ava as an actress, and he complained of her habit
of checking her makeup and hair right before each take. "She gives me
nothing," he said. "I have to lift her every time." If he felt a scene was not
playing right, Bogart would muff a line deliberately. Ava knew what was
going on, but never uttered a complaint to Mankiewicz. "Bogie knew
every trick in the book to fuck up a scene and get a retake," she said.

Bogie often made remarks about Ava's personal life when she was
within hearing distance. If there was a newspaper reference to Luis
Miguel or to Sinatra, he made certain that it was brought to her attention.
He could be brutal. "I don't know why you want to two-time Frank with
a goddamn fruit," he said. "I never had you down as a dame who'd go for
a pantywaist."

"I still admired the sonofabitch on the screen, but I just didn't like him
very much as a man—and he had no respect for me at all," said Ava. "Luis
Miguel was definitely no fruit, I can tell you that. Bogie knew it, too." She
grew resentful. When not needed on the set, she did not fraternize; she
retired to her portable dressing room and slept. Bogart found this "stand-
offishness" annoying, but that is the way of a diva. The crew never lost
their awe of her.

He called Ava "the Grabtown gypsy," after the Carolina hamlet where
she was born, and said the reason she didn't drink with him was because
her southern accent slipped out when she had a few rounds, and her bullfighter admirers would discover that she was just a "li'l hillbilly girl."

"That's what attracts 'em, honey chile," said Ava.

"That's nuts," Bogie grumbled. "One Sinatra is worth a dozen bull-fighters."

. . . .

During a break in the filming, Bogie met Ingrid Bergman, his costar from *Casablanca,* whose romance with Rossellini had caused such scandal in 1949. "You were the top of the heap," he said, berating her for throwing away her career. "You were a great star, and now look at you. What are you now?"

"A happy woman," she replied.

. . . .

In the early months of 1954, tension mounted as both Ava and Frank were nominated for Oscars—Ava for Best Actress in *Mogambo;* Frank for Best Supporting Actor in *From Here to Eternity.*

According to George Jacobs, Frank went to the Good Shepherd Church in Beverly Hills for the month before the Oscars. "He didn't even see any girls that much, he wanted God's help so bad," said the valet.

Eternity won eight Oscars, tying the record held by *Gone With the Wind.* All five leading players were nominated for Academy Awards. Harry Cohn had electrified the industry with a film in black and white at the normal screen ratio at a time when studios were experimenting with wide screens and three dimensions. The movie became the biggest moneymaker in Columbia history.

"*From Here to Eternity* provided a golden touch to the careers of all the principals connected with it, especially Sinatra, whose Academy Award as supporting actor dramatized his conquest of failure," said Cohn biographer Bob Thomas. "Ava paid for the ticket that enabled Frank to fight for the role of Angelo Maggio," said Sheilah Graham. "It proved to be a good investment, especially for Frank, who accepted a total salary of $8,000 for a performance that won him the Oscar. After that, there was only one way for him to go. Up."

Ava lost to Audrey Hepburn, who starred in *Roman Holiday* with Gregory Peck. During the making of *Contessa,* Bogie developed a small cough, which became more noticeable as the shooting progressed. Tricks aside, the cough ruined many takes, a prophetic indicator of the cancer that would claim him in less than three years.

....

After *Contessa,* Ava and Dominguín returned to Madrid, where they lived in a small hotel, "he and I in one room and Bappie in another." One evening, Ava started to experience pain, "like the worst menstrual pains only low in the stomach." At the hospital, the diagnosis was kidney stones.

A cot was put in the room for Luis Miguel, who stayed with her around the clock, eating all his meals with Ava for two weeks.

Bappie and Dominguín had been to a bullfight one afternoon and came back with Mary and Ernest Hemingway. As they entered the hospital room, Ava was on the phone to Hollywood, talking in a commanding voice about a movie that would eventually be called *Love Me or Leave Me.* Journalist A. E. Hotchner, traveling with the novelist, described the scene in his memoir *Papa Hemingway.*

"I don't give a goddamn how many scripts you send," said Ava, "I am not, repeat, not, *not, NOT* going to play Ruth Etting!"

Another singing role, just what she didn't want. Ava was still smoldering from the miming scenes in *Show Boat.* "I stand there mouthing words like a goddamn goldfish while you're piping in some goddamn dubbed voice! I said a dramatic part, for Christ's sake, and you send me Ruth Etting!" shouted Ava. "It's no wonder I've got this attack. I ought to send you the bill."

Ava hung up, smiled beautifully, and held her hand out to her visitor. "Hello, Ernest," she said in a soft, lyrical voice. "Sit here on the bed, Papa, and talk to me. I'm absolutely floored you could come."

They visited for a couple of hours, drinking and chatting. He called her "Daughter," which reminded her of her father, who always called her that.

"Are you going to live in Spain?" asked Hemingway.

"Yes. I sure am. I'm just a country girl at heart. I don't like New York or Paris. I'd love to live here permanently. What have I got to go back to? I have no car, no house, nothing. Sinatra's got nothing either. All I ever got out of any of my marriages was the two years Artie Shaw financed on an analyst's couch."

Hemingway said analysts spooked him, "because I've yet to meet one who had a sense of humor."

"You mean, you've never had an analyst?"

"Sure I have," said Hemingway. "Portable Corona number three. That's been my analyst. I'll tell you, even though I am not a believer in the Analysis, I spend a hell of a lot of time killing animals and fish so I won't kill myself."

"That's too deep for me, Papa."

Doctors and their friends came by Ava's room to visit all of the celebrities, "puffing their cigars, drinking, looking at me and saying, 'Oh, isn't she beautiful,'" said Ava. "It was like a fucking nightclub!"

....

Later that month, when Ava left the hospital, she, Papa, and Dominguín drove to a bull-breeding ranch in the high country near El Escorial, where Luis Miguel worked with some yearling calves. Hemingway biographer Carlos Baker described Papa as "pleasurably captivated to be photographed in the distinguished company of a famous film actress and the best bullfighter alive." Ava had appeared in two of Hemingway's movie adaptations—*The Killers,* which Papa considered his only good movie, and *The Snows of Kilimanjaro* (which Hemingway called "The Snows of Zanuck"). Ava stood with Papa at the ring wall and watched Dominguín work. "He's a lovely man, isn't he?" Ava said.

"Are you serious about him?" asked Hemingway.

"How do I know? I speak no Spanish, he speaks no English, and so we haven't been able to communicate yet."

"Don't worry," said Papa, "you've communicated what counts."

....

Ava was suspended by MGM that summer during a contract spat. She took a cottage on Lake Tahoe with Dominguín to establish Nevada residence and get a divorce from Sinatra. Introducing the bullfighter to visitors, she suggested drinks. "Get a piece of ice," she told Miguel. Laughing, she added, "That's not the same as a piece of *ass*." She explained, "He's trying to learn English."

She made rare visits to Tahoe, and no one knew her phone number, if indeed the house possessed a phone. When she and Dominguín weren't in bed, they were battling. Following a drunken shouting match in one of the casinos, the lovers parted. Howard Hughes had been spying on Ava, and he arranged a flight to Madrid on a private plane for the toreador. Meanwhile, Ava's husband and her two exes were appearing in Vegas that summer. Frank was back, bigger than ever, singing at the Sands and making serious money. Through her lawyer, Ava requested some reimbursement for all that she had spent on his upkeep during their two years together. No way.

The day after completing her residence requirement, photographers were waiting at the courthouse, but Ava did not appear to pick up divorce papers. She decided to leave the divorce an open issue, while her lawyers pursued some payment for the high cost of loving Frank Sinatra. Instead, she left Tahoe with Howard Hughes for Florida; from there, she went to Cuba to visit Hemingway, then back to New York for a final rendezvous with Dominguín.

The bullfighter asked Ava to marry him, and she refused. Their great romance was over. When Luis Miguel Dominguín was asked what he intended to do, now that the chase was over, he said, "I'll do nothing, and rest afterward."

Afterward can be a very short time in the bullfighting trade. That year, Dominguín started chasing Italian actress Lucia Bosè, who was in Madrid to star in the film *Death of a Cyclist*. She had recently separated from her fiancé, the Italian comic actor Walter Chiari, whose attentions began to falter after he made the acquaintance of Ava Gardner in Rome.

Lucia, who had been Miss Italy of 1947 (Gina Lollabrigida was runner-up), knew little Spanish and less about bullfighting, but she and Dominguín were both on the rebound from Ava encounters, and so began an accelerated courtship. They still had not kissed when Dominguín asked her to marry him, which she did—in Las Vegas on March 1, 1955. She retired from the movies to raise their children. "It never ceased to amaze me the incalculable force of his sexual incontinence," said Lucia. Ava knew how to pick 'em.

. . . .

On one of her return visits to Hollywood that year, Ava had a drink with old MGM stable mate Peter Lawford. Louella reported it in her column as a "date," which Frank considered a breach of loyalty. He called Lawford at three o'clock in the morning. "Do you want your legs broken, you fucking asshole?" he said. "Well, you're going to get them broken if I ever hear you're out with Ava again. So help me, I'll kill you."

❧ 9 ❧

Of Rats and Men

In early June 1955, Frank Sinatra led an expedition from Hollywood to Las Vegas, where Noël Coward was opening at the Desert Inn. Everyone met at the Bogarts', climbed aboard a chartered bus to the airport, and then a private plane took them to the Sands, where Frank had rooms and a nice line of credit. The gang included Bogie and Betty, the Mike Romanoffs, the David Nivens, Swifty Lazar and Martha Hyer, Jimmy Van Heusen and Angie Dickinson, Charles Feldman and Capucine, Judy Garland and Sid Luft.

After four days of gambling and gamboling (including a room-service order for three hundred Bloody Marys one morning), Betty Bacall surveyed the wreckage of the party and said, "You look like a goddamn rat pack." With that, the Rat Pack was born. To be an upstanding rat, explained Bacall, "one had to be addicted to nonconformity, staying up late, drinking, laughing, and not caring what anyone thought or said about us." Frank was named pack leader, Betty was den mother, and Bogie was in charge of public relations. He promptly created the Pack's motto: Never Rat on a Rat.

One month later, a few of the Rat Pack and pals celebrated Independence Day on Bogie's boat, *Santana,* for a sail to Catalina. Bogie, an old navy hand, loved his boat. When he left New York and settled in Hollywood in the 1930s, one of the first things he did was buy a sleek motor launch, which he named *Sluggy* during his marriage to Mayo Methot. Bogie volunteered for civilian patrol during the war years, and cruised the Pacific coast looking for enemy submarines, which he did not encounter. After the war, both *Sluggy* and Mayo were retired, and Bogie bought *Santana*—a handsome fifty-five-foot sailboat with a galley, three cabins, and a comfortable sleeping capacity of eight—from actor Dick Powell.

The Bogarts, the Nivens, and Richard Burton were on board for the Fourth of July festivities; Sinatra pulled up alongside in a motor cruiser he had chartered with a piano on board. As Frank sang that evening, other boaters paddled over in dinghies and floated in a quiet circle around *Santana*. Lauren Bacall sat at Frank's feet as he sang, and everyone got rather drunk.

Bogie and Richard Burton went out lobster potting, with Bogie "making cracks about Betty sitting on Sinatra's feet," recalled Burton in his journals. The next day, things intensified. "Bogie and Frankie nearly came to blows about the singing the night before," said Burton. He thought that Frank was "peculiarly vulnerable and Bogie was unnecessarily cruel." Lauren Bacall was so angry about her husband's behavior, she asked Burton to drive her home the next morning.

"It was also a situation that was not helped by the fact that Bacall had started an affair with Sinatra, and Bogie, a heavy smoker who by now had cancer of the esophagus and was becoming increasingly thin and frail, may well have known about it and was devastated," said David Niven's authorized biographer Graham Lord. Bogie was "aware of his wife's roving eye," said biographer Stefan Kanfer. "There were rumors about a fling with Sinatra."

"Bogart didn't seem to care—but there was no doubt he knew about it, too," said *Time* magazine's Ezra Goodman. "He spent his time before the cameras, at Romanoff's and on his boat. He was philosophical about it all." There was also his wig maker, Verita Thompson, to keep in mind. Never rat on a rat, remember.

In September 1955, at the Rocky Marciano championship bout—where Bogie had ringside seats, in training for his final movie, *The Harder They Fall*—he told Lauren that he'd heard an old friend of Sinatra's say, ambivalently, "Frank's a last-rites pal. If you get hit by a truck, he's right there with an ambulance, everything, but how often do you get hit by a truck?"

Sinatra's valet, George Jacobs, said, "I think he worshiped Bogart enough to keep his impulsive lust in check. I say I *think,* because as Mr. S himself often said, 'a hard dick has no conscience,' and whenever he and Betty would be alone together at the house for some innocent reason, like picking up a script or showing her a painting, he would usually send me away. But I'd bet he was loyal to Bogart, if no one else."

. . . .

On March 1, 1956, Humphrey Bogart underwent a nine-hour surgery in Good Samaritan Hospital. Entering from Bogie's back, the surgeons removed two inches of his esophagus, raised his stomach twelve inches, and discarded one rib. "I hope that the operation has checked the cancer," said the lead surgeon. "But only time will tell."

Bogie came home in an ambulance and was taken on a stretcher to the front door, where Betty greeted him. "People say why do you get married," said Bogie, his eyes moistening, "and look what I've got here."

. . . .

On April 19, Ava Gardner was in Monaco for "the wedding of the century," Grace Kelly's marriage to His Serene Highness Rainier III (born Rainier Louis Henri Maxence Bertrand de Grimaldi). Ava's escort was Rupert Allan, whom she introduced to Grace in 1953, when they were in London completing interiors for *Mogambo*. Rupert would become Grace's publicist and escort her to the 1955 Cannes Film Festival, where a *Paris Match* photo op with the prince led to their engagement. Thus, if you traced the origins of the royal couple back to a starting point, for Grace, Ava was the "reign maker." They had become fast friends.

The entire operetta was filmed in 35mm and color under contract to MGM, complete with hairdressers, klieg lights, cameras, and publicists. "It looked to Ava as though half of Culver City was in Monte Carlo," said Lee Server. "It was a goddamned MGM movie."

Although the press made the story seems like a storybook romance, it was more like marriage by design. The plan had been crafted years earlier, when Rainier was advised to take a high-profile American for his bride in order to reap the rewards of publicity and American investment in his impoverished little principality. After Vatican City, Monaco was the smallest independent state in the world, measuring some 499 acres along 2.5 miles of the French Riviera, close to the Italian border. It was smaller than the back lot at MGM. It was little more than half the size of New York's Central Park. The goal was to transform it into a money machine for hotel owners and casino operators. The right bride could do for Monaco's tourism what the coronation of Elizabeth II did for Great Britain.

According to Robert Evans, the first candidate was Marilyn Monroe. The prince? "Is he rich? Is he handsome?" she asked. "Give me two days alone with him and he'll be on his knees wanting to marry me!" The timing for Marilyn was not right, however; and royal acceptance might have been an issue.

Grace was willing. Yes, she could bear an heir, no problem. "Assuring them she was a virgin? That was another story," said Evans, one of Grace's lovers in the early days. In Hollywood, Grace had affairs with most of her leading men, including James Stewart, Ray Milland, William Holden, Bing Crosby, and Clark Gable. Her specialty was older married men. Gary Cooper said that the pristine and elegant actress was "a cold dish until you got her panties down. Then she couldn't stop exploding."

"Giving another Academy Award–worthy performance," said Evans, Grace conceded that she was not a virgin. "But she was Catholic! She was fertile! She was rich! And she was a big fuckin' movie star! Four out of five was good enough to close the royal deal."

The wedding—totally ignored by all of the royal houses in Europe, with no major nation sending a significant dignitary—became the world's first media superblitz as sixteen hundred journalists showed up in Monaco to cover the event, when only forty had been expected. "No one looked, dug, or played the part with greater aplomb than Grace," said Evans.

Frank Sinatra was invited to the wedding, and he flew into London but then decided against attending. During the filming of *High Society,* he was in pursuit of Grace, but she declared that she would not be intimate with him unless he was "the last man on earth," adding, "and even then I wouldn't do it."

So thankful was Princess Grace for Rupert Allan's skill in controlling the media that she appointed him Monaco's consul general in Los Angeles, and Prince Rainier made Rupert a Chevalier of the Order of Grimaldi, whatever those honors mean. The façade went on and on.

....

On April 17, Frank Sinatra arrived in Spain, where he would be starring in *The Pride and the Passion,* a costume drama about an episode in the Napoleonic Wars. Earlier that year, Stanley Kramer, the award-winning producer of *High Noon,* thought that Marlon Brando and Ava Gardner would be his costars, but Marlon backed out and Frank signed on, thinking that this was opportunity knocking loudly for a reconciliation with Ava. But then Ava backed out.

Still, she was in Madrid, and Frank would costar with Cary Grant and newcomer Sophia Loren in this strange story about Spain's war for independence and a patriot who leads a ragged band of partisans across the country, pulling a huge cannon. Frank didn't think much of the movie, but he and Ava had been having long phone conversations.

Frank told Stanley Kramer in advance that if a newspaperman showed up at the airport, he would take the next plane back. When he arrived, however, Frank was friendly and gracious toward photographers, smiling broadly, with young singer Peggy Connelly, his date at the Oscars that year, at his side, and later at a cocktail party at the Castellana Hilton in Madrid, for pictures that were on the front pages of Spain's newspapers next day.

Frank refused to stay in a local inn while Kramer shot the numerous outdoor scenes, insisting on a suite at the Castellana, a two-hour drive to and from the location every day. Peggy Connelly was in the suite when Frank got a call from Ava.

"You going to see her?" Connelly asked.

Frank said yes, and within hours Peggy left on a brief trip out of the country.

....

"In the script, Grant and Sinatra compete for Sophia's favors," said Stanley Kramer, "but in real life the story was even more interesting because she was actually the special friend of Italian producer Carlo Ponti. That didn't stop Grant from courting her and even falling in love with her, while Sinatra, at the same time, was openly lusting after her."

Cary Grant and Sophia had an affair during the making of the movie, and he proposed marriage. She said no, and returned to Ponti. As for Frank, "she was so scornful throughout the filming that he began resorting to taunts and gibes in an effort to provoke her attention," said Kramer. In the large mess tent where meals were served to cast and crew, Frank would stand up at his table and, using his old Jimmy Cagney imitation, shout, "You'll get yours, Sophia!"

"She steadfastly ignored this," said Kramer, "until once, at a midnight supper after a late shooting, she decided she had heard enough. Sinatra again shouted across the room, 'You'll get yours, Sophia!' This time she stood up and shouted back, 'But not from you, Spaghetti Head!'"

....

When Peggy Connelly returned to the suite after her trip, Ava was sitting on the living room couch, wearing Frank's bathrobe, reading a newspaper. "This is an uncomfortable situation, isn't it?" said Connelly. Ava looked daggers and said nothing. Peggy departed for lunch with Frank on location.

"How were things at the hotel?" he asked.

"Crowded," said Connelly.

"Oh, was she still there?"

Something had happened. Something had gone wrong for Frank.

"There was no drama," Connelly told Sinatra biographer Anthony Summers. "From the way he spoke Ava could have been any girl he'd left at the hotel, a prostitute even."

Frank and Ava had spent a night together, but she was now involved with Walter Chiari, the handsome young comic actor she had met in Rome after attending his revue, which included an imitation of Sinatra. Frank could not get out of Spain fast enough.

In late July, Frank flew back to the States weeks before his scenes were completed. Grant and Loren shot scenes with a Sinatra stand-in. "The rumor was that he had learned that Ava Gardner would not take him back, and she was the reason he'd accepted the part in the first place," said Sophia in her memoir. Kramer cut a deal where Frank would do a week on the back lots at United Artists, and the movie was patched together with scenes that barely resembled Spain.

. . . .

Despite failing health, Humphrey Bogart had kept busy after doing *The Barefoot Contessa* with Ava in 1954. He masterfully portrayed the unstable Captain Queeg in *The Caine Mutiny* that year, then the escaped killer in *The Desperate Hours* the following year, and a weary sportswriter in *The Harder They Fall*.

Now, in the summer of 1956, he gave the performance of his lifetime in a wheelchair in the den of his home, smoking and drinking and acting as if he were on the road to recovery. His longtime routine was cocktails with friends from 5:30 to 8:00 P.M.—he called them "freeloader gatherings." Bogie dressed each afternoon in his scarlet velvet smoking jacket and gray Daks slacks, and at 5:30 he'd be seated in the den, drink in hand, waiting for the freeloaders to arrive.

Regulars included Spencer Tracy, Katharine Hepburn, David Niven, John Huston, Swifty Lazar, Nunnally Johnson, Harry Kurnitz, Truman

Capote, Richard Burton, and Frank Sinatra. They talked about parts, personalities, studio gossip, everything but illness and mortality. Everyone acted as though things were going to be fine.

....

Ava Gardner visited Ernest Hemingway that summer in Zaragoza, an industrial city in northern Spain. She carried with her the shooting script, by Peter Viertel, for *The Sun Also Rises,* in which she would play Hemingway's most memorable heroine, Lady Brett Ashley. "You have to read it," she told Papa.

"I know you weren't paid, since they could remake the original for nothing, but for your own pride you have to read it and change things. Everyone in the script runs around saying, *'C'est la guerre,'* and peachy things like that."

Hemingway would receive no payment because the book had been sold outright, with no provision for remakes. Producer David O. Selznick took advantage of the same loophole when he announced a remake of *A Farewell to Arms* with his wife, Jennifer Jones, starring as the novel's heroine, Catherine Barkley. For publicity purposes, Selznick announced to the world press that, although not legally obligated to, he was pledging to pay Hemingway fifty thousand dollars from the profits of the picture, if and when it earned any profits.

Hemingway's colleague A. E. Hotchner wrote, "Ernest, who had never kept secret his lack of affection for Mr. Selznick, dictated a telegram in reply saying that if by some miracle, Selznick's movie, which starred 41-year-old Mrs. Selznick portraying 24-year-old Catherine Barkley, did earn $50,000, Selznick should have all $50,000 changed into nickels at his local bank and shove them up his ass until they came out of his ears."

"Ava stayed all evening," said Hotchner, who was still in attendance. "We drank an impressive amount of champagne, and Ava was lively and funny and beat both of us in an impromptu olive-pit-flipping contest at the bar. Ernest enjoyed himself and said that Ava was one of the good ones."

············

For a brief period after recovering from the operation, Bogie felt strong enough to lounge around the pool and go to Romanoff's for an occasional lunch. Then came a relapse, another operation, cobalt treatments, and by the end of summer visitors could see that he had lost more weight—he was down to ninety pounds now—and his gray Daks were too big for him. "I must put on some weight," he would say, scolding himself, always in good spirits.

············

In April, the big question at the wedding of the century had been, "Will Grace Kelly ever make another picture?" She was still under contract to MGM, and her next scheduled film, *Designing Woman,* costarring Gregory Peck, was ready to start. The role of Marilla Brown Hagen had been written for her. While MGM could insist that Grace report, or even sue Her Majesty—the studio would look "more stupid than usual," one wag observed. A deal was made. In exchange for Grace's not being required to do *Designing Woman,* MGM had obtained exclusive film rights to the wedding in Monaco. Who would replace Grace?

"I fought for that part," said Lauren Bacall. "I wanted it badly. I took a lower salary, I did everything. She got the prince, I got the part."

Lauren called the role a "godsend." "That movie was one of my happiest film experiences," she said. "It was a romantic movie and I seemed to be constantly running toward Greg or away from him, so I had emotional and physical release to compensate for keeping everything inside at home." You have to think that Bogie, the consummate pro, was proud of his wife's work under battlefield conditions.

In October, to celebrate Lauren's recent thirty-second birthday, Frank again flew some of the Rat Pack and friends to Vegas, where he was playing at the Sands. Bogie stayed home. He and his son, Steve, were joined by friends for a couple of days' sailing to Balboa and Catalina. Aboard the

Santana for a final voyage, Bogie spent most of the time alone in the cockpit, relaxing with his scotch and cigarettes, dozing and studying the sea and the sky. "Sailing. That was the part of him no one could get at," said Truman Capote. "It was some kind of inner soul, an almost mystical hideaway."

In her memoir, *By Myself,* Bacall said that Bogie called her at the Sands, wishing her a happy birthday. "I hadn't expected it and screamed with excitement and pleasure. Should I have gone with him? I kept wondering. I was escaping from reality until that call."

She returned home, to find Bogie a bit edgy but calm enough to hear who'd been there and what they'd all done. "He was somewhat jealous of Frank—partly because he knew I loved being with him, partly because he thought Frank was in love with me, and partly because our physical life together, which had always ranked high, had less than flourished with his illness," she said. "Yet he was also crazy about Frank—loved having him feel that our home was his home."

. . . .

After five days in a hospital in late November, Humphrey Bogart was sent home to die. He could no longer handle the stairs. In order to host the freeloaders, he modified the dumbwaiter that ran between the first and second floors and used it as an elevator. Nurses took him to it on the second floor by wheelchair and helped him onto a small stool inside. They lowered Bogie to the first floor, where he was assisted into another wheelchair and wheeled to the den. He sat and talked to his friends, acting as if there were no pain.

One day, Bogie called Verita Thompson and asked her to check out *Santana* to see if everything was all right. "Don't drink all my scotch," he said. "I'll be down there soon." Verita discovered that the boat had been repainted. In order to be sold, *Santana* had to look her best.

On a Saturday afternoon shortly after the holidays, Bogie and Bacall watched *Anchors Aweigh,* Frank's first movie at MGM. The following morning, as Lauren left to take the kids to Sunday school, he said "Goodbye, kid." When she returned, he had slipped into a coma. Bogie died at 2:10 A.M., Monday, January 14, 1957.

The call to Frank came in the wee small hours at the Hampshire House, where he stayed during his gigs at the Copacabana. Tony Consiglio answered. "Is Frank there?" asked Bacall. Tony said Frank was resting. "Tell him Bogart just died," she said, and hung up.

Frank stayed in his room all that day watching television and making phone calls. Sammy Davis, Jr. and Jerry Lewis stepped in at the Copa. That evening, Abbey Lincoln, the beautiful black actress and jazz singer, came to visit Frank and spent the night.

....

On Thursday, January 17, a minute of silence was observed on all the movie lots in Hollywood and three thousand people lined the streets outside All Saints Episcopal Church in Beverly Hills, where services were held for Bogie. Inside, the famous of Hollywood paid homage while Bogie was being cremated at Forest Lawn; a large-scale model of his beloved *Santana* was on view where the coffin would normally have been positioned, and John Huston delivered a eulogy. The only close friend missing was Frank Sinatra.

Designing Woman opened in April 1957, three months after Bogie's death. That summer, Frank and Lauren became a steady pair. They flew to Las Vegas for *The Joker Is Wild* opening, then to the *Pal Joey* opening in L.A. "She is lonely since Bogie left us," said Sinatra. "I'm a lonesome guy, too." Louella Parsons wrote that it was part of Frank's friendship with Bogart "to see that she didn't mourn in loneliness."

....

In the spring of 1957, Ava Gardner arrived in Mexico to begin filming *The Sun Also Rises.*

In May, she filed for divorce in Mexico City. Frank was notified, and he replied by wire: "I wish you every happiness and will do nothing to stand in your way." On July 5, the divorce was granted.

As they moved on to the rest of their lives, they thought it was over between them. It wasn't.

············

Sadie Vimmerstedt, a fifty-eight-year-old grandmother who worked at a cosmetics counter in a Youngstown, Ohio, department store, had followed the Sinatra marital saga for years. She was pleased that "Frankie boy" had gotten his just desserts for abandoning Nancy and running off with Ava. She sent a letter to songwriter Johnny Mercer asking him to write a song about romantic vengeance. She even had an idea for the lyric: "I want to be around to pick up the pieces when somebody breaks your heart." Sadie addressed her letter simply to "Johnny Mercer, Songwriter, New York, NY." She heard nothing for five years.

The postal service delivered the letter to the ASCAP office in New York, and eventually it reached Mercer, who responded, with apologies, in 1962. He had written a song called "I Wanna Be Around," and he wanted to split the royalties with her, since she'd had the idea. Sadie was thrilled.

The song became a hit for Tony Bennett, but that was only the beginning, for, on June 9, 1964, Frankie boy himself, none the wiser, made a great recording of the song he had inspired with Count Basie and his orchestra, arranged by Quincy Jones, for an album called *It Might As Well Be Swing*. Frank needed seven takes to get it down, but there it was—a lyric that resonated with anyone who'd been cast aside for another:

> *And that's when I'll discover that revenge is sweet;*
> *As I sit there applauding from a front row seat,*
> *When somebody breaks your heart like you broke mine.*

Sadie wrote to Mercer, telling him about being interviewed on the radio in Cincinnati. People were coming into the department store to get her autograph. "I'm getting to be very famous," she wrote. "It's like a Cinderella story." After a few more appearances on radio and TV, though, she wrote to Mercer again. "I'm *tired,*" Sadie said. "I think I'm getting out of show business."

. . . .

On location in Mexico, Ava spearheaded the campaign to remove Robert Evans from *The Sun Also Rises* and replace him with her boyfriend, Walter Chiari. Evans was cast as a matador, something that Ava knew about; and she thought she could use her diva power to enchant producer Darryl F. Zanuck.

Robert Evans started out in the fashion business, running Evan-Picone clothiers. On a business trip, he was spotted at the Beverly Hills Hotel by Norma Shearer, queen of old Hollywood. She thought he would be perfect playing her late husband, Irving Thalberg, in a new movie, *Man of a Thousand Faces.* Now, with Evans cast as a bullfighter in *The Sun Also Rises,* his fellow cast members said his acting was so bad, they wanted him replaced.

Darryl F. Zanuck stood only about five foot three, but he was imposing where it counted. It was said that he liked to expose himself in front of starlets he was pursuing, "to get those broads' juices running." Ava may or may not have been treated to the exhibition, but she seemed to know the legend. "The only thing bigger than his cigar is his cock," she liked to say, "which he's not shy to show or put into use."

Ten days before shooting was to begin, a cable was sent to Zanuck in London: "With Robert Evans playing Pedro Romero, *The Sun Also Rises* will be a disaster." Ava, Tyrone Power, Mel Ferrer, Eddie Albert, Peter Viertel, and director Henry King signed it.

Within a week, Zanuck arrived on the set in Morelia, Mexico, and walked down the steps into the bullring to take them on. With a large cigar in his mouth and a bullhorn in his hand, Darryl F. Zanuck said, "The kid stays in the picture. And anybody who doesn't like it can quit!" He turned, walked up the steps, and was gone.

· · · · · · · · · · · ·

At Frank's small dinner parties, Lauren was the hostess. "It seemed to everyone—to his friends, to mine—that we were crazy about each other, that we were a great pair; that it wouldn't last; that Frank would never be able to remain constantly devoted, monogamous—yet that maybe with me, he would," Lauren wrote in her memoir. "I was the center of his life at the moment. At least I thought I was—I felt I was. It seemed perfect, no way for it not to work. And I was happy. Surface happy."

On September 14, 1957, eight months to the day since Bogie's death, columnist Thomas Wiseman, in London's *Evening Standard,* reported that Frank and Lauren Bacall would marry within six months, "barring an act of Providence or Ava Gardner."

Under Lauren's influence, said Wiseman, Humphrey Bogart "became as mellowed as the scotch he liked to drink." Marrying Sinatra, he said, would be taking on an even tougher assignment. "It will be like trying to mellow wood alcohol."

"Betty Bacall may have confused sex and love," said George Jacobs. "Aside from the ghost of Bogie, she had baggage, two kids, and her own career. Mr. S hated careers if they conflicted with his happiness. Ava's was bad enough. Moreover, Betty was jealous of Ava and the continuing trance she had put Frank in." Even for Lauren Bacall, Ava Gardner was a tough diva to follow. "Who wouldn't be jealous, given Frank still called Ava every week, and had his bedrooms festooned with her photos," said Jacobs.

Lauren sold her house. "I knew Bogie's ghost would always be there, always coming between us." She had her gardener dig out all of the clivia plants and replant them at Frank's house—they were his favorite color, orange.

One night, Frank came over to see her. There had been an impasse in their relationship, and he had been drinking heavily. "He didn't know how to apologize, but he was fairly contrite, at least for him," she said. "He said

he had felt somewhat trapped—was 'chicken'—but now could face it."
"Will you marry me?" he asked.

"He said those words and he meant them. Of course all my barriers fell. I must have hesitated for at least thirty seconds. Yes, I thought to myself, I was right all along—he couldn't deal with it, was afraid of himself, but finally realized that he loved me and that marriage was the only road to take. I was ecstatic—we both were."

Frank said, "Let's go out and have a drink to celebrate—let's call Swifty, maybe he can join us."

They met Swifty Lazar at the Imperial Gardens, a Japanese restaurant on the Strip. In a booth at the bar, they started to plan the wedding. A young girl came to the booth, asking for autographs. Frank handed Lauren the paper napkin and pen. "Put down your new name," he said. Lauren wrote, "Lauren Bacall," followed by "Betty Sinatra."

Frank was leaving for Miami the next day. They would work out everything on his return. In the meantime, mum was to be the word.

....

One fateful evening, a fiesta was given in honor of Zanuck at *The Sun Also Rises* location in Mexico. The producer sat, large cigar and all, with Ava by his side. Robert Evans approached the table and, without asking, took Ava onto the dance floor. "The Barefoot Contessa was somewhat shocked, but not for long," said Evans. "For the next forty minutes we danced as one. In a total sweat, without a single word between us, we made it back to Zanuck's table. The silence was eerie; so were the stares. She sat. I left. From that moment, it wasn't only Zanuck who thought I was Pedro Romero."

And so the movie was shot, and the affair began. For two weeks, Evans thought it was love, but no. "Ava, the professional, was just trying to make our onscreen chemistry more convincing. Not that she lorded it over me. Ava was wide open about Ava, blaming herself for her failed love affairs, telling me the most bizarre stories about how she'd screwed up her marriage to Frank Sinatra. I think she was still madly in love with him. Was I nuts about her? Who wouldn't be?" After shooting their interior scenes together in Mexico City, they would go to the bullfighters' hangouts. When Ava walked in, she got a matador's cheers.

In October 1957, Ava fell from a horse in a bullring at a friend's estate in Spain. She was drunk. Initially, there were reports of a scarred face, as well as paralysis of her lip and right cheek. She flew to New York for possible surgery, and Frank came to her side, recommending a plastic surgeon. Ava decided against surgery. Lauren Bacall was angry, according to her biographer Howard Greenberg. Lauren dined out with Spencer Tracy one evening. A reporter asked, "Where's Frankie?" "Frankie who?!" she said. "I'm not his keeper. Who knows where he is? Or who cares?" Ava returned to Europe and consulted in England with Dr. Archibald McIndoe, a pioneering plastic surgeon, who told her to "do absolutely nothing to it." The lump and the bruise gradually faded, but Ava always checked a mirror, ran a finger across the area, feeling the firm tissue just beneath the surface, sensing an imperfection in her right cheek not visible to others.

············

While Frank was out of town, Swifty Lazar took Lauren to see Emlyn Williams in his Dickens evening at the Huntington Hartford Theatre. During the intermission, Louella Parsons stopped Lauren and Swifty and asked the actress if she and Frank were going to get married. Lauren's heart leaped. "Why don't you ask him?" she replied, and kept moving. By "him," she meant Sinatra. Louella turned to Swifty and asked *him*.

That evening, after theater and dinner, Lauren and Swifty pulled up to a newsstand for the early edition of the morning *Examiner* and saw the headline for Louella's story: SINATRA TO MARRY BACALL.

Swifty laughed. "I didn't know she'd do this," he said. "I just said I happened to know that Frank had asked Betty to marry him. So what? He did! What's wrong with saying it?"

Plenty, according to Frank. A few days of silence, and then a phone call.

"Why did you do it?" Frank asked Lauren. He thought that she had given away their secret.

"I didn't do anything," she said.

"I haven't been able to leave my room for days—the press are everywhere—we'll have to lay low, not see each other for a while."

"What?" She suppressed a scream. "What are you saying, Frank?" He was three thousand miles away, his attitude remote. "What do you mean?"

"He felt trapped," she said. "I tried to rationalize his feelings—couldn't—but he'd be back in a couple of weeks and we could figure it out then."

She never heard from him again.

. . . .

After hearing the news, Ava called Frank and asked about the breakup. "I was never going to marry that pushy broad," he said.

"I had never seen the famously courtly Mr. S be so vicious about any woman," said George Jacobs, "not even the whores he would pay off and ship out because they were wearing too much makeup or cheap perfume."

As a neophyte actress, in 1944's *To Have and Have Not,* Lauren had delivered the most memorable line: "You know how to whistle, don't you, Steve? You just put your lips together and blow." Frank complained that Lauren spurned his need for oral sex. "All she does is whistle," he said.

In rejecting Bacall so venomously, Frank may have been acting out the self-loathing that one might experience for having an affair with one's best friend's wife while the man was on his deathbed. Betrayals didn't get much worse than that.

. . . .

In December 1958, Ava toasted her thirty-sixth birthday with Robert Evans at the Harwyn Club in New York. They had been lovers on and off since the movie wrapped six months earlier. "Ava, the world's most beautiful woman, was a haunted soul," said Evans. "She was haunted by her poor childhood, stormy romances, fading beauty."

"It's over, Pedro," Ava said that night, ever the femme fatale.

"It was never really anything to begin with," said Evans. "You were just using me."

"Don't flatter yourself, I wasn't even thinking of you."

Evans raised his glass. "Happy thirty-six, Lady Brett."

"Happy!" she said. "I'm over the hill. I know it, you know it, and the industry knows it."

She's right, thought Evans. It was a business with a very short memory, where beauty had a very brief shelf life. It was over for any leading lady brushing against her mid-thirties. Beauty was also the beast.

Ava closed her eyes.

⊰ 10 ⊱

Top of the Heap

Ava's departure, at the risk here of sounding crass, would be perceived by many as a great career move for Sinatra. As George Bernard Shaw observed, a great actor can have only one love—himself. "Frank had every conceivable reversal and disappointment socially, professionally and privately," said Bing Crosby. "Very few people in our business can rally from something like this. But he did—and big!" After Ava left, he threw himself into work and achieved what some have called the greatest comeback in show business history. "Frank Sinatra was the most powerful person in the entertainment industry from 1954 to 1965," said Guy McElwaine, a leading agent of the era. Paradoxically, Frank could not have done it with—or without—Ava.

After winning the Oscar, Frank Sinatra decided to shape his career on his own terms, and nobody else's. On a movie set, for instance, only a short part of each day was spent acting; the rest was a technical game of patience, and that was not Frank's specialty. The endless takes, followed by endless waits—while the camera and lighting were adjusted, the script revised, the makeup restored—pillaged the spontaneity so vital to his performance. The man was not designed for waiting.

In October 1955, Jerry Lewis and Dean Martin were visiting Frank on the set of *The Man with the Golden Arm,* where Otto Preminger was directing Sinatra in a scene they had been rehearsing all morning—the climax of the story, where Frank's character, Frankie Machine, goes through heroin withdrawal. "Everyone was a little anxious, as people get when a big scene is about to explode," said Lewis.

It was going to be a rare long take. That's what Frank liked. "Keep the cameras rolling," he told Preminger. "You'll get what you want." "The set got extremely quiet," said Lewis in his memoir. "Prop men moved materials into place. The cinematographer checked last-minute light. Preminger called the roll, then cried, 'Action!' . . . Frank was in the corner of his bedroom, screaming at the top of his lungs as he underwent his horrific ordeal. Dean and I were standing directly beside the camera, and as close as we were, and as well as we knew that it was just a movie, we both had gooseflesh watching Frank's incredible performance. It ran for the better part of four minutes, and was simply explosive. He hit every beat and every nuance."

Preminger yelled, "Cut!" Sinatra arose and lit a cigarette. He walked toward the director. "That was great, Frank," said Preminger, "but we need one more take!"

Frank whirled around. "Another take? For what, if that one was so good?" He walked to his dressing room, sat down, and poured a Jack Daniel's. Lewis complimented Frank on the scene. "I knew it was perfect and that I'd never get it that way again!" he said.

Preminger stuck his head in the doorway. "Frank, are you sure you want me to print that last take?"

Frank took a sip of his drink. "Uh-huh," he said.

. . . .

As the studio system unraveled, Frank was in free fall, along with other stars—but he had an advantage: He had been dumped by MGM. He was a free operator, a partner, producing as well as starring in his own films, with full creative control and copyright ownership. This represented a sharp departure from the old notion of stars as "hired hands." The studios were on their way to becoming distribution companies.

When they hired "One-Take Frank," producers knew they were getting a handful. But he was good box office. He learned his dialogue, rehearsed as much as the director wanted (not always happily), and was ready for the camera. On *Guys and Dolls,* he told director Joseph L. Mankiewicz to call him to the set only after rehearsing with "Mumbles," his grudging name for method actor Marlon Brando.

Sinatra earned an Oscar nomination as Best Actor for his 1955 portrayal of Frankie Machine in *The Man with the Golden Arm.* Critics and movie historians still cite the drug-withdrawal scene as Sinatra the actor at his best.

....

In 1955, Frank signed on to play Billy Bigelow in the Rodgers and Hammerstein musical *Carousel,* considered by many as the perfect role for him, with songs that would become part of the Sinatra repertoire. Neither Rodgers nor Hammerstein was engaged by that thought, but this, after all, was Hollywood, not Broadway. As shooting time approached, Frank harbored some doubts, as well. Was he muscular enough to play the brawny Billy Bigelow? And then there was that distance to Boothbay Harbor, Maine. "What the hell are we going on location for?" He thought *Carousel* could be shot on soundstages.

Twentieth Century–Fox announced that because of the adoption of a new wide-screen process (Todd-AO), the movie would be shot in both 35mm and 55mm processes. Musical prerecordings were laid down that summer in Los Angeles. On August 16, Frank sang "If I Loved You" with Shirley Jones. "I'd always thought that no one could read a lyric the way Frank could," said producer Henry Ephron. "He didn't disappoint me."

Then came the tough one—the quarter-hour operatic "Soliloquy." Conductor Alfred Newman proposed that Frank record the last sixteen bars first—"I've got to get ready before she comes . . . I've got to be certain that she . . ."—and then, after a break, they would start from the beginning with a fresh voice and intercut the two. "I offered up a prayer for one good take," said Ephron. "God was elsewhere."

Frank struggled through several repeated takes. Mild panic followed in the recording booth. Was the vocal range too much, or was he just not in top voice? "Let's try it another time," said Frank. "I've had it for tonight."

Ephron walked him to his car. "What's Henry King doing on this picture?" asked Frank. He was not happy with the choice of director. As Ephron recited King's credits, Frank snapped, "If you had any sense, you'd get Jean Negulesco."

"Sinatra!" lamented Ephron in his memoir, *We Thought We Could Do Anything.* "He couldn't sing 'Soliloquy,' but he was telling me how to produce the picture. He was a hard man to like."

....

Frank flew into Portland, Maine, on August 24, with Hank Sanicola and sportswriter Jimmy Cannon, a drinking buddy along for the ride. There they met Tony Consiglio and drove to Boothbay, where a camera crew, electricians, propmen, seventy dancers, and all the players except Frank were waiting. It was early morning when they arrived, still dark. Frank told Tony to check out the set—where he was arrested for trespassing. From jail, Tony called in. Indeed, there were two different cameras installed for shooting the movie.

"Don't unpack the bags," ordered Frank at the house the studio had leased. His first meeting was with producer Henry Ephron.

"What's this crap I've been hearing?" demanded Frank. "If I make two pictures, do I get double salary?"

Ephron explained the plan. The movie would be shot in standard 35mm CinemaScope and then again in the 55mm wide-screen process. "Do both cameras shoot at the same time?" asked Frank.

"No," said Ephron. This was all new to him, as well. "Unfortunately, they need different lighting, or something like that."

"Well, forget it, kid. It's the cameras or me. One of us has got to go."

"Frank, for Christ's sake—"

"Listen, Henry. You've heard me say it—it's been printed a thousand times—I've only got one good take in me."

Ephron called Darryl F. Zanuck, no fan of Frank. "Do we need the fifty-five camera?" he asked.

"Skouras said it will add three million to the gross," said Zanuck.

Next day, Abe Lastfogel called on Zanuck, reiterating the ultimatum: It was either Frank or one of the cameras. "I'll sue Frank for five million dollars," said Zanuck.

"He's been sued before," said Abe warily. "It doesn't mean a thing to him."

Like another bad marriage, Frank wanted out. "It's a long production schedule, and I suspect that he didn't *want* to do it," said Scott Eyman. "Also, by 1955, his career was heating up again. He had plenty of other work to consider."

Between rounds, Zanuck had been talking with Gene Kelly, who was available. Another candidate was Gordon MacRae—"His tongue is hanging out to do it," said Zanuck. The idea began to form: You loved them in *Oklahoma!* Now, Jones and MacRae in *Carousel*!

Zanuck called Henry Ephron in Maine the next day. "I've sent Frank a telegram that I'm sure will straighten everything out," he said. He read it to the producer: "Dear Frank, Even though Rodgers and Hammerstein didn't want you for the picture, I persuaded them that you were exactly right and that you will be wonderful. Best, Darryl."

The following morning, Frank and his entourage drove to the Portland airport in the rain.

....

Time put "The Kid from Hoboken" on its cover for August 29, 1955. "Sinatra can be a difficult and sometimes impossible person," said Ezra Goodman. "He has been called 'a middle-aged delinquent.'" The story concluded with a quote attributed to Sinatra: "I'm going to do as I please. I don't need anybody in the world. I did it all myself."

"Sinatra stated that he had never made that remark to me, to anyone from *Time* magazine, or to anyone at any time," said Goodman years later. "And, to tell the truth, he was right. Some creative writer or editor in *Time's*

New York office had helpfully put the words into Sinatra's mouth. I am afraid that *Time*'s story, for all its merit, did not do much to allay Sinatra's suspicions about journalists."

When Ezra Goodman walked on the set of *Pal Joey,* for a *Time* cover story on Kim Novak in 1957, the actress's costar informed director George Sidney that either Goodman or Sinatra was leaving the set. Exit Ezra.

....

Two weeks into shooting *Carousel,* the Skouras plan was abandoned and *Carousel* was shot in the standard 35mm format. Theater owners had revolted at installing and investing in new equipment for the wide-screen process. Years later, when he saw Gordon MacRae at a party, Sinatra pointed a finger and said, "He does my outside work."

....

Twin Palms was "the only house we really could ever call our own," said Ava. "It was the site of probably the most spectacular fight of our young married life, and honey don't think I don't know that's really saying something." (To this day, one of the sinks in the master bathroom bears a crack from a champagne bottle thrown during one of their brawls.)

After their divorce, Frank sold the Palms and moved to a new home in Rancho Mirage, alongside the seventeenth fairway of the Tamarisk Country Club. It started out as a cozy two-bedroom with a small kitchen and dining area, and had a swimming pool off the living room and master bedroom. A golf course meant risks, of course; a golfer once shanked a cart into the pool.

It evolved into what became known as "the Compound," with cottages that had nameplates—"High Hopes," "New York, New York," "My Way"—plus a "caboose" for Frank's elaborate toy train collection, and a tennis court he had built for Ava. It was not lavish by resort hotel or spa standards. It was just very comfortable. Richard Burton archly described it as "a kind of super motel in shape and idea, a series of elaborate suites with every possible modern gadget, surrounding a small swimming pool."

Frank chose the towels, the soaps, and the liquors for the bar personally. Here he was able to host and entertain and lead a private life, to play golf with princes and vice presidents, when he was not shuttling between residences in London and New York, where he had a spectacular duplex on East Seventy-second Street overlooking the East River, and, later, suite 2500 at the Waldorf Towers. In Hollywood, he maintained a Japanese-modern bachelor pad high above the city, with views of the Pacific Ocean, the San Fernando Valley, and downtown L.A.

Ava had visiting rights to all of Frank's homesteads, whether he was there or not. (When he sold the vacation home at Las Brisas, in Acapulco, she was heartbroken.)

. . . .

In the early 1950s, as the impertinent rock and roll started to dominate radio playlists, the market for easy-listening singles began to shrink. Then, along came a new musical format: the long-playing album. Sinatra's shift from singles to albums, in response to the commercial realities, was astutely timed for the man and his music. "LP's made singles seem like foreplay," said record exec Stan Cornyn. "Very non-doo-wop. Record companies now sold twelve songs per sale, not just two. . . . From albums came bigger profits."

Frank had a new deal with Capitol Records. It wasn't lavish—one year only, no advance, and Frank had to pay for the cost of recording sessions. Whereas most albums were like anthologies, collections of singles, Sinatra pioneered the "concept" album, in which each song was part of an overall musical theme. His partner in this endeavor was Nelson Riddle, an arranger Frank met in April 1953. Riddle, like Sinatra, was born in New Jersey. He also served an apprenticeship with Tommy Dorsey, joining the band's trombone section in 1945, and then (when he lost his front teeth) turning his talent toward arranging. In early sessions with Sinatra, Nelson crafted soaring, brassy arrangements for "Don't Worry 'Bout Me" and "I've Got the World on a String," far removed from the old Sinatra choirboy sound.

Frank's voice had deepened, in part from the effects of his lifestyle—
cigarettes and Jack Daniel's, long nights with (and without) Ava. "I didn't
care for his original voice," said Nelson. "I thought it was far too syrupy.
To me his voice only became interesting during the time when I started
to work with him. . . . He became a fascinating interpreter of lyrics, and
actually he could practically have talked the thing for me and it would have
been all right."

Later that year, Nat King Cole rejected "Young at Heart," calling it "a
song for old ladies." Yet when Jimmy Van Heusen heard it, he said, "Frank,
you got to do this one." On December 9, 1953, he recorded the song, art-
fully arranged by Riddle, which rose to number two on the charts, the first
million-selling record of his career, and hit the heights as he was getting
attention for his acting in *From Here to Eternity*. The Sinatra and Riddle col-
laboration was sealed.

On February 17, 1955, Frank recorded "In the Wee Small Hours of the
Morning," a song written by Dave Mann and Bob Hilliard for Nat King
Cole, but intercepted by Frank and Nelson Riddle while going up an elevator in the NYC Capitol building with the songwriters. This would be
the anchor tune for an album of love-gone-bad songs ("ballads of desper-
ation," Riddle's biographer called them), which Frank directed from the
outset. He selected the songs, and rehearsed them night after night with
pianist Bill Miller at his home in the Springs.

Frank met Miller in 1951 at the Desert Inn, where the pianist, a veteran from the great Charlie Barnet band, had a trio in the lounge. Frank
liked what he heard and asked Bill, born in Brooklyn, a few months
older than the singer, to accompany him on TV shows and club dates.
They clicked. Miller was now his musical shadow on retainer; where Frank
went, Miller followed, often hiring musicians for gigs and recording
sessions.

If a problem arose with any of the arrangements, Nelson Riddle would
be summoned to spot-weld. For Sinatra, a performance might be an
evening, but a recording was forever. He went over each song until every

nuance, pause, inflection had been totally mastered by him and the musicians as they laid down the tracks through February and early March of 1955. "In those days he had a voice to burn," said Nelson. He got inside such songs as "Mood Indigo" and Cole Porter's "What Is This Thing Called Love?" Musicians at the sessions said that Frank wept openly while listening to the playback of "When Your Lover Has Gone." After the tracks were mastered, he sequenced them for what he called "the Ava album."

In the Wee Small Hours rose to number two on the album charts and remained there for eighteen weeks. Like the Maggio role, it was a "comeback" for the singer. Frank was living his music, his voice reflecting a lingering sadness but wistful resignation over Ava. "A public that had at first been titillated, then offended, by the Gardner-Sinatra relationship, was now ready to recognize its validity once they heard it expressed as poignantly and painfully as this," said *New York Times* critic John Rockwell. When Nelson was asked to describe Sinatra's voice during this period, he said, "It's like a cello. Ava taught him the hard way."

. . . .

Although he neither read music nor played an instrument, Frank Sinatra nonetheless had a keen musical intelligence. "Frank knew a lot more about music than he let on," said arranger Billy May. "He could hear chord changes a lot of instrumentalists couldn't hear." Frank invited Billy and his wife to dinner at Chasen's and a performance of the Los Angeles Philharmonic one night. "The program included something by a remote Russian composer, Reinhold Glière," said May. "It takes a musician to know about him. He was a contemporary of Rimsky-Korsakov early in the twentieth century. I was surprised that Frank knew all about him—some of his other works, the whole thing. He was very knowledgeable."

Frank heard musical arrangements (not just tunes) in the studio. "He was a good judge . . . 'Take the brass out, they won't hear me . . . put the strings in, let the saxes in there,'" said Lee Herschberg, the recording engineer who worked with him for twenty-five years. "His diction was the best I ever heard. You hear every syllable of every word. He was the best at using a microphone, when to get in close, when to back away. You never heard him breathe." Andy Rooney wrote, "People who understand music hear sounds that no one else makes, when Sinatra sings."

Frank could be high-handed during a recording session. "He thinks nothing of turning around and conducting the orchestra himself to get the exact tempo he wants," said Nelson Riddle. In addition to Nelson, he was blessed with other arrangers who knew how to couch his unique voice and vocalizations, notably Billy May, Gordon Jenkins, and Don Costa. Many songs Frank sang were standards he had recorded in the 1940s, but new arrangements rendered them fresh, different, exciting. Like any great vocal artist, Frank never sang the same song the same way twice, which made his rerecordings more than embalmed souvenirs of times gone by.

....

Nelson Riddle's arrangements became the aural impetus behind Sinatra's musical comeback. His interpretive range was remarkable, from the subdued tones of *In the Wee Small Hours of the Morning* to the hard-charging jazz ethos in the standout album *Songs for Swingin' Lovers!* "He used different instruments—the flute, the bass trombone, the Harmon-muted trumpet bleats of Harry 'Sweets' Edison, vibraphonist Frank Flynn—and the sounds of the woodwinds, and driving brass counterpoint with a lush string background," said Riddle biographer Peter Levinson. "He used the brass and the strings in counterpoint, with the band romping along, and then suddenly cutting off the brass while the rhythm kept going and the strings provided a soft cushion." The Riddle sound was unique and distinctive. "You could recognize it immediately," said pianist Al Lerner. "He used a lot of auxiliary chords and harmonic structures for the strings, which, to my knowledge, hadn't been heard before." Classical musicians often sense echoes of Debussy, Mahler, even Brahms in those Riddle charts.

"Most of our best numbers were in what I call the tempo of the heartbeat," said Riddle. "Music to me is sex—it's all tied up somehow, and the rhythm of sex is the heartbeat. I always have some woman in mind for each song I arrange; it could be a reminiscence of some past romantic experience, or just a dream-scene I build in my own imagination." Riddle's son Chris told Peter Levinson of a heated argument he overheard between his mother and father. "All you think about is music and sex!" said Doreen, ending the squabble. "Is there anything else?" asked Nelson.

During the recording sessions for *Songs for Swingin' Lovers!* in January 1956, the Capitol execs sensed in this a special album, and that there should be more than the usual twelve songs. Producer Voyle Gilmore called Frank, who called Nelson, telling him that he had to arrange three more songs. "Nelson got out of bed and started writing," said Frank Sinatra, Jr. "By seven o'clock the next morning he got two songs to the copyist. He then had a few hours sleep and started writing again at one o'clock in the afternoon." According to Riddle, the arrangement for "I've Got You Under My Skin" was finished in the back of a cab to the studio, where Vern Yocum, the copyist, had ten of his associates ready to roll. Sinatra recorded the first two tunes with Nelson and the orchestra while they were copying the last arrangement, which was what Sinatra, in concert, called "Nelson Riddle's shining hour." Cole Porter's "I've Got You Under My Skin" became synonymous with Sinatra "more than any other arrangement of his entire career," said Peter Levinson. "Milt Bernhart's epic trombone solo on the tune, recorded on January 12, 1956, was one for the ages. It followed on the heels of George Roberts's repeating, burping nineteen-bar bass trombone chorus, which served as its introduction." After the band ran through Nelson's arrangement the first time, the musicians applauded.

Nelson Riddle transformed Sinatra from pious choirboy to hip saloon singer. Frank unearthed a new sound, one he could take from the studio to the nightclub and, later, the concert venues. "As far as I'm concerned, the sound that I got behind Sinatra is *my* sound," said Riddle. "He brought his voice to the picture; I brought my orchestra." André Previn applauded: "I personally think they're Nelson's records with a vocalist on!"

When Dorsey heard *Songs for Swingin' Lovers!*, arranged by his old trombonist, he said, "That son of a bitch is the greatest singer ever! He knows exactly where to go and what to do. The little bastard used to look at me and watch what I was doing when I was playing and he'd ask me, 'How do you hold notes so long? How do you hold that phrase so long?' I have to give Frank credit. He's got good taste. He won't let anybody push him around." When trumpeter Lee Castle said, "I wonder where he got that from," Tommy started laughing.

....

Between April 1953 and April 1957, Nelson Riddle directed over forty Capitol recording sessions for Sinatra. One weekday afternoon, Frank asked him to assemble an orchestra for a late-night session. Nelson started calling in the regulars. "That means paying triple scale, you know," he reminded the musicians, who were puzzled at the late hour. By 11:30 P.M., the band had run through eight or ten numbers, and Frank entered the studio with his lady of the moment, Kim Novak. The actress sat at the rear of the studio while Frank serenaded her in a concert for one. When it ended, he thanked the musicians, took Kim's hand, and the couple departed for adventures in the night.

....

Shortly after signing a new seven-year deal with Capitol in 1960, Frank Sinatra opted to start his own label, Essex Records. Capitol and Frank would each own 50 percent. Alan Livingston told him it was a great idea but not possible. If he afforded Frank such a deal, Nat Cole, Peggy Lee, and others would expect the same consideration.

Frank was upset. But how to get out of his new deal? Enter Mickey Rudin.

Frank may have been all about making music, but his agent and attorney was all about making money. Milton A. "Mickey" Rudin, five years younger than Frank, had gone to Hollywood in the late 1940s by way of Brooklyn and the *Harvard Law Review*. "A heavy man with a deep voice made raspy by ten thousand cigars, Rudin moved slowly, talked slowly, and thought quickly and incisively," wrote David McClintick in his landmark

Hollywood exposé *Indecent Exposure.* "There were few important people in the entertainment communities of Hollywood, Las Vegas, and New York whom Mickey Rudin did not know, few parts of the entertainment industry with which he was unfamiliar, few kinds of information to which he did not have access." Rudin's clients included Marilyn Monroe; Lucille Ball; moguls Marvin Davis, Steve Ross, Stephen Wynn; Elizabeth Taylor; Norman Lear; the Jackson Five; and the Aga Khan. But Sinatra was the big account. Rudin had so much responsibility that they never flew together.

Warner Bros. Records' creative director, Stan Cornyn, called Rudin "a man born to twist arms." The jowly lawyer had portrayed a judge in two cameo roles in movies. Thus, Frank called him "the Judge." When asked about Frank's Mafia connections, Rudin would just smile and look wise. "It never hurt, I wouldn't deny it," he said.

Mickey Rudin explained to Capitol execs that his client had grown hoarse. "He had not too many cards to play against Capitol, but laryngitis was one," said Cornyn in his engaging *Exploding: The Highs, Hits, Hype, Heroes, and Hustlers of the Warner Music Group.* Frank's throat problem could persist for years and years, said Rudin. Might never heal. Who knows?

After months of throat lozenges and silence in the recording studio, the disputing parties worked out a separation agreement. Frank agreed to do four albums for Capitol, and set about creating his new label, now called Reprise, "to play and play again." "Almost everyone pronounced it 'Repreese,'" said Cornyn. "Frank, who was slow to forgive, was the only one to pronounce it 'Re-prize,' as in 'reprisal.'"

Billy May did the arrangements for *Come Swing with Me,* among Frank's last albums at Capitol. "When we went into the studio it was like doing a live album," said May. "One-take Frank. Music While U Wait. But he never gave me a hard time. I could see that Frank was having a problem as we ran a tune down, and I said, 'Is something wrong with the lead sheet?', and he said, 'Yeah, I can't even see it.' He'd been out drinking at a restaurant before coming to the studio. When the session was over, he said, 'Come on fellows, let's go to my place'—and we went to Frank's for two hours to party."

....

After thirty years of making records for others, Frank Sinatra now worked for himself. In January 1961, he launched Reprise Records, which issued its first single on Valentine's Day, Frank singing "The Second Time Around," which climbed to number fifty on the *Billboard* Hot 100. On March 27, Reprise released its first album, Frank's *Ring-a-Ding Ding!,* which reached number four on the charts. But one singer does not a musical roster make. Frank couldn't do it alone. Starting a label is like building a fire: You need enough wood for a real blaze; one or two big sticks were not enough. The company started losing money immediately—Frank's money.

Reprise had signed contracts with many of Frank's old pals, including Duke Ellington, Count Basie, Jo Stafford, Rosemary Clooney, Ethel Merman, Joey Bishop, Art Linkletter, Alice Faye, Danny Kaye, and, yes, Dodgers pitcher Don Drysdale. There was also an act called Arturo Romero and His Magic Violins. Of the sixty-two artists on the roster, only one (apart from Frank) had amounted to anything commercial: Trini López. No rock and roll allowed, of course. Musicians of Frank's generation looked on rock and roll the way brain surgeons espy chiropractors.

Mickey Rudin knew that Essex Productions, which incorporated all of Frank's finances, was in trouble. He talked with Frank, who had been talking with Jack L. Warner. Sinatra was hot from the 1960 film *Ocean's 11,* which he both starred in and packaged for Warner Bros. When Warner suggested doing a multipicture deal, Rudin quickly realized the one asset that Essex could leverage for fresh cash was Frank's acting. Warner's studio also had a struggling record label, so Rudin combined a movie deal for Frank's acting services with the sale of his record company. Reprise called it a merger. Warners called it a "rescue takeover."

Reprise was heavily in debt, and the Warner Bros. Records' management team was pushed back into the red by the acquisition, but show business is all about relationships, and Jack Warner wanted the deal done. As part of the multipicture deal, Frank sold his two-thirds interest in money-losing Reprise and received a one-third share in the combined record company, as well as a seat on the Warner-Reprise board—and Warner did all the funding. (Previously, Frank's funding of Reprise was like throwing his money from a moving car.) In the closing days, Rudin tossed in a small proviso: If Warner ever wanted to sell the merged labels, Frank had veto power. Not a problem, we're all friends here.

"Giving up on Reprise bothered Sinatra not for a moment," said Stan Cornyn. "He'd had it. With his quick passions, Sinatra had craved his own label—the same as he'd other times craved that broad over there, or his own leather booth and bottle of Jack. Quick passion: You do it, you forget it."

In November 1966, the Warner group was taken over by and merged with Seven Arts Productions. In late 1967, when Warner Bros.–Seven Arts purchased Atlantic Records, Rudin steered the deal along so that Sinatra's 33 percent was exchanged for 20 percent interest in a bigger company. Then, in 1968, along came Steve Ross, the tall, silver-haired, silver-tongued deal maker, who was buying and merging his way into the entertainment business, which would eventually land him in the catbird seat as CEO of Time Warner. Known as "the last great pasha of American business," Ross could relate to the ordeals and oddities of the entertainment world; he had sent the company plane across the country to bring Steven Spielberg's dogs to East Hampton, L.I., or back to New York City from the Caribbean to fetch some Nathan's hot dogs.

There was only one obstacle to Steve's $400 million deal in progress—20 percent of the Atlantic and Warner record labels was still owned by Frank Sinatra. That had to be bought out separately. "They had a tremendous position," said Ross's tax lawyer, Alan Cohen. "Sinatra really had veto power." Reenter Mickey Rudin. "Mickey asked me for the world," said Cohen, "and ended up getting nine-tenths of the world." For tax reasons, Steve Ross and Frank Sinatra met and signed the papers in New Jersey over a major Italian dinner at the home of Martin and Dolly Sinatra. Frank had cautioned Ross about his mother's penchant for squirreling away any of her son's money that she could get her hands on. Ross brought along two checks, just in case—one, which he held out as they were closing the deal, and which Dolly grabbed, in the amount of one thousand dollars.

Later, the big check passed to Frank, who folded and slipped it into the headband of his hat, and was surely feeling ring-a-ding as the limo returned him to Manhattan with the biggest paycheck of his life: $22.5 million.

....

"Frank knew he was the king and he played that role," said Eddie Fisher. "I remember him saying, 'I'd rather be a don for the Mafia than President of the United States,'" and that's the way he acted. Frank liked to come on in the manner of a godfather, the *capo dei capi* to the stars. "With my luck," Johnny Carson—himself accustomed to being a star among stars—told a friend, "I'll be on a plane flight with Sinatra that goes down, and the headlines will read 'Sinatra and Others Perish in Crash.'"

Dick Van Dyke recalled the time he and his wife, Margie, were invited for dinner with Hope Lange, his costar on *The New Dick Van Dyke Show,* and Sinatra, who was dating Hope—and was cooking. "Margie was all excited about meeting Frank," said Van Dyke. "It was funny, because it wasn't like she'd never met big stars before. We had attended every major awards show. I'd made movies with some pretty famous people."

Dick reminded Margie that she disliked Hollywood, its stars, and its emphasis on status. She looked at him as if he had started to speak in a strange language. "But this is Frank Sinatra," she said.

....

In the mid-sixties, Frank joined his daughter Tina in several sessions of analysis. "My father fit the mold of the classic overachiever," she said in her memoir, *My Father's Daughter.* "He had his own void inside, the product of his emotionally meager childhood. As long as he kept working, kept moving, he might outrun his loneliness. The void gaped widest when he lacked a special woman in his life, as in the early sixties, when Dad and Ava moved permanently from turbulent romance to entitled friendship, and no one had replaced her."

He dated women, including some who bore a striking resemblance to

Ava. "Before bed, he would be so charming," said Jimmy Van Heusen. "The girl was 'mademoiselle this,' 'darling that,' and 'my sweet baby.' He was cavalier, a perfect gentleman. You never saw anything like this man in your life. He'd jump across the room to light a cigarette. He'd fill her glass with champagne every time she took a sip.

"It was the next day that we'd always find the other Frank, the one who wouldn't speak to the girl, who had been the most beautiful woman in the world the night before. Sometimes he wouldn't even go near her, nor would he tolerate any affectionate overtures from her. Humped and dumped. The minute the conquest was achieved, kaput. The girl could pack her bags. I saw so many of them leave his house in tears."

....

At the height of his career, earning millions a year now, Frank Sinatra seemed to have a talent for everything but happiness. Frank was not what anyone would call introspective. He made no attempt to understand any link between his demons and his mood swings. He functioned on impulse and instinct. His intimates believed him unhappy because second success had cost him Ava. Old loves die hard, if they die at all.

In P.J. Clarke's one rainy evening in 1970, Frank was closing the place with Jimmy Cannon, Jilly Rizzo, and Pete Hamill. Somebody played the jukebox and Billie Holiday filled the room, singing "I'm a Fool to Want You." "A song out of Sinatra's past," said Hamill. "Out of 1951 and Ava Gardner and the most terrible time of his life. Everybody at the table knew the story."

Frank Sinatra, meanwhile, stared at the bourbon in his glass. Then he shook his head. "Time to go," he said. They knocked back their drinks, rose as knights from the Round Table, and followed Frank out a side door and into the rainy night.

⊰ 11 ⊱

Twilight of the Goddess

When Ava moved to Spain in 1955, she lived briefly in a modest three-bedroom brick house on the outskirts of Madrid, where she was almost unreachable. No telephone. Her mail came through a friend, at another address. In December of that year, Ava moved into a large home in La Moraleja, an expensive residential development near Madrid. The house, on two groomed acres, had four bedrooms, three baths, two sitting rooms, large fireplaces, a patio and a swimming pool said to be the largest private pool in the country. Betty and Ricardo Sicre, the latter a successful financier, also moved into La Moraleja, not far from Ava, who was godmother to their son.

Ava was still in demand, but the movie business was changing hourly as the studios continued in free fall. Despite her unhappiness with Hollywood, clearly the old system had benefited her and made her the last of the great love goddesses. Now she lacked regular news (or gossip), had no coaching or guidance, and—even though her agent Charles Feldman was one of the best—there could be long blank stretches between opportunities, even for a goddess.

On a rainy midsummer evening in 1956, Ruth Waterbury, the highly regarded editor of *Photoplay,* met Ava in the bar of the Castellana Hilton in Madrid. Ava arrived in a hostile mood, one that the editor knew well. "It is not a personal hostility, but one that Ava holds against the world in general," said Waterbury. "From the day Ava first landed in Hollywood, she's always had it, and now it's getting worse. Why does Ava who has everything—beauty, youth, fame, fortune, freedom—hate everything?"

The actress's mood went beyond being "merely angry." Ava blasted MGM and the producers who had misused her. "One more year on my MGM contract and I'm free," she said. "Free to do exactly what I please, when I please and nothing else but." Or so Ava hoped. Initially, every-one thought the stars would have some creative freedom after the end of the studio system. But along with the freedom came the difficulties of redefining and reselling themselves to a shifting audience. Unless you have a savvy marketing team behind you, this can be self-defeating. All that Ava had was her sister Bappie and her maid, Reenie, and they would often come and go.

"She seems to think that life, reporters and MGM are all trying to put something over on her, as, for instance when the studio tried to talk her into making *Love Me or Leave Me,*" said Waterbury. "She said they weren't going to stick her with that one. You know what a hit that turned out to be—for Doris Day. It's all such a shame. Ava has such warmth, when she wants to turn it on."

....

In January 1959, Ava—free from MGM at last—departed for Australia with Bappie and former studio publicist (now her manager) David Hanna to star with Gregory Peck in *On the Beach,* a bleak story of Australian sur-vivors facing global contamination after a nuclear war. When she arrived, a remark attributed to her in the press enraged many in that nation. "I'm here to make a film about the end of the world, and this seems to be exactly the right place for it," she was reported to have said. Of course, throughout her life, Gardner was known for her imprudent talk and down-to-earth quips, sometimes cutting to the quick. Of Clark Gable—once her teen idol—she is reported to have said, "Clark is the sort of guy that if you say, 'Hiya, Clark, how are you?' he's stuck for an answer."

"The Melbourne press really gave her a bad time," said director Stanley Kramer. "They asked questions about her tax situation, whether Frank Sinatra was coming to see her, how often he phoned her."

In one of their phone conversations, Frank mentioned a concert he had given, and Ava said she wished she could see him. "So why don't I come down there and sing to you?" he said.

"I would love that, baby."

"Then you got it," said Frank, just like that.

Ava sat in the front row at the West Melbourne Stadium the night of March 31, 1959, when Frank sang his heart out, backed by the Red Norvo Quintet, which he brought with him from Los Angeles. The concert, recorded—but not released—became an underground favorite among Sinatra connoisseurs, especially for the vibes work by Norvo as Frank sang the closer, Cole Porter's "Night and Day."

Afterward, Melbourne photographers and reporters chased Frank, quizzing him about a reconciliation with Ava. "You slobs," he snarled. "If I see you again, you'll never forget it. They'll find you in the gutter." The press wars intensified. Years later, the infamous quote attributed to Ava would be exposed as a fabrication by (Sydney) *Sun-Herald* reporter Neil Jillett. Exasperated at being denied an interview with Ava, he added the phony quote as a joke, he later claimed. His editors, failing to see the humor, printed it as a statement, and it became an Ava quote heard 'round the world. If the press ever asked her that question again, said Ava to director Kramer, her revised response would be, "I'm here to make a film about the end of the world, and I hope all you fellows are there when it happens."

. . . .

After Australia, Ava returned to Madrid, where, after seventeen years in MGM's harness, she could go her own way with no studio to watch over her, no morals clause to frustrate her inhibitions. Ava was free to choose a life of her own. She chose a dissolute one.

In the past, stories had proliferated of her adventures with toreadors. "In the bull ring of the ancient town of Alcala de Henares, slight, curly-haired matador Cesar Giron, 21, was so inspired by Ava's presence in the stands that he dispatched his bull in high style, won both ears and the tail, presented his bloody trophies to Ava, who clutched an ear to her lips for a long kiss as the crowd cheered," reported *Time* magazine. It was said that she so overwhelmed a novillero—one who has never fought bulls in Madrid—named Chamanco that she ruined his career at twenty.

Now the tales about the most glamorous expatriate in Madrid escalated as Ava, amateurishly, became consumed by flamenco. Flamenco dancing sessions usually started after midnight and rarely ended before dawn. Flamenco sessions may take one guitarist or ten to begin with, one dancer or two dozen to respond to their rhythm, and a steady supply of wine. In Madrid, where she had been banned from many of the flamenco clubs, Ava's entourage consisted of Gypsies who vagrantly worked the bars as entertainers, performing for tips, or playing at parties where they might drink and carry off items of value. Ava's notorious flamenco sessions at her house became the talk of Madrid. They often continued until noon the next day; and then she slept for a day afterward.

Ava was still struggling with Spanish, unable to manage a conversation. Driving was an uncertain pilgrimage. One morning, she tried to locate a Madrid physician, whose address was "Santa Barbara," which could mean a plaza, a square, or a street in the city. After several false starts, she was recognized by a group of young street children, who ran in front and alongside of the car, with loud cries—"Ava, Ava"—leading her to the intended Santa Barbara physician.

. . . .

In Madrid, Ava found ephemeral solace in the arms of many lovers. Peter Duchin, a young pianist on holiday to celebrate the release of his first album, met Ava at a flamenco club one evening. "While I tried to look cool, Ava Gardner let go with her great horselaugh and checked me out with her almond-shaped eyes," he said. "Before long I was coming on to her, and she was coming on to me." Ava was "as real a woman as I've ever known," he would later recollect in tranquility. "The pain in her life had outweighed the joy, and she wasn't afraid to show it. Apparently, she hadn't recovered from her breakup with Frank Sinatra, about whom she talked often and fondly." She asked Peter to play songs that Frank had sung for her. When he played "Lush Life," one of her favorites, she leaned on the piano and sang the lyrics softly and cried.

"I was half her age, but I must have appealed to her because of my energy, even though it wasn't quite a match for hers," said Duchin. "Every night, five nights running, we hit the flamenco clubs. All the musicians and dancers knew her. The moment she walked in, they exploded."

Peter's great adventure ended abruptly at seven o'clock one morning when Ava's Ferrari spun out on a wet country road. "While we whirled to a stop in a hay field, my life passed before me," he said. "Ava just laughed and laughed."

. . . .

During the summer of 1961, MGM star Esther Williams and husband, Fernando Lamas, were invited to a party at the Madrid home of Luis Miguel Domínguín and Lucia Bosé. Suddenly, Ava arrived, trailed by an entourage of drunken Gypsies. She was barefoot, wearing a bright blue-and-red Gypsy-style dress, with Spanish earrings and her hair long and brushed straight. She looked stunning. As she lapsed into her flamenco routine, she riveted everyone's attention.

"Obviously they'd all been drinking sangria by the gallon," said Williams. "They also had not been invited. Nevertheless, Ava decided to get up on a table and dance flamenco." As she twirled, atop the table in front of her former lover, everything was revealed, for she was not wearing panties. Lucia told Domínguín, "Get her out of here!"

"My heart went out to Ava and what she had become," said Esther. "If you wanted to see someone who had lost the golden halo that came with Hollywood stardom, all you had to do was look at Ava Gardner, my old MGM friend. She had gone from famous to infamous to notorious and was now regarded as something of a menace to polite society in Madrid."

. . . .

"There were reports that Ava had relieved herself in the lobby of the Ritz in Madrid," said Bob Thomas. "When that got back to Hollywood, which was a small company town, it did tremendous harm to her reputation. She was putting herself out of the business." Ava's biographer Lee Server said, "She had openly urinated in the vestibule between the reception lobby and the bar, witnessed by startled staff and passing guests. As a result, she was forbidden to ever enter the hotel."

When James Stewart signed in at the Ritz as "film actor," the receptionist told him the hotel did not allow actors to stay there. The unwritten law had expanded to include *all* singers and movie stars at both the Ritz and the Palace hotels. Taking advantage of his military status, Stewart signed in as "Colonel, U.S. Air Force." That was acceptable. For director Billy Wilder, however, there was no room at the Ritz, despite his plea. "I swore to God I would not pee in the vestibule," he said.

. . . .

Next to the Eiffel Tower and the Folies Bergère, one of Paris's most desirable (and expensive) attractions was La Tour d'Argent, a restaurant known for its haute cuisine, and the company it kept, including presidents and premiers, statesmen and celebrities. After her first visit to La Tour d'Argent, in the 1950s, Julia Child wrote, "The restaurant was excellent in every way, except that it was so pricey that every guest was American." Among those American guests were Frank and Ava, who were still together at the time.

Now, in 1961, Ava returned alone to the restaurant one evening for a late supper. The kitchen was closed, but Claude Terrail, the tall, imposing owner, remembered her well. He cooked a steak for Ava, and an affair blossomed. Claude was no stranger to Hollywood; he had been married to the daughter of Jack Warner, and he had squired Jane Fonda, Jayne Mansfield, and Marilyn Monroe over the years. Errol Flynn and Orson Welles were friends. When not overseeing the restaurant, he kept himself busy as a playboy. "There is nothing more serious than pleasure," he said.

It became a jet-set romance, "for seven months, eight months, all over the world I went with her. My fantastic time with Ava, the most divine person I have ever met," he told Lee Server. "Such highs and such lows, this was Ava. Nothing between. Like a queen one moment, a scared child the next. At times so romantic, so sweet, like a girl of seventeen years old."

For his birthday, Ava wrote out a check, payable to Claude "in the amount of a million kisses." In the evening, when he came home late, he would follow a trail of small notes Ava had written, leading to where she awaited him. "The things she did were not those of an ordinary person," he said. "She would put on one of Frank Sinatra's records and have a private talk with him, as he was singing. She would sit and listen and say, 'Yes, yes, I know . . .' or another song and she would say, 'No, don't say that . . . you must forget . . .' She would have a talk with the record itself. It was something almost mystical."

Ava wore Claude out. Life became a series of ups and downs. Her drinking worsened. It began to frighten him, the personality change once the liquor began to flow. "I had to give up," he said. "She was too dangerous for me."

. . . .

After not working for nearly three years, Ava happily accepted $500,000 from producer Samuel Bronston in 1962 to play Baroness Natalie Ivanoff in *55 Days at Peking,* a story of Americans in China during the Boxer Rebellion. The picture would be shot near Madrid, where an almost full-scale model of the Forbidden City had been built on the plains. It would be blown up in the final scene in the movie, which also starred David Niven and Charlton Heston. Heston opposed casting Ava. Her stardom was starting to fade, but Bronston insisted that she was still "very big in foreign release."

Charlton Heston had come into films as the studio system was breaking down, but he understood how it functioned—"very efficiently, but with not much care for its people," he said. "Ava had not been treated well, I think—not by the studio that made her, or the several famous men who married her as a trophy wife, nor the larger number who used and abused her as a star-fuck. That's an ugly word, but nakedly honest."

Ava soon meant trouble on the set. "Like many very beautiful actresses (and there were none more beautiful than Ava), she was very insecure about her acting, though she was in fact perfectly capable," said Heston. The problem was alcohol. "Ava's security trembled on the rim of a vodka glass, into which she often slipped." She had also begun an affair with David Niven, which was more like a romp between old friends than a real romance. Back in the 1940s, Ava had had a dalliance with David and learned about the kinky side to his sedate British demeanor—including a one-way mirror installed between the men's and women's changing rooms in the swimming pool cabin at his Beverly Hills home. "You could see through into the ladies' changing room," said actor John Mills, "so the men's changing room was always crowded!"

In *55 Days at Peking*, Paul Lukas was playing the doctor in charge of the hospital in the foreign compound. Lukas, a Hungarian actor, had played the role of the father in Lillian Hellman's play *Watch on the Rhine*, and was admired by all. In 1944, he won the Best Actor Oscar for the same role in the movie version, beating out Humphrey Bogart in *Casablanca*. Ava approached him one day. "Mr. Lukas, I have great respect for your acting, and I'd certainly appreciate any tips you could offer me about my acting," she said, perhaps patronizingly. Lukas glared at her. "Yes, Miss Gardner, I think there is something that would help a lot," he said, nodding and shaking his head agreeably. "If you could manage not to start drinking before noon every day."

. . . .

Frank and Ava, cheek to cheek in early 1953 when things were going strong. Later that year they split, and the war continued for better and for worse, until death did them part. *Sunset Boulevard/Corbis*

Frank with pal Tony Consiglio and trumpeter Ziggy Elman a few weeks before the December 30, 1942, Paramount Theatre show that would launch him as the original American idol. *Photo courtesy of Franz Douskey*

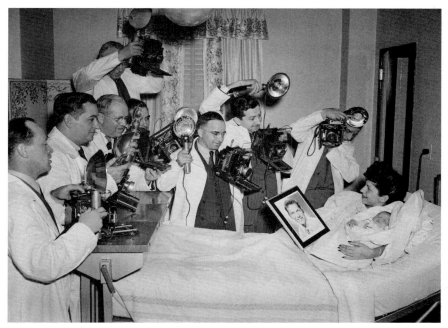

Nancy with Frank Jr. in a Jersey City hospital shortly after his birth in January 1944. Frank Sr. was in Hollywood making a movie. *Bettmann/Corbis*

Frank and Nancy in their Toluca Lake homestead with young Nancy, baby Tina, and Frank Jr., late 1948. *Bettmann/Corbis*

Ava and Mickey Rooney married on January 10, 1942, in the village of Ballard, California. Sister Bappie and Les Peterson, from MGM's publicity department, attended the ceremony. *Bettmann/Corbis*

The bride wore a navy blue suit and a corsage of orchids. The groom stood on a stool and appeared as tall as Ava in press pictures. *Bettmann/Corbis*

MGM mogul Louis B. Mayer with Jean Harlow, the "blonde bombshell" who costarred with Clark Gable in *Red Dust*, which Ava saw as a youngster. Ava played her part in the remake, *Mogambo*, with Gable. *Bettmann/Corbis*

Ava and Mickey study a banquet program as Louis B. Mayer holds a cigar, and his tongue. Before their marriage, he warned Ava, "He just wants to get into your pants." *Bettmann/Corbis*

Ava and Artie Shaw at the Stork Club in New York, March 5, 1945. They married in October that year—she was Artie's fourth wife. (There would be eight.) "These love goddesses are not what they seem," he said. *Bettmann/Corbis*

Ava and Burt Lancaster take a photo-opportunity break between scenes of *The Killers* in 1946. For Burt, it was his first movie. For Ava, after years of walk-ons and bit parts, it was a breakthrough role. *Sunset Boulevard/Corbis*

Hoboken celebrated Frank Sinatra Day in October 1947 as Captain Martin Sinatra put his hat on the head of his son and they rode through town on a fire engine while 50,000 cheered. *Bettmann/Corbis*

Ava in London, making *Pandora and the Flying Dutchman* with actor/toreador Mario Cabre, who romanced her with wine and poetry. Frank flew in from the States, and Mario returned to the bullfighting trade. *Bettmann/Corbis*

Ava and Frank were members of MGM's Class of '49 that posed for a portrait to celebrate the studio's twenty-fifth anniversary. *Front row L-R:* Lionel Barrymore, June Allyson, Leon Ames, Fred Astaire, Edward Arnold, Lassie, Mary Astor, Ethel Barrymore, Spring Byington, James Craig, Arlene Dahl. *Second row:* Gloria DeHaven, Tom Drake, Jimmy Durante, Vera-Ellen, Errol Flynn, Clark Gable, Ava Gardner, Judy Garland, Betty Garrett, Edmund Gwenn, Kathryn Grayson, Van Heflin. *Third row:* Katharine Hepburn, John Hodiak, Claude Jarman Jr., Van Johnson, Jennifer Jones, Louis Jourdan, Howard Keel, Gene Kelly, Alf Kjellin, Angela Lansbury, Mario Lanza, Janet Leigh. *Fourth row:* Peter Lawford, Jeanette MacDonald, Ann Miller, Ricardo Montalban, Jules Munshin, George Murphy, Reginald Owen, Walter Pidgeon, Jane Powell, Ginger Rogers, Frank Sinatra, Red Skelton. *Back row:* Alexis Smith, Ann Sothern, J. Carroll Naish, Dean Stockwell, Lewis Stone, Clinton Sundberg, Robert Taylor, Audrey Totter, Spencer Tracy, Esther Williams, Keenan Wynn. *John Springer Collection/Corbis*

July 18, 1951. Frank and Ava at the Los Angeles premiere of *Show Boat*, which was also the premiere showing of the scandalous couple in public. *Bettmann/Corbis*

Frank and Ava, returning to New York from Philadelphia, where they applied for a marriage license but were unable to marry. The nearly-weds would spend the cooling-off period quarreling at the Hampshire House. *Bettmann/Corbis*

On November 7, 1951, a rainy Wednesday in West Germantown, Pennsylvania, the couple was married in a friend's home as reporters and photographers clustered outside the house. "Well, we finally made it," said Frank. *Bettmann/Corbis*

In Miami, two days after the wedding, a photographer grabbed a lonely shot of Frank and Ava, holding hands as they barefooted along a cold, windy beach dressed in an odd mix of clothes. Ava wore one of Frank's jackets. Her trousseau bag still had not arrived. *Bettmann/Corbis*

After spending their first wedding anniversary in Africa, where Ava was costarring in *Mogambo* with Clark Gable and Grace Kelly, the couple posed for a getaway photo as Frank returned to Hollywood to begin work on *From Here to Eternity*. *Bettmann/Corbis*

On location in Hawaii, director Fred Zinnemann coaches Montgomery Clift and Frank for a scene in *Eternity*, which was an enormous success for Sinatra the actor, but not for Sinatra the husband. *John Springer Collection/Corbis*

While Frank's career faltered, Ava's was on the ascent. In October 1952 (shortly after their Palm Springs battle that brought police to the house), Ava was all smiles as she left her footprints in soft concrete at the famed forecourt of Grauman's Chinese Theatre in Hollywood. *Bettmann/Corbis*

Ava, alone, at the Los Angeles premiere of *Mogambo,* October 8, 1953. Frank was performing at the Sands in Las Vegas. MGM would announce their separation later that month. *Michael Ochs/Corbis*

Frank and Ava, arriving in Rome on December 28, 1953. Frank's effort to reconcile during the holidays would fail. Ava was having a torrid affair with toreador Luis Miguel Dominguin. *AP Photo*

Luis Miguel Dominguin and Lucia Bosé, the Italian actress he married shortly after parting with Ava. During her flamenco madness days, Ava crashed one of their parties. *Bettmann/Corbis*

Humphrey Bogart kisses Ava's cheek at a party before the start of their film, *The Barefoot Contessa*. They both loved Frank, but disliked each other. *Bettmann/Corbis*

Frank and Tommy Dorsey reunited in August 1956 for a show at the Paramount Theatre. When Dorsey heard Frank's *Songs for Swingin' Lovers*, arranged by his old trombonist Nelson Riddle, he said, "That son of a bitch is the greatest singer ever!" *AP Photo*

Frank in the Capitol recording studio, Los Angeles, 1956, when he was creating a remarkable series of "concept" albums. "He thinks nothing of turning around and conducting the orchestra himself to get the exact tempo he wants," said arranger Nelson Riddle, behind Sinatra to the right in this photo. *Bettmann/Corbis*

The origins of Frank's rat pack have been traced to this gathering at the Sands' Copa Room in Las Vegas, June 1955. Left to right: Humphrey Bogart; Sid Luft; Lauren Bacall; Judy Garland; Ellie Graham; Jack Entratter; Mike Romanoff (partly hidden); Frank Sinatra; Gloria Romanoff; David Niven; and Primmie Niven. *AP Photo*

Frank Sinatra on stage at the Sands, early October 1956, during the belated celebration of Lauren Bacall's thirty-second birthday. Guests include (left to right) Jack Benny, Mary Livingston, John Ireland, Kim Novak, Cole Porter, and Lauren Bacall. Bogie, gravely ill, stayed home to sail with his son. *Bettmann/Corbis*

Ava talking with U. S. Ambassador John Davis Lodge in choice seats at a Valencia bull-fight. Betty and Ricardo Sicre, next to Ava, were the actress's closest friends in Madrid. *Bettmann/Corbis*

Frank and singer Peggy Connelly at the Academy Awards in March 1956. Frank took Peggy to Madrid that summer, where he attempted another reconciliation with Ava, which failed, to the surprise of no one. *Bettmann/Corbis*

Ava at the Rome airport in 1956 with Italian comic Walter Chiari, who did an imitation of Frank in his act. They traveled together for years, including a trip to her family in North Carolina. *AP Photo*

Ava on the set of *The Sun Also Rises* in 1957 with Tyrone Power, Robert Evans, and Mel Ferrer. Ava led the campaign to kick Evans off the movie. He later became her lover. *Genevieve Naylor/ Corbis*

Lauren Bacall with Frank leaving the Pantages Theater after viewing the closed-circuit fight between Carmen Basilio and Ray Robinson in September 1957. At the time there were rumors of marriage in the Hollywood air. *Bettmann/Corbis*

Ava on the set of *The Naked Maja*, in 1957, when she was under contract to MGM and the demand for love goddesses was still profitable for the studio. *Sunset Boulevard/Corbis*

Ava on the streets of Rome in 1964 with George C. Scott, who beat her savagely. When asked how she could stand this guy, Ava replied, "Oh, I've fallen for him." *Bettmann/Corbis*

Frank Sinatra and Mia Farrow on their wedding day, with Jack Entratter, at the Sands Hotel in Las Vegas, July 21, 1966. Ava wept. *Bettmann/Corbis*

Frank with Dolly and Frank Jr. at Marty Sinatra's funeral, January 28, 1969, at the Madonna Church in Fort Lee, New Jersey. The cortege and burial afterward turned the event into a travesty. *AP Photo/Anthony Camerano*

Ava and Reenie Jordan, her lifelong maid and travel companion, in Rome, where Ava shopped for a trousseau when it appeared she and Frank would remarry. *Photo courtesy of Flora Cunningham*

Frank and Barbara Marx slice cake at their wedding on the Annenberg estate in Palm Springs, July 11, 1976. "I told Frank he should marry Barbara," said Ava. "It's better for all of us." *Bettmann/Corbis*

Frank escorts Barbara as they arrive at the White House to attend the seventieth-birthday celebration of President Ronald Reagan, February 6, 1981. *Bettmann/Corbis*

On August 5, Ava was shocked when Frank telephoned with the news that Marilyn Monroe had been found dead. Frank wasn't convinced it was the suicide the police were calling it. He was going to launch his own investigation. Frank and Marilyn had lived together and consoled each other in 1954, when he was despondent over the loss of Ava, and Marilyn was still recovering then from the break with Joe DiMaggio. Both were still in love with their estranged spouses.

"Frank said that Marilyn was like a shooting star, and you couldn't help but be fascinated by her journey," said Esther Williams. "While you knew she was going to crash and burn, you didn't know how. The only reason Sinatra wouldn't allow himself to become more serious about Marilyn, was because he was still so wracked with pain about Ava."

Ava commiserated with David Niven, who was guilt-ridden, too. He recalled waking up in the morning after a party at a friend's house, and lying next to him was "this starlet called Marilyn Monroe." Now it haunted him, to think she might have killed herself over the way she had been treated, like a passed-around sexual toy. It was a death due at least in part to the ordeals of stardom, an occupational hazard.

....

Ava's difficulties continued as the *55 Days at Peking* shoot moved along. She was usually a half hour late to the set, and a no-show one morning, insisting she was ill. Scenes had to be rearranged, shots switched, actors called in, actors sent off the set, and the frustration grew in the heat of a Spanish summer. One day, Ava showed up late, did one shot, and walked off when an extra took a snapshot of her. Aside from assigned and credentialed professionals, no one was supposed to take her picture, certainly not on the set. Ava returned after a three-hour lunch, and walked off again when she heard the click of another camera. No one else did. "She insisted that the offender be found, fired, and stripped of his film," said Heston. "In her fury, she made the Dowager Empress of China seem like your favorite aunt." Ava retired to her dressing room to compose herself, and director Nicholas Ray wrapped the company for the day.

And so it went into the blazing month of September, when Ray collapsed with a major coronary. Ava was shaken. "I think she even accepted some responsibility for it," said Heston. "It's been as difficult a working relationship as I've ever known, but you have to feel some sympathy for a sick and lonely person. I suppose she feels ill equipped for the situation in which she finds herself, and reacts with suspicion and hostility because she has no capacity for richer response."

At the end of the shoot, Ava attended a party, looking marvelous in white satin with appropriate and obviously genuine emeralds. There was music and dancing and drinking. As Charlton Heston left the party that night, he saw Ava standing alone in the middle of the Avenida Generalissimo in her white satin evening gown, with her red satin cape, performing matadors' passes on the taxis speeding by. "She was incredibly beautiful," he said.

Nicholas Ray never directed another feature.

. . . .

In 1964, John Huston and producer Ray Stark met Ava in Madrid to discuss casting for *The Night of the Iguana*. This was the first time Huston had seen Ava since working on the script (without credit) of *The Killers* in 1946, when, rather than jump into his arms, she jumped into his swimming pool. Now, eighteen years later, she was a different Ava. "Before, she had been shy and hesitant in her delivery, having to overcome a Southern accent which prompted her to speak slowly and carefully; now she spoke freely—I might even say, with abandon," said Huston. This, combined with her beauty and her maturity, made her perfect for the role of Maxine Faulk, the hotelier who lusts after the defrocked priest played by Richard Burton.

Ava had misgivings about her ability to do the part. "I knew damned well that Ava was going to do it; she did, too—but she wanted to be courted," said Huston. "So Ray and I stayed on in Madrid another week and played the game. . . . Because of my earlier strikeout, I let Ray take the lead."

Stark was a small man, with light hair and blue eyes. He laughed at himself a lot but was relentless in his pursuit of an objective. The nightlife of Madrid proved to be a test. "The first night we went out, I left the scene around four in the morning," said Huston. "Ray stayed on with Ava. This went on for three or four days—through most of the nightspots and flamenco dance groups in Madrid—and I started leaving at midnight. Ray became more haggard and gray-faced. Ava blossomed. She was just pursuing her regular routine. When we left, poor Ray was a shattered wreck, but Ava had agreed to do the picture."

"The tangled web of relationships among the principals set something of a record," said Huston. "Elizabeth Taylor, who was still married to Eddie Fisher, accompanied Richard Burton. Michael Wilding, Elizabeth's ex-husband, handled the job of publicizing Richard Burton. Peter Viertel, Deborah Kerr's second husband, had once been involved with Ava Gardner."

Ava gave what many thought was her finest performance on film. Her "attendants" on location in Mexico were two local beach boys, who followed her every place she went.

. . . .

For Dino De Laurentiis, *The Bible* was to be the mother of all epics: two six-hour films with five auteurs—Orson Welles, Federico Fellini, Robert Bresson, Luchino Visconti, and John Huston—and a budget of ninety million dollars.

After a few cuts in the budget, only one director survived—John Huston—and the story was trimmed to the first twenty-two chapters of Genesis. George C. Scott was cast as Abraham, and Ava was the choice for Sarah, with some trepidation on her part after struggling through that epic turkey *55 Days at Peking*.

Ava met Huston and Scott at the Grand Hotel in Rome, and everything was cordial and businesslike. Scott was with his family—Colleen Dewhurst and sons—and Ava had spent a few days with Frank Sinatra, who was filming *Von Ryan's Express*—about a mass escape by Allied prisoners from an Italian prison camp—and living in an eighteen-room villa that Twentieth

Century–Fox had provided outside Rome, with a heliport from which he was flown each morning to the movie's mountain location.

Actor Brad Dexter joined them for dinner at the villa one evening. Dexter was better known now as the guy who had saved Frank from drowning off the coast of Hawaii during the filming of *None But the Brave,* rather than as one of the leads in *The Magnificent Seven,* and the husband of Peggy Lee. "Frank was still trying to revive the relationship," he said, "but it was painful for Frank to see the woman he adored destroying herself with booze." "She's the only woman I've ever been in love with in my whole life, and look at her," said Frank after Ava staggered from the table. "She's turned into a falling-down drunk."

....

George C. Scott, a former marine, was a much-admired actor with a long-standing, lamentable reputation for heavy drinking and terrible tantrums. He was called the "Wild Man of Broadway" after a conflict with a costar in an Off-Broadway production of *Richard III,* tearing apart his dressing room, punching his hand through a mirror and opening an artery, and breaking three knuckles.

After dinner and a few drinks one evening, the affair was under way. Ava, now forty-two, saw Scott, thirty-eight, as a jovial bedfellow. What she overlooked was that he was falling in love with her. The actor soon had visions of marriage, and he became insanely jealous at the mention of any of her previous lovers or husbands. "If I even mentioned Frank Sinatra's name, he would boil over," she said. "Talk about obsessive! His rages were terrifying." He would awaken in their bed after drunken rages, unaware that he had left Gardner bloody and bruised. "We both drank a fair amount," said Ava, "but when I drank I usually got mellow and happy. When George got drunk, he could go berserk."

....

Sinatra heard about Ava's latest difficulties and called Tom Shaw, assistant director on *The Bible,* at three o'clock one morning. "He wanted to know if it was true what he heard: that George Scott beat the shit out of Ava," Shaw told Huston biographer Lawrence Grobel. Shaw didn't want to get caught between Sinatra and Scott. "No," he said, but Sinatra knew better.

One evening while Ava and Scott were fighting in a restaurant parking lot, three bruisers surrounded George, and then drove him off in a waiting car. The next morning, he was rueful and apologetic. The beatings ceased for a while.

Ava, ever loyal to John Huston, refused to quit the movie—which would have been costly for all—but she also refused to quit Scott. Initially, her bruises could be covered with makeup, but then the beatings escalated. Scott fractured her collarbone, putting her in a neck brace, which they covered up in biblical robes. After Ava dislocated her shoulder— saying she had slipped on a rug—Huston changed the shooting schedule so that Ava could see a doctor in Madrid, who bandaged her with a harness, which she wore beneath her costumes until the end of the location work in Rome.

Scott's wife left Rome with the boys and returned home to Connecticut. Ava and Scott began drinking heavily and fighting in public. "I mean, two people drunk don't make for a good love affair," said Tom Shaw. "I'm almost convinced he never fucked her. I don't know why. But I've been in that position where you're loaded . . . and it was going on constantly."

Frank called Ava as he was packing to depart. "Angel, why don't you and Reenie come and stay out here at this villa?" He was finished shooting the movie. "There's a big pool, and it's all paid for and there's a car." Ava said yes, telling only John Huston.

Scott showed up at the villa one evening around midnight, thinking that this was Sinatra's place, which intensified his anger. "He started hitting and punching Ava, and she wouldn't resist," said Reenie. "But he had wakened the two big guys Sinatra had left for Ava, just in case." Scott was escorted ungently off the premises and hauled back to where he'd come from.

. . . .

Stephen Birmingham, the author Ava befriended on the set of *The Night of the Iguana,* was staying at Ava's house in Madrid with his wife, Nan, while Ava was in Rome. When she returned, one arm was in a sling. Scott had yanked out a hunk of hair on the back of her head, and she had double vision in both eyes. "How can you stand this guy?" asked Birmingham.

"Oh, I've fallen for him," she said. "I've fallen for him."

A few days later, Scott came to Madrid, and Birmingham was invited for drinks at Ava's. "I walked in and George's face looked like raw hamburger, sort of oozing and awful," said the writer.

Ava pulled him aside into the kitchen. "You see George's face?"

"My God, what happened?"

"Last night he got drunk, he had a fire going in the fireplace, and he threw himself face-first into the live coals," said Ava. "I had to pull him out."

....

Ava seemed a willing victim, and had suffered verbal abuse during her marriage to Artie Shaw, and physical encounters with Howard Hughes, who had dislocated her jaw during a fight. But Scott's pattern of abuse was more dangerous. It would start with a drunken rage, a quarrel, the beating, followed by apologies and remorse the next morning, along with a declaration of undying love and the blackmail of what he would do to himself if she left him. "Women believe this sort of junk," said Reenie, who watched in horror from the sidelines and commiserated with Ava the morning after.

Stephen Birmingham theorized that Ava stayed in the relationship because she came "from an environment, kind of redneck, where men beat up women. If you weren't happy with what your wife or your girlfriend did, you let her have it; you slammed her across the face. So I think she thought that was part of the way men and women interact. Or at least it wasn't strange to her. Also, she had a tendency toward liking violence. She obviously liked bullfighters, and she liked the bullfight itself, its kind of physical excitement."

Frank was quoted in *Photoplay,* April 1965: "If there's one guy I don't tolerate, it's a guy who mistreats women. They are the real bullies in life and what they need is a real working over by a man their own size."

....

During the holidays, Ava and Reenie were staying at the Regency in Manhattan. (Ava had been banned at the St. Regis.) George Scott called and invited her to his home, a farmhouse in Greenwich, Connecticut. He promised not to drink.

Reenie was appalled. "Miss G, you are mad!" she said. "He might kill you!"

"He is fine if he doesn't drink," said Ava. "We will get along. Everything will be all right."

They agreed that if Scott behaved badly, Ava was to call Reenie. Next afternoon, the phone rang. "Reenie, could you give me that recipe for fried chicken with dumplings?" said Ava. Reenie could tell by Ava's voice that it was bad.

"Miss G and her sister Bappie had been raised on Southern fried chicken—not with dumplings! She was in deep trouble!"

Reenie had read in the newspaper that Frank Sinatra was in town, staying in his suite in the Waldorf. She got through to him. "Mister Sinatra," she said, "I think Miss G is in bad trouble, and I don't know what to do." She told him about the situation. She didn't have a phone number or an address in Connecticut.

"Don't worry, Reenie," said Frank. "I'll take care of it."

Later that day, two massive men visited George C. Scott at his farmhouse in Connecticut and advised him to say good-bye to Ava. She returned to her suite at the Regency. When Reenie asked what had happened, Ava refused to talk about it.

....

In January 1965, Ava Gardner was in London to visit her friend the poet and novelist Robert Graves, who was lecturing at Oxford. She stayed at the Savoy Hotel. As it happened, George Scott was also in London—ostensibly for the premiere of *The Yellow Rolls-Royce*—and staying at the Savoy. He asked her to an evening at the theater. He had tickets for *Othello,* probably not the best choice, given George and Ava's history. Othello: "Get me some poison Iago, this night. I'll not expostulate with her, lest her body and beauty unprovide my mind again . . ." Iago: "Do it not with poison. Strangle her in her bed . . ."

Afterward, Ava said good night to Scott in the hotel lobby and went to her suite. Later that night, roaring drunk, he broke down the door and burst into the room, holding a broken bottle. Ava and Reenie hid in the locked bathroom and escaped through a transom into the hallway, fleeing down the corridor as Scott returned to his room and trashed it. Security was called; the British police took him to the lockup. On January 8, 1965, London's *Daily Express* reported that Scott had pleaded guilty to charges of being drunk and disorderly. When Ava paid her bill, the Savoy manager said that the hotel would no longer accept any reservations from her.

. . . .

In November 1965, George C. Scott met a friend in a bar in New York City. He was alone now; earlier that year, Colleen Dewhurst had divorced him. After a few drinks, Ava's name came up. "Yeah, she's in Hollywood at the Beverly Hills," said George. "Let's give her a call." When he finally got Ava on the phone, it was just like old times: They quarreled and Scott hung up in anger. That night, Scott told his friend Tammy Grimes that he was going to drive across the country to beg for Ava's hand.

The next day George C. Scott purchased two bottles of vodka, a Lincoln Continental, and drove to Los Angeles. In her bungalow at the Beverly Hills Hotel, at one o'clock in the morning, Ava heard the sounds of someone forcing his way through the back door. Scott, in a drunken rage, pinned Ava down and started hitting her. If she didn't marry him, he said, he would kill her. He smashed a bottle and waved the jagged glass at her face. "I thought this time it was all over for me," she said. She kept talking to him, trying to calm him down. "Listen, honey, you're in bad shape," she said. "Let me call a doctor." Gradually, he began to fade.

"I called my doctor to give him an injection so he could be peacefully removed from the premises," Ava said. "And let me tell you, *that* wasn't easy. Jesus, that was a scary time. Probably the scariest."

"Scott had tracked Miss G from Rome to London to New York to Beverly Hills," said Reenie. "He was exhausted, unshaven, defeated, the victim of his own raging madness. He just sat there with his head in his hands."

Ava never saw George C. Scott again. She told hair stylist Sydney Guilaroff that if she saw Scott on television she would start to shake all over again.

. . . .

In September 1966, Ava was in New York for the much-delayed premiere of *The Bible*. Rex Reed, then a movie reviewer for *Cosmopolitan,* hung out with her at the Regency, where she would not allow him to take notes (he scribbled furiously in the bathroom) as she stalked around like "an elegant cheetah," eating Nathan's hot dogs (rushed from Coney Island by limo), with champagne flutes of cognac (in one hand) and Dom Pérignon (in the other), sipping them alternately, he remembered, "like syrup through a straw."

Ava hated the movie. "All the way through it I kept punching Johnny on the arm and saying, 'Christ, how could you let me do it?'" she said. "Then Johnny Huston takes me to this party where we had to stand around and smile at Artie Shaw, who I was married to, baby, for Chrissake, and his wife Evelyn Keyes, who Johnny Huston was once married to, for Chrissake. And after it's all over, what have you got? The biggest headache in town. Do you think for one minute the fact that Ava Gardner showed up at that circus will sell that picture? Nobody cares what I wore or what I said. All they want to know anyway is was she drunk and did she stand up straight. This is the last circus. I am not a bitch! I am not temperamental! I am scared, baby. *Scared.* Can you possibly understand what it's like to feel scared?"

Reed asked Ava if she hated all of her films as much as she did *The Bible.* "Christ, what did I ever do worth talking about?" she said between sips. "Every time I tried to act, they stepped on me. That's why it's such a goddam shame, I've been a movie star for twenty-five years and I've got nothing, *nothing* to show for it. All I've got is three lousy ex-husbands."

Ava declared that she hated her "seventeen years of slavery" at MGM. "I mean I'm not exactly stupid or without feeling, and they tried to sell me like a prize hog. They also tried to make me into something I was not then and never could be. They used to write in my studio bios that I was the daughter of a cotton farmer from Chapel Hill. Hell, baby, I was born on a tenant farm in Grabtown. How's that grab ya? Grabtown, North Carolina. And it looks exactly the way it sounds. I should have stayed there. The ones who never left home don't have a pot to pee in but they're happy. Me, look at me. What did it bring me? The only time I'm happy is when I'm doing absolutely nothing. When I work I vomit all the time. I know nothing about acting so I have one rule—trust the director and give him heart and soul. And nothing else." Reed: "Another cheetah roar."

Although *The Bible* received a yawn from most critics, moviegoers made it a box-office winner. Rex Reed didn't think much of the movie but loved Ava madly. "At a time when religion needs all the help it can get, John Huston may have set its cause back a couple of thousand years," wrote Reed in his review. "The film runs three hours (plus intermission) and in that time the only real surprise is Ava Gardner, who plays the barren, childless Sarah with staggering beauty, control, and dimension. She is no longer the beautiful female wolf the MGM press agents taught her how to be in 1950, but she has matured beyond all expectations into something much more exciting: a real person, able to bring real levels of emotion to roles that deserve her."

....

After completing *The Bible* and recovering from George C. Scott, Ava did not work for more than three years. In 1966, she was one of many actresses under consideration by director Mike Nichols to play Mrs. Robinson in *The Graduate*. Other candidates included Patricia Neal, Geraldine Page, Deborah Kerr, Lana Turner, Susan Hayward, Rita Hayworth, Shelley Winters, Eva Marie Saint, Ingrid Bergman, and Anne Bancroft.

In Madrid, Ava threw the script to Betty Sicre. "Take a look and see if you think I should do this," she said. After reading it, Betty said, "Ava, this is great!"

In New York later that year, Nichols received a call from Ava. "Come and see me," she said. "I'm at the St. Regis. Come at five." Nichols was excited. "She was Ava Gardner . . . the source of a million fantasies," he said. At thirty-four, Mike Nichols was a fledgling director who had stepped behind the camera for only one movie—but it was to direct Richard Burton and Elizabeth Taylor, the two biggest stars in the world, in *Who's Afraid of Virginia Woolf?* The movie was nominated for thirteen Academy Awards, including one for Best Director. Nichols didn't win, but, after a successful stage career, his film debut was auspicious, and it was said that he was an enforcer, unafraid to shred the feelings of cast and crew.

As he prepared for his meeting with Ava, he received another call. "Mr. Nichols, we're at the Regency," said Ava's secretary (probably Bappie). Ava had forgotten—she *used* to stay at the St. Regis.

To some directors, it might have seemed like typecasting, Ava Gardner—now forty-three, infamous for hard-drinking and partying with youthful suitors—in the role of Mrs. Robinson, a forty-five-year-old well-heeled, predatory alcoholic who seduces Benjamin Braddock, the twenty-one-year-old graduate who falls in love with her daughter. Nichols told Hillel Italie of the Associated Press he was attracted to doing the movie because he could relate to Benjamin's awkwardness, to his sense of always being at least a little embarrassed. For Mike Nichols, nine years younger than Ava, his visit to her suite would be like a Mrs. Robinson encounter of his own. "The main thing is—she's Ava Gardner!" he said. "Not the youngest, but incredibly sexy and gorgeous—almost superhuman in that way. My heart was pounding."

When he arrived, Nichols was a bit taken aback by Ava's retinue of resolute admirers hanging around the suite, "a group of men who could only be called lounge lizards: pin-striped suits, smoking in the European way—underhand—with greased-back hair." Then, Ava saw him. "Out, out, everybody out!" she shouted. "I want to talk to my director." Nichols was deeply embarrassed.

Ava sat at a little French desk with a telephone. "I've been trying to call Papa all day!" she said. Ava seemed to be going through every movie-star cliché, thought Nichols. He wasn't sure he could go through with the meeting, especially since Papa Hemingway had been dead since 1961.

"The first thing you must know is I don't take my clothes off for anybody," she said.

"Well, I don't think that would be required," said Nichols.

She then confided, "The truth is, you know, I can't act. I just can't act! The best have tried, but it's hopeless."

Nichols replied, "Oh, Miss Gardner, that's simply not true! I think you're a great movie actress."

"You're very sweet but I can't act." Nichols quickly grasped the impossibility of working with Ava. Her lifelong habit of putting herself down, as if acting were a series of successes or failures, never a middle ground, only extremes, could not have been more untimely for her cause. Anne Bancroft was not only a better actress; she was also, at age thirty-five, playing a woman forty-five, a more attractive MILF at that point. While actually closer to Mrs. Robinson's age, Ava's stardom was slowly fading along with her looks.

When Ava returned to Madrid, she told Betty Sicre that Mike Nichols had booked her into a hotel and that a door connected their rooms. "Oh, I turned it down because Nichols was coming on to me, and he expected me to unlock the doors," she said. She was very insulted.

"But I doubt Mike Nichols would do that," Betty told Lee Server.

"Why would he do that? I think probably what happened was she just got drunk in their evening interview and he decided she'd be too iffy to work with. I think she blew it herself there."

Here she was, again being the diva, a role Ava played commandingly. She is not of your world, friends out there in the dark. You are in *her* world, possibly as an uninvited guest. With Ava, it was hard to tell: Was this diva role manufactured, or something she had arrived at or evolved into, where she felt free to do what she did best.

Apart from the role of diva, Ava had rarely been an actress. She was more like an attraction.

. . . .

In May 1964, Ava had vacationed with Betty and Ricardo Sicre cruising around the Mediterranean on their yacht. Adlai Stevenson, the former presidential candidate, whom she and Frank had backed after their Palm Springs battle in 1952, came on board with Marietta Tree, and took a fancy to Ava, a "strange, lovely, lush girl," he said. The press claimed that they were an "item," which a flattered Stevenson laughed off.

In July 1967, Ava traveled with Ricardo Sicre to Switzerland, where young Ricardo Sicre, Jr., was graduating from a private school. He was now bound for the Ivy League. One evening a year or two later, when Stephen Birmingham was on the town with Ava in New York, they started with dinner at Trader Vic's, then went on to Jilly's—Frank's favorite hangout, where Jilly Rizzo and his attentive staff fussed over Ava, who was in a long dress and a mink coat. She kissed the life-size cutout of Frank as Pal Joey and declared, "My guy."

Jilly, born Ermenigildo Rizzo to Italian immigrant parents on New York's Lower West Side, had one eye and an arrest record for assault before meeting Frank and becoming his enforcer. "Frank had something to do with Jilly's marriage breaking up," said Bill Miller. "Jilly was having more fun with Frank. I like the line that Frank said Jilly said to him about his wife: 'I love her, but *fuck her.*'" He had bit parts in three movies. Frank changed the lyric in "Mrs. Robinson" to include the line, "Jilly loves you more than you can know." He was family. Dolly even had a term of affection for Jilly. She called him "Fuckface."

Ava and Birmingham moved on to Christo's on Third Avenue, where the owner presented Ava with a special bottle of aged tequila. Suddenly, Ava remembered she had promised Betty Sicre that she would "get together with her son Ricardo, who's at Princeton." Ava was his godmother.

"Hell, let's take a taxi," said Birmingham, matching Ava drink for drink. It was, after all, only a sixty-five-mile drive. "Wonderful idea," said Ava.

Snorting tequila, they arrived in Princeton at 7:00 A.M. as students were heading toward class. "Where does little Ricardo live?" asked Birmingham. "What's his dormitory?" Ava had no idea. "We'll just go up and down the streets here and we'll ask people."

They drove around the campus, and Ava—in long gown and mink, clutching the bottle of tequila—jumped out of the cab and asked, "Do you know my friend Ricardo Sicre?" Nobody did. As word spread that Ava was cruising the campus in a New York taxi, students began following—it was like the streets of Madrid—running and shouting, "Ava, Ava!" They stopped in front of a dormitory, where Ava ran into the entrance hall. "Ricardo! Ricardo!" she shouted. "Where are you?" No sign of Ricardo. Back in the cab, she directed the driver: "Take us to the president's house."

At the president's house, Ava, still clutching the bottle of tequila, emerged from the cab. "Ava, let's think about this now," said a now discomfited Birmingham. "You're very fond of your friend Ricardo and you're very fond of his parents. You, on the other hand, *are* Ava Gardner, and you have had, uh, a little bit to drink tonight. . . . I have a terrible feeling that if you barge into the president's house at this point in the morning, you may have little Ricardo bounced right out of this college."

"Yeah, I guess you're right," Ava conceded.

They got back in the cab to return to New York, stopping at a Howard Johnson's for breakfast. Then they returned to the cab, and Ava suddenly remembered. "Jesus Christ!" she said. "It's Yale!"

$\prec$ 12 $\succ$

There Are No Third Acts
in American Lives

Over dinner at the Fontainebleau one evening in February 1968, Frank Sinatra told Paul Anka that he was thinking of retiring. The young singer wasn't surprised. Frank was not oblivious to the rapid changes going on around him in pop culture. Certainly, he didn't want to make a spectacle of himself, though he was on record for dismissing rock 'n' roll as something "written for the most part by cretinous goons." To Frank, it was "the martial music of every side-burned delinquent on the face of the earth. It is the most brutal, ugly, desperate, vicious form of expression it has been my misfortune to hear."

Despite Frank's apocalyptic misgivings, rock and roll had proved very profitable to him and the Warner/Reprise group, where it flourished and proliferated. Beginning in 1967 with the signing of the Grateful Dead, the company had steadily built a lineup of rock and pop artists that, by the end of the decade, would make it one of the world's leading rock labels, with a roster that included Fleetwood Mac, Van Morrison, Alice Cooper, the Doobie Brothers, Little Feat, Van Halen, Deep Purple, Jethro Tull, Black Sabbath, and King Crimson.

Paul Anka, of course, was no rocker. He didn't wield a guitar. He held a big band–style microphone and sang. Anka was playing Vegas five years before anyone had even heard of the Beatles. He and Frank had met in 1958, at Trader Vic's, where they were sitting at tables next to each other and Frank joked about having Paul write him a song. "I didn't have the balls to give him 'Lonely Boy' or whatever else I was writing at the time," said Anka in his memoir. "What would he do with that stuff anyway?"

They socialized at the Sands, where Frank gave health-club robes with embroidered nicknames to his coconspirators: Sammy Davis, Jr., was Smokey the Bear, Dean Martin was Dago, and Paul was the Kid. "That's where the kibitzing went on in the early hours of the morning," said Anka. "That's where the fun was. The girls were hot, tiptoeing into the steam room giggling. We'd be sitting around talking, bullshitting, and all of a sudden a couple of showgirls would come in, and they're naked, too. Frank would have women of the night brought in now and then. They would come in, take their clothes off, these beautiful women, standing there stark naked. There were little rooms, massage rooms, off the main steam room and that's where you'd go if you wanted to have sex with them."

Now, over dinner in Miami, Anka thought Frank vulnerable. The Rat Pack thing was over. Gone was the Sands, where Frank had lost two front teeth to casino manager Carl Cohen the previous September during a drunken rampage. ("Never fight a Jew in the desert," Frank was now joking from the stage during his shows.) And he had lost his gaming license at Tahoe because of the Sam Giancana connection and all the mob stuff. The Mia thing was in a state of collapse, and there was always the specter of Ava, a name you didn't mention around Frank.

....

Casino owner Steve Wynn told Paul about one night when he was having drinks with Frank and Dean after a show and he had asked, "Frank, of all the women you've known, who was the best in bed?"

"Easy question!" Frank and Dean said in unison. "Angie!" Both had done amorous time with Angie Dickinson.

"I would have thought Frank would say Ava Gardner," Wynn told Paul.

"A beautiful, remarkable creature, drank in the Hall of Fame category—she was too ornery for Frank."

"Even a decade after the divorce was official, Mr. S was seriously in love with her," said George Jacobs. "Dreams don't die. His greatest fantasy was that she would marry him once again."

Frank and Ava often talked by phone into the late hours. On an earlier trip to Miami, Frank suspected that Fontainebleau operators were over-hearing his calls. He had a private line installed—one independent of the Fontainebleau switchboard—so that he could talk to Ava in London.

The private phone number was delivered to him in a sealed envelope. Within half an hour, the phone rang. Frank picked up the receiver. "Hello, Mr. Sinatra?" Someone had given out the number. "Mr. Sinatra, is that you?"

Frank ripped the phone off the wall, opened the terrace door, and threw the phone into the pool.

....

"Kid, I'm fed up," said Frank. He was going to do one more album—"and then I'm out of here." He asked Paul about a song he'd promised to write for him years ago.

"I gotta think about that."

"Don't take too long!" said Frank.

He's in his mid-fifties now, thought the songwriter, with a lot of living already in the rearview mirror.

....

Frank Sinatra was shooting another Tony Rome movie in Miami by day—*Lady in Cement,* with Raquel Welch—and singing at the Fontainebleau nights, keeping long hours after the show. He was never in bed before 5:00 A.M., and rarely slept more than a few hours.

He was also going through marital withdrawal symptoms. In late November 1967, Mickey Rudin had met Mia Farrow, unannounced, on the set of *Rosemary's Baby,* the gothic movie that would transform her from a

TV actress to a movie star, much to Frank's frustration. Mia, who was supposed to costar with Frank in *The Detective,* had been replaced by Lee Remick when *Rosemary's Baby* ran into overtime. It was all so familiar, like Ava redux: problems with a wife who had a mind and a career of her own. The joke was that Frank might sue for divorce on grounds of insubordination. Rudin had prepared separation documents, drawn up in the first person, ready for her signature. Mia was heartsick, in shock. She signed. It was the beginning of the end of a sad little romance that had begun two years earlier, when Mia was the twenty-year-old star of TV's *Peyton Place,* and the love of Frank Sinatra's life.

Tina Sinatra said that her father, at fifty, "had a crying need to nurture," and, after getting over "the last pained chorus of his romance with Ava," he was ready to settle down and try marriage again. As for the age difference, perhaps Frank was thinking of Bogie, who had been twenty-five years older than Bacall, and that had worked out, sort of.

They married on July 19, 1966, a burning 110-degree day in Vegas. Frank and Mia climbed into a limousine at the Vegas airport as security guards held back hundreds of fans trying to capture a glimpse of the betrothed couple. Farrow's hair was short-cropped. The previous year, the young star of *Peyton Place* had made worldwide headlines by chopping off her waist-length locks.

In the Sands Presidential Suite, Mia wore a simple silk beige brocade jacket, a knee-length skirt with matching shoes. Frank wore a plain blue suit with a white carnation in his lapel. The couple did not exchange wedding bands. Mia wore her $100,000 diamond engagement ring. Before the ceremony, Frank had George Jacobs call Ava in London. He didn't want her to find out after the fact. He had kept the wedding plans secret, not even telling his former spouse Nancy or any of his kids (who were Mia's contemporaries) "because he didn't want to hear what he already knew," said Tina—"that he was nuts." Dean Martin would less than playfully joke that he drank scotch that was older than Mia, who was twenty-one.

Frank and Ava were both familiar with Mia's father, the movie director John Farrow, who had died three years earlier. He was "an Australian boozer and womanizer," Frank told Jacobs. One of Farrow's conquests was Ava, whom he directed in *Ride, Vaquero!* in the late summer of 1952. It was an affair so torrid that Farrow's wife, Maureen O'Sullivan, had a special late-night entrance constructed to his bedroom so that he could come and go without disturbing her sleep. This all went down "at the height of Ava's turmoil with Mr. S," said Jacobs, wryly suggesting that if Frank had a score to settle, here was his chance to do it over John Farrow's dead body.

"I think that Dad looked at Mia and saw this frail little waif, and thought, maybe *this* one would be more malleable," said Tina in her memoir. "Only later—too late—would he realize that Mia's frailty was all on the surface. She was just as career-driven as Ava, and probably more independent."

When the marriage was announced, Ava put on a brave face and kidded, maliciously, off the record, about Mia being "a fag with a pussy," as if Frank was a latent homosexual finally coming out. But, after George's call from Vegas, she felt deeply wounded. "Ava had wanted to be untouched by the news," wrote her biographer Lee Server. "But she had not been able to hold it together that first night, and the sense of loss had overwhelmed her. She cried and could not stop crying."

After they married, Mia was careful never to mention Ava. At the Springs, "there were many lovely photographs of her around the house," she recalled in her memoir. "He looked so pained when he talked about her that it was a relief when he changed the subject." There was also a striking portrait of Frank, painted by Paul Clemens, a gift from Ava in the sixties. It was more reflective-looking than other paintings of Frank that had been done over the years, usually to promote an album or a movie. This one "captured Dad's spirit best," said Tina. It had an honored place in the Compound for the rest of his years.

Later that year, Frank was in London shooting *The Naked Runner*. He was cast as a retired CIA-type assassin whose son is kidnapped to blackmail the killer into going back to work. Frank visited Ava, who was perched in an apartment and considering a move from Madrid, where she was being hassled for back taxes. Ava knew that Frank was not a happy husband; but, as Ava later told George Jacobs, "He made his bed, let him sleep in it."

Ava told Frank that her heart belonged to her corgi, Rags. "Mr. S even walked Rags for her to show what he'd do to win her back," said Jacobs. "It wasn't enough. If she had only said she would give their love one last try, Mr. S would have dumped Mia then and there."

The shoot in London did not go well. After a few weeks, Frank wanted to get back to Palm Springs. They could finish the movie there. Brad Dexter, who was titular producer of *The Naked Runner*—and who had been Frank's sidekick since saving his life in the waters off Hawaii—said it would be a real stretch, substituting the Springs sunny skies for the green and gray of East Germany that the story required.

"It's my picture and I'll shoot it where I want to," said Frank, who never spoke to Dexter again.

. . . .

It was clear that Ava, in her mid-forties, was no longer attracting starring roles. After losing out on Mrs. Robinson, and watching Anne Bancroft's star rise in the heavens over Hollywood, Ava returned to movies, playing second fiddle to Catherine Deneuve in *Mayerling*, which Rex Reed called "a ghastly misfortune." In 1968, she was on location in Austria for three months, in the unlikely role of Austrian Empress Elisabeth, playing opposite James Mason as Emperor Franz Joseph.

"The best thing about *Mayerling* is the brief appearance of Ava Gardner, who plays the sixty-year-old mother of Omar Sharif with the kind of magic and mystery appropriate for the most illustrious woman in 1888," said Reed. "She resembles a bruised flower now, but she gives the only interesting performance in a film which, without her presence, would be stagnant as a swamp."

As *Mayerling* was winding down, and Ava was in London doing interiors with director Terence Young, she received a cable from Frank, reported columnist Sheilah Graham: "I need you. Come at once. You will know why when you read the headlines in the morning papers." He and Mia were getting a divorce. Frank was seriously ill, battling pneumonia, and calling for her. "Mr. Young took Ava to the airport," said Graham. "She was happy and excited, thinking perhaps this would mean a reconciliation and remarriage."

....

Frank had contracted pneumonia just before he was set to open at the Fontainebleau. He refused to be hospitalized; instead, he was confined to bed in his suite at the hotel, where his entourage surrounded him. He hated being ill. He was lashing out at everyone.

"I was very worried about his health," said George Jacobs in his memoir. "His skin was sallow, greenish. He was too weak to insist on wearing a hairpiece. He seemed to have given up. He looked frail and old and helpless, as well as furious at himself, and the heavens, for letting him get this way."

Mia flew in, but the vibe was not good. "When she got there, Frank's so-called Dago Secret Service made her miserable," said Sinatra biographer J. Randy Taraborrelli. "All of Frank's hangers-on blamed Mia for the boss's condition. . . . They told her he was near death and couldn't see anyone, scaring the hell out of her. They also told her that the divorce was to blame. 'And it's all your fault,' they said." One of the guys, probably Jilly, pulled Mia aside and said it wasn't as bad as she was being led to believe but that she should just go home. "Appearing to be ravaged, with a frozen look in her eyes, Mia got on the next plane back to Los Angeles," wrote Taraborrelli.

....

Dolly and Marty came to their son's sickbed. For Marty, it was a difficult trip. His asthma had grown worse. The atomizer spray—his "trumpet"—wasn't always strong enough to open his bronchial tubes. Dolly often gave him an adrenaline injection to ease an attack when he couldn't breathe. Nancy Sinatra told of the time when her grandparents came out of a restaurant, were waiting for a cab, and Marty became ill from the exhaust fumes. Dolly yelled at him for forgetting his trumpet. Of course, she had forgotten the adrenaline.

....

Ava suddenly, farcically, appeared at Frank's bedside, disguised in a blond wig and dark oversize glasses for traveling. "They told me you were dying, Francis," she said. "I've been traveling for 24 hours to get here."

She loathed the Sinatra entourage of tough guys. They disliked her in return. She was not what a good Italian wife ought to be. She hated Frank's playgrounds—Hollywood, Las Vegas, Florida. And now here she was, jet-lagged and stressed out in Miami.

"You glad to see me, baby?" asked Frank.

Ava got angry. He was his same old miserable self; it was all tough talk and dirty jokes and rants about the hippies ruining the country, playing to his goons.

"Jesus Christ, you're not dying, are you?" she roared. "Faking it again. Here we fucking go. What the hell is *really* wrong with you? You got a cold or what? What am I doing here, anyway? Do you know what I had to go through to get here?"

"Hey, lady, I been sick. What you come here for if you're gonna give me a hard time . . ."

He started coughing and hacking. There was a time when Ava saw all the flaws in Frank, his wardrobe, and his arrogance. But now it was Frank who saw the flaws. Ava's face and her figure had started to surrender to gravity. Her sloppy, casual attire, consisting of shirts and slacks, turned Frank off. Even her language dismayed him.

"I'm sick, lady," he said dismissively. "This ain't like Lake Tahoe. Fuck you, anyway. Scram."

Ava went back to her suite, packed, and returned to London. Frank would survive. Her dream would not.

A week later, Frank did one show a night at the hotel. He resumed movie work on March 5. Looking through the script, he asked the director to make a line change, so that Tony Rome cracks, "I used to know a broad who collected bullfighters."

....

Any hopes for a reconciliation with Mia evaporated that summer when *The Detective* opened to marginal reviews on May 28 and *Rosemary's Baby* opened two weeks later, on June 12, and became the number-one hit in America. "A great deal of the credit for this achievement must go to Mia Farrow," Roger Ebert said of the film.

Frank and Mia's divorce was finalized on August 19, 1968, in Juárez, Mexico. Mia told the court, "I don't seem to be able to please him anymore." Frank didn't show. They had been married for twenty-five months. *Rosemary's Baby* was a success and Mia was now a bona fide movie star. In his memoir, Robert Evans, the head of Paramount, recalled Mia's asking him to have the studio take out "a double-page ad in the *New York Times, Los Angeles Times, Variety* and *Hollywood Reporter* comparing the dual openings of their pictures, in terms of box-office dollars and critical acclaim. I gave her request the heaviest thumbs-down I've ever given. Thanks but no thanks, Mia. I'm not looking to wake up with a vacancy between my legs."

....

Later that year, Paul Anka sat down to write a song. The previous summer, while traveling in Mougins, a small town in the south of France, he had heard a beautiful little pop tune, "Comme d'habitude," which meant "as usual," about a couple breaking up. The song, recorded by Claude François, was a small hit in Europe, and Anka acquired the rights. Now he set about working on new lyrics for the tune, in response to Frank's morose monologue that for him the end was near.

The title came first, "My Way"—embracing Sinatra's swagger, a theme that was unapologetically "chauvinistic, narcissistic, in-your-face, and grandiose." That would be Frank. "I started typing like a madman—forget the craft, I told myself, just write it the way he talks: 'Ate it up . . . spit it out.'" In four hours, Anka had it his way.

In November, Frank Sinatra returned to Caesars big-time—the first entertainer to get $200,000 a week, one show a night, six nights, a day off—reunited with his old bandleader Harry James.

Paul Anka flew into Vegas and met with Frank and Don Costa, who was conducting and doing arrangements for Frank. Anka played the demo for "My Way."

"That's kooky, kid," said Frank. "We're going in."

Was Frank low-key in his response? Nah. "Coming from him, you have to understand, that meant he was ecstatic," said Paul.

When alone, Frank told Don Costa he did not like the song. Costa, who had discovered Anka, urged Frank to reconsider. He thought it a perfect song for the older Sinatra to record. Frank often made Costa's life miserable, but their bickering seemed to clear the air. And his arrangements were beautiful.

Frank met Don Costa, a guitarist at the Latin Quarter in Boston, in January 1953. Don became an arranger and producer in the fifties, working with Sarah Vaughan, Tony Bennett, and Steve Lawrence and Eydie Gormé, and recording his own million-selling single, the theme from *Never on Sunday*. After launching Reprise, Frank hired him for the much-praised *Sinatra and Strings* album, which included magnificent renditions of "Come Rain or Come Shine" and "Stardust," consisting of only the introductory verse. He had also arranged Frank's hit "Cycles." "Don Costa was the best writer of brass and strings I ever heard," said recording engineer Lee Herschberg. "Once, during dinner in Paris at a restaurant, Don had an idea for a song. He began to write on the tablecloth, which he took to his hotel room, worked through the night, and came to studio next morning where we recorded it."

After much coaxing, Costa devised a chart for "My Way," and Frank reluctantly agreed to rehearse it with pianist Bill Miller during the stay at Caesars.

. . . .

In the early sixties, Ava had sold her home outside Madrid and moved to a modern duplex apartment at 11 Avenida Doctor Arce in the city. The partying continued and complaints proliferated about the noise, the yapping corgis (Ava now had two), and the late hours. Some complaints came from Ava's neighbor in the apartment directly below—Juan Perón, the exiled former dictator of Argentina, who had settled in Madrid with his young wife, two poodles, and the embalmed corpse of his infamous first wife, Eva Duarte de Perón, the Evita of Andrew Lloyd Webber musical fame. Journalist Reid Buckley, working with Ava on the script for *The Bible,* observed Ava stepping out to her terrace one day to water her carnations—something she did whenever she heard her downstairs neighbor step out on his terrace—and making sure the pots overflowed, crying in a theatrically loud voice, "Now, quit pissing, Rags. Quit pissing on my flowers, you terrible dog!" The water, meanwhile, spilled onto the terrace below, spattering on the rail.

The complaints escalated, including some to the U.S. ambassador, and soon an auditor from the Spanish revenue department called to discuss back taxes owed, perhaps as many as a million American dollars. Ava's business manager tried to negotiate a settlement with the Spanish government, showing receipts and arguing that she had been a big attraction for Spain, that the publicity she received was good for tourism.

A meeting was scheduled with Ava, her business manager, and Señor Manuel Fraga Iribarne, the minister of tourism. The meeting dragged on, for Spanish protocol says that you engage in small talk before you get down to business. Ava grew impatient as the small talk went on and on.

Finally, Señor Fraga—whom Ava called "Señor Bragas," the Spanish word for underpants—attempted to offer her a way out, "Ah, Señorita Gardner, yes, we are now here to discuss your indebtedness to the Spanish government of ten thousand dollars."

"What the fuck?" she rashly shouted. "I thought it was a million!"

"You're quite right, Miss Gardner," the minister replied indifferently, withdrawing the offer. "It is a million dollars."

London, here she came.

. . . .

During a stopover in Hollywood, Ava commiserated with George Jacobs, who had been dismissed after dancing with Mia at a nightclub, which was not valet protocol, according to the book of Frank. "We talked about Frank and Mia, which Ava knew was a ridiculous match from the outset," said Jacobs in his *Mr. S: My Life with Frank Sinatra.*

"Everything she predicted had come true. However, she wasn't the slightest bit pleased with the accuracy of her predictions. She felt as bad for Frank as I did. I urged her, as always, to try to get back together with him."

It seemed to Jacobs that the entire fifteen years that he had been with Frank were "a kind of crazy odyssey on his part to do everything in the world, and I mean the entire world, to get over losing her." Ava laughed it off. "She would always love Frank, but it was more as a friend, or actually a wayward son, than as a grand passion he once had been for her, and, alas, she remained for him."

. . . .

At three o'clock on Monday, December 30, 1968, Lee Herschberg was setting up his equipment for a recording session at Reprise: Frank Sinatra, one song, "My Way," one arrangement, by Don Costa. Bill Miller had hurt his hand; the piano would be played by Lou Levy. Miller would conduct. There could be many takes.

For a typical Sinatra session, Frank would rehearse a tune and run over the key changes while Herschberg was doing sound checks and testing microphones, fine-tuning the gear. Then, after half an hour or so, they would start recording and do a song repeatedly until they got it right.

This would be different. After Caesars, Frank had retreated to Palm Springs, where he rested and rehearsed the song—"woodshedding," he called it. There was very little drinking and smoking, so that by the time he walked into the recording studio with his daughter Nancy, Frank was ready, and, after a few hellos, he declared, "Let's do it."

Bill Miller hit the downbeat, and Frank started singing "My Way."

"About halfway through the take, I looked at the tape machine and the needles were laying on the pin," said Lee Herschberg. "The calibration was not right. I thought, Oh my God, we're recording at too-hot a level. But then I figured, We'll get through this and do another take."

When the song came to an end, there was a pause. Then Frank said, "That's it."

"Frank was great," said Herschberg. "The band was great. It *was* a great take." But the engineer started to sweat. On playback, he could hear a couple of spots where Frank's vocal was a little bit edgy—he often had what he called "shot glass throat"—but it came out fine. One song, one arrangement, and one take was it. There was applause.

. . . .

In January 1969, Marty Sinatra was in Houston, under the care of Dr. Michael DeBakey for a heart condition. Marty's asthma had become emphysema, and his condition progressively worsened. For five days, Frank Sinatra stayed by his father's side.

"He caressed his face and he wiped his mouth," said his daughter Nancy in her memoir. "They had always been openly affectionate, men of few words, understanding each other easily. To lose your father . . . that must be wrenching enough. But to be at his side, holding his hand, hearing him gasp for air . . . To watch him die. . . . I don't know what they went through individually. But they went through it together."

Marty Sinatra could not read and could not write much more than his name. Frank would read things to him. He liked to watch TV. "He was a very quiet man, a lonely man," said Frank years later, speaking to a Yale Law School gathering. "And shy. When I'd bring people over to the house in Fort Lee, years later, he'd cook for three days for us. And he wouldn't sit down. 'Come on, Dad,' I'd say, 'sit with us. These people have never met you.' 'No, no, no,' he'd say; 'you go ahead. I have to take care of things in the kitchen.' . . . Oh, but he was a lovely, lovely man. I adored him. In some ways, the greatest man I ever knew in my life."

Although Marty and Dolly had been living in Fort Lee, New Jersey, Dolly chose a grave site in another town, which turned Marty's funeral into a theatrical parade. The cortege required a drive through the city, which led to a traffic jam and took hours as uniformed firemen stood at attention at side streets when the hearse passed, and townspeople jammed the streets.

"At the gravesite there was bedlam," recalled daughter Nancy in her memoir. "So many people. . . . Dolly tried to throw herself on the coffin, wailing, 'Marty, Marty, don't leave me.'" Frank urged the priest to hurry things along. "Father Bob jumped to an Amen and we placed flowers on the coffin and managed to get Dolly into the car. . . . There had been no time for a decent service, a proper goodbye." For Frank, his mother had turned his father's burial into a Neapolitan travesty.

. . . .

"My Way," released in early 1969, rose to number twenty-seven on the *Billboard* charts and lingered for eight weeks, but it was not the hit that was anticipated, not another "Strangers in the Night."

Privately, Frank claimed to disown the song—perhaps because some of his act was now self-referential, and the lyrics cut *too* close to the bone. "God how I detest that song," said Boston critic Lee Grove. "The lyrics were so self-congratulatory, so falsely self-deprecatory, so awful. Biting off more than you can chew, eating it and spitting it out—it was a song about mastication and expectoration."

For Sinatra, the lyrics—"Regrets, I have a few . . ."—must have been torturous. He said the words were not subtle enough, too "on the nose"— the first-person anthem of an older man, looking back on his life and declaring victory as he loved and laughed and cried, approaching the finish line. Stoicism, not surrender. A song of reflection for an older man, a song of aspiration for a younger one.

Onstage it became a song that would not go away, as fans hollered for it. "My Way" had become "the national anthem." Knowing that he'd have to sing it at every concert, he'd sometimes poke fun at the lyrics. When he got to the words "my way" for the first time, he'd sing instead, "I did it . . . sideways!" But then he would turn serious, and bring it home with a stirring anthem finish. It became his finale for years.

············

In August 1969, Frank recorded an album called *Watertown*. Earlier that year, his *My Way* album had gone gold. *Watertown* was quite different, a somewhat artistic song cycle about a man who falls in love, has a family, and then his wife takes off. She says she is coming back, and he goes to the train station and waits for her, but she doesn't return.

Watertown looked like a winner to the marketing squad at Reprise. On January 9, 1970, the final revision and label were done; 450,000 copies were pressed. *Watertown* was released in March 1970.

"*Watertown* was one of the first albums Frank did not sing live," said Lee Herschberg. "They did the tracks in New York, sent them to L.A., and Frank put on earphones and did the overdubbing. Nobody liked the songs. It was a chore for him, like singing while his jaws were tightly gripped. It was a different kind of recording, and he wasn't comfortable with it."

For a multitude of reasons, *Watertown* was a disaster, selling only 35,000 copies. How could Frank have been so wrong?

············

On March 23, 1971, at age fifty-five, Frank Sinatra announced his retirement, saying that after three decades of work, there had been "little room or opportunity for reflection, reading, self-examination, and that need, which every thinking man has, for a fallow period, a long pause in which to seek a better understanding of changes occurring in the world."

To most, it looked like depression. Since his father's death, he had been downsizing his life, pulling in the walls. He bought a home near the Compound for Dolly and gave his mother "an allowance check." She loved the horses, spending mornings with Jilly studying the racing forms, and the month of August in an apartment in La Jolla, near the track in Del Mar.

Frank sold the flat in London. He sold the East Seventy-second Street apartment in New York City, moving to a suite at the Waldorf Towers. After a "retirement" concert in June, he said good-bye to performing for a while.

"My check, a thousand dollars, arrived every week," said Bill Miller, his pianist, who had been on retainer since the mid-1950s. "For me it wasn't a question of if Frank would be back—it was only a matter of when."

❧ 13 ❧

Down and Out in London

After pausing at several pubs one day in early 1972, Ava Gardner, feeling just a bit tight, decided not to haggle. "I'll buy it now," she told the owner of a second-floor apartment at 34 Ennismore Gardens, which would become her sanctuary for life. It had a magnificent view, with windows opening onto a long terrace across from the beautifully maintained gardens. A living room ran from front to back, and there was an excellent kitchen, a fireplace, and a comfortable, cozy feel. So cozy, in fact, "I had a hard job tearing Miss G away to go off and be a film star again," said Reenie, "but she went."

It was a good time for Ava, now four years removed from Spain, the land of sun, and happily at home in the city of rain. "I like rain," she said. "London rain is not a slashing torrent that wipes you out. It's fine rain. Thin rain. Nourishing rain. It gives me tranquility. I can grow." She sounded like a travel agent. "What does it matter?" she said. "I sleep all day anyway." People even spoke English here.

The nameplate on the door was Morgan, after a favorite corgi, named after her financial adviser. (Rags was now gone.) When someone tracked her down and called, she would answer the phone saying, "Mrs. Baker isn't here. She's out right now." The apartment was also a short walk from

Hyde Park and Harrods, where she had an account that Frank reportedly tended to.

....

Ava no longer called Hollywood, but occasionally Hollywood called on her. Fame meant being escorted to the head of the line, or being told, "No check, compliments of the management"; it also meant, in the later years, charging more for less of your services. Major actors were playing smaller parts—cameos—and getting their standard salaries, some working only a few days for seven-figure paychecks.

John Huston cast her as Lillie Langtry in 1972's *The Life and Times of Judge Roy Bean,* opposite Paul Newman, who played the corrupt, flamboyant judge who built a town in honor of Lillie, the performer he worshiped but had never met. Ava, playing Lillie, finally arrives in the town and is greeted by Huston's great diminutive friend, Billy Pearson, a jockey in real life. Since this wasn't a speaking part, Pearson could say anything he wanted and there would be no sound track. "He kept trying to get me to break character," said Ava.

"Miss Gardner was at her most graceful and elegant," said Huston. There is a glimpse of her perfect beauty through the train window, and then she steps off the train with Billy Pearson's help. He puts up his hand, which she takes, and they walk up the street toward town.

"Well, Miss Langtry, you don't know how nice it is to see you," said Billy. "All I can think about is eatin' your pussy!" Ava said, "Oh, really?" Pearson said, "Hector and me been out here so long, all we do is jack off dreamin' about ya." Ava went right on saying her lines exactly as if what Pearson said was in the script. "She was such a professional, I could not shock her," said the charming Billy. John Huston was wiping tears from his eyes.

Ava, ever the diva, was a hit with the cast. "We had a small dinner for her and she was over two hours late," said actress Victoria Principal. "She arrived in white jeans and a white shirt that fit her magnificently. And she didn't walk into the room; she came in like a cat. I had never seen a woman move like that or have that kind of presence, before or since. I've never seen a woman electrify a room sexually like she did. You were aware that she was on the prowl."

In 1974 Ava had an expanded cameo (and second billing) in *Earthquake,* a "successful disaster" in the era of disaster movies. The movie had Sensurround, the first new film effect since CinemaScope, with vibration effects created by a fifty-cycle audio track played just below the range of human hearing. It scared audiences. When the picture opened at Grauman's Chinese—where it set a Hollywood record—the system shook some plaster out of the ceiling.

Charlton Heston again groused about Ava not knowing her lines— "She tends only to approximate the exact text," he said—and requiring fourteen takes on one fairly simple scene. By the thirteenth take, Ava was growing restive. Director Mark Robson talked to her softly and did one more take. "Cut! Print! That's very good, Ava. Much better. We won't need you now till the dolly shot." As she left the stage, Robson noted Heston's quizzical look. "Sometimes," he said quietly, "you have to know when you've gotten all there is."

"Gardner was one of the last of the woman stars to make it on beauty alone," wrote *New Yorker* reviewer Pauline Kael. "She never looked really happy in her movies; she wasn't quite there, but she never suggested that she was anywhere else, either. She had a dreamy, hurt quality, a generously modeled mouth, and faraway eyes. Maybe what turned people on was that her sensuality was developed but her personality wasn't. She was a rootless, beautiful stray, somehow incomplete but never ordinary, and just about impossible to dislike, since she was utterly without affectation."

. . . .

After two years in retirement, Frank Sinatra came back in 1973. His advisers said he needed some cash flow to maintain his lifestyle; so, the money was nice, but, more than that, he needed the love and approval of an audience. "His destiny was to be a legend that lasted long after his time," said Shirley MacLaine. "But the source of his energy was unfathomable.

I don't think it comes simply from drive, or ambition, or the pulsating fear of being left behind. It has more to do with remaining a perpetual performing child who wants to please the mother audience."

Frank again started recording songs, an eclectic mix, with no "concept" in mind. Joe Raposo had written for Frank—"You Will Be My Music" and "There Used to Be a Ballpark"; and "Let Me Try Again," from Paul Anka, plus Sondheim's "Send in the Clowns." Warner/Reprise art director Ed Thrasher—whose wife, the undiscovered, gorgeous Linda Gray, watched from the engineering booth—shot photos of Frank in the studio, then set about designing the comeback album cover. As deadlines approached, and the music was mastered, Thrasher had an idea. He met with Frank's people and said, "How about ol' blue eyes is back"?

Frank's people cringed. Oh no no no. "Old? Frank would *never* want to be called 'old,'" they said. Frank was a performer with failed hair-plug procedures, numerous hairpieces, and skin tightening in all the right places.

"No, not o-l-d," said Thrasher. "You know, O-L-apostrophe . . . like ol' pal." Ed showed them a cover comp he had prepared, using his studio shots.

When Frank saw it, he *loved* the idea. So did his people.

. . . .

"With 'Ol' Blue Eyes,' Sinatra had reinvented himself again," said film director Peter Bogdanovich, "as he had when he went from being the almost femininely vulnerable mama's boy-crooner of the forties to America's top swinger of the fifties and sixties." Frank thought he would record an album and do a few concerts and club dates each year, but somewhere along the way he met Jerry Weintraub, Elvis's promoter and Paul Anka's pal, who said go huge.

After the release of the *Ol' Blue Eyes Is Back* album, the concert tour began at Madison Square Garden (televised as "The Main Event") and then moved on to venues where Frank had never gone before—stadiums and arenas with seating capacities of twenty thousand and more all over the world. Weintraub told Frank that a million middle-aged men would pay to hear him sing "My Way," and you can throw in a million middle-aged spouses and dates, too. Weintraub was right.

On the tour, Frank was outdrawing Led Zeppelin, Elton John, the Rolling Stones, and even Elvis. His ticket prices were higher, too. The clamor for "My Way" would usually begin mid-show and build to a crescendo just before Frank announced, with the subdued opening strains of Costa's Bolero-like arrangement, that he was going to sing "the national anthem." The place would explode. He tried to retire the song a few times, but the concertgoers had come to hear it, so Frank would reluctantly put it back in the act.

"Opinion about 'My Way' is mixed," said Ed O'Brien, author of *Sinatra 101*. "Some view it as a personal anthem of great strength, others as an embarrassing self-congratulatory statement. I don't believe that there is any middle ground regarding the song." Many fans and concertgoers felt it was more about the man than his music. Frank Sinatra, Jr., now conducting for "the old man," said the "five words of plain English" in the refrain—"I did it my way"—summed up his father exactly.

. . . .

Ava was a lifelong tennis player, and, though her visits were fleeting, Frank had built a court for her at the Compound. During an Ava stopover, he asked Barbara Marx—a neighbor, who would later become his fourth wife—to organize a doubles match for Ava. The next day, Barbara and Bill Davis, the Palm Springs Racquet Club pro, joined in the match. Afterward, over drinks, Ava flirted openly with her tennis partner. "Frank had the strangest expression in those eyes of his, which swirled with every emotion," recalled Barbara in her memoir, *Lady Blue Eyes: My Life with Frank*. "I think he held a torch for Ava his whole life."

Frank was soon dating Barbara Marx, who thought she manifested some of Ava's qualities. "Frank liked strong women," she said. "That was what first attracted him to Ava, I think. And as with Ava, whenever he and I argued, it was sudden, noisy, and temporary. For several months at the end of 1974 and beginning of 1975, we even dated other people, although I'm sure we did it just to make the other one jealous." On one occasion, Frank took Jacqueline Onassis for dinner at "21," and the papers speculated wildly that he was in full pursuit, though Jackie—then working for the publisher Doubleday—was only in editorial pursuit of Frank's memoirs, which he would never write.

"As soon as Frank felt he had suffered enough or was booked to go on tour again and didn't want to go alone, his ardor intensified," said Barbara. And so would hers. In midsummer 1975, she was with Frank in London for a highly successful concert in Albert Hall, where the audience included Princess Grace, Mia Farrow, and Ava. "This is one of the best nights of my career," said Frank.

Backstage, Barbara met her old tennis foe again. "Ava was very polite, and we got along fine, but I noticed that there was even more drinking going on this time."

....

It was a time when Frank and Ava were rarely together but often in touch. For her birthday each year he sent her a glorious floral bouquet, which she placed in her bedroom, where it bloomed, then faded, and remained until the next year, when a fresh bouquet arrived, replacing it on Christmas Eve. "We might have been in different cities, different countries, but we were never apart," she said. "And every once in a while, Frank would call me in Madrid, London, Rome, New York, wherever I happened to be, and say, 'Ava, let's try again.' And I'd say, 'Okay!' and drop everything, sometimes even a part in a picture. And it would be heaven, but it wouldn't last more than twenty-four hours. And I'd go running off again, literally running. We could never quite understand why it hadn't and couldn't work out."

Once, when Ava was staying in Frank's suite at the Waldorf Towers, author Stephen Birmingham came by for a visit. Frank was there, looking up an address in the phone book, which he couldn't read because he didn't have his glasses. "Here, try mine," said Ava, handing him her Ben Franklins. Sinatra put them on. "Hey, they work for me!" he said. "That's another reason why you and I should get back together." They laughed.

Afterward, when they were alone, Birmingham asked Ava, "Why don't you get back together?"

"We'd be at each other's throats in five minutes," she replied.

. . . .

In 1975, when Ava was in Rome, the phone calls grew in frequency and intensity.

"You know as well as I do that if I'm ever going to marry again it will be with Frank," Ava told Reenie. "If I don't marry Frank, I'll be alone for the rest of my life, because nobody else interests me."

"Miss G, when it comes to second-time-around, it's usually with a different fella."

"Not with me, hon'," said Ava. "It's Frank or no one."

"Is that what Frank wants?" Reenie asked.

"He's been on the phone for weeks saying he loves me, and why don't I go back and we start all over again. We're older and wiser now."

That's the theory, thought Reenie. "But what about Barbara?"

Long pause.

"Frank says that if I'm sincere in my intention to go back and marry him, he will tell Barbara what we're going to do."

Longer pause, with glass of wine in hand.

"I've made up my mind. I'm going back. I'm going to marry Frank."

. . . .

Ava would need a trousseau, of course. Off they went to Fontana for daytime dresses, evening dresses, cocktail dresses, sports clothes, casual outfits, negligees, and peignoirs. "They were really happy to see us," said Reenie in her memoir. Ava had them delivered to the Grand Hotel.

Ava did not inform Frank about the trousseau, however, and this gave Reenie pause. "She did not sound like a woman who was totally happy about the whole thing," she said. "I got the impression that Frank was saying, 'Angel, come across here and we'll get married. Yes, of course, I'll talk to Barbara, but if you don't want to come back, I'll marry Barbara.'"

It was more like a deal than a proposal.

"Barbara had been around a long time, and she was plainly in love with Frank," said Reenie. "Now Frank was giving Miss G not so much an ultimatum, but an option. It worried her."

Everything had become so confused over the years, and there was no clear path back to the past. And what sort of past had it been? Would this be a fresh new start? Or just another temporary truce until they resumed their old warring ways?

You can never bring back time. It's like trying to hold water in your hand.

More phone calls.

And then came that final decisive conversation, with wineglass in hand. Ava put down the phone and gave a long sigh.

"It's over," she said. "I told Frank he should marry Barbara. It's better for all of us."

. . . .

Dolly, like many of Frank's friends, was against the marriage to Barbara, a former Vegas showgirl. "We don't want a whore in the family," she said. "Barbara was a big mistake," said Tony Consiglio. "Somehow Frank loved her, but it was no Ava love. Nothing that fiery. If you opened Frank's heart, you'd see 'Ava' written inside." When asked what he saw in Barbara, Frank told George Jacobs, "Grace Kelly with my eyes closed."

On July 11, 1976, a blazing Sunday morning in the desert sun, Francis Albert Sinatra married Barbara Ann Blakeley Oliver Marx at Sunnylands, the Walter Annenberg estate, surrounded by some of the most famous paintings in the world, and two hundred selected guests. During the vows, when Judge Walsworth asked Barbara to take Frank for richer or poorer, the groom leaped in, saying, "Richer, richer!" which cracked everyone up—"even Dolly, who was there to give us her support," said Barbara in her memoir, *Lady Blue Eyes*.

When Ava was told of the wedding, there were no tears, just a depression that lifted quickly.

By Tina Sinatra's account, Barbara set out to seduce a famous man, then proceeded to isolate him from his friends and children, while he continued laying his golden eggs with the same awesome regularity. Later that year, the statue of Ava, created for the opening scene in *The Barefoot Contessa*, that had stood on the Compound grounds since 1957 was hauled away and never seen again.

....

On Thursday morning, January 6, 1977, Frank and Barbara boarded a chartered jet in Palm Springs and flew to Las Vegas, where Frank would open at Caesars that night. It was a violent, stormy day. Dolly was supposed to be with them, but she said she would take a later flight. Frank cautioned her to leave before dark. The visibility was getting worse by the minute.

Late that afternoon, on her way to the airport, Dolly told Angel, the driver, "If anything happens to me, everything goes to my grandson." Frankie Jr. was her favorite. At five o'clock, she boarded the Learjet with her old friend Anna Carbone. At 5:30, the plane departed. Four minutes later, it had gone off the radar screen.

Frank went onstage in shock that night, knowing that the jet carrying his mother was missing. Back in the Springs next day, Frank went up in a helicopter as the search began. Temperatures dropped, and a cold, fierce rain made visibility worse. "We didn't find her," said Frank when he returned.

On Sunday morning, searchers found the crumpled fuselage and the bodies at the nine-thousand-foot level of the east slope of Mount San Gorgonia, Southern California's highest mountain. The plane, flying 375 mph, slammed into a sheer cliff, scattering wreckage over half a mile.

The Federal Aviation Administration said the jet appeared to be heading in the wrong direction at the time of the crash, which occurred during a snowstorm after darkness had fallen. There may have been some confusion between the flight crew and Palm Springs Tower.

Frank was prepared, and there was sadness and acceptance when he received the news by phone. "I didn't get a chance to say good-bye," he said.

Dolly was eighty-two.

. . . .

In late June 1978, Ava was invited to the wedding of Princess Grace's daughter Caroline and Philippe Junot, seventeen years older, in Monaco, where royalty from across Europe mingled with movie stars and celebrities. David Niven hosted a small prewedding lunch, where Frank sang "My Way" to the couple.

At the wedding reception, Frank noticed that Ava was drunk. He spoke with Cary Grant, who took Ava gently by the arm and walked her out. "Ava needed to go and lie down," Grant later explained as he smiled sadly. "Frank asked me to make sure someone drove her back to her hotel."

. . . .

In November 1979, Ingrid Bergman returned to Hollywood as the Variety Club of America's guest of honor at a television program to raise funds to build a hospital wing for underprivileged children—to be named the Ingrid Bergman Wing.

The event was held at Warner Bros. stage 9, where she had made *Casablanca,* and where they still had the sets of Rick's Café Américain. On the set, pianist Teddy Wilson smiled and Ingrid was asked to hum "As Time Goes By." She started to, and then a voice behind her took up the song. It was Frank.

Frank Sinatra and Ingrid Bergman hardly knew each other, but they had a lot of front-page experiences in common. Both had gone through scandals that rocked the entertainment industry and became symbols of changing moral values in the United States. Now they were together in song near the finish line. He had flown three thousand miles from Atlantic City, where he was opening the next night, to sing one song, and fly straight back.

"I want to be part of Ingrid's tribute because I've always wanted to sing

'As Time Goes By' to her," said Frank. Bergman, in a battle with cancer, was deeply touched.

....

In January 1983, Don Costa was in New York, where Sinatra had scheduled sessions for an album, and he began to experience chest pains. He called Paul Anka, who called an old friend, Ben Dreyfus, who arranged for an ambulance. "Ben called me after they had put Don on a gurney," said Anka. "He told me that Costa wouldn't leave until they handed him the musical scores for the arrangements he was writing for Sinatra."

Shortly after they got Don to a hospital, he was gone. "Don had recently recuperated from open-heart surgery, but unfortunately was a cocaine user, heavy smoker, and drinker—as well as being one of the sweetest guys on earth and a genius musician," said Anka.

"Don did a lot for Frank," said Billy May. "He was a good musician, a wonderful guy, had a record company, made a lot of money, and went through a bad divorce, lost it all."

"He worked himself to death," said Bill Miller. "He wouldn't turn down *anything*. And he was warned, slow down." He was fifty-seven.

....

On August 6, 1984, Lena Horne opened her show *The Lady and Her Music* in London, where she played to packed houses for a month. "Horne's happiest moments in London were spent with Ava Gardner," said biographer James Gavin. "Long a recluse, the actress came to the Adelphi Theatre midway through Horne's run."

Afterward the two old MGM starlets laughed together at Downes Wine Bar, where photos were taken. Someone asked Ava about her "wonderful" time in the movies. "It wasn't wonderful," she said. "It was shit."

....

In the spring of 1978, Frank Sinatra and Nelson Riddle had a falling-out. Several charity foundations were honoring Nelson at a testimonial dinner at the Century Plaza Hotel on March 18. Frank agreed to present the award to Nelson, but he had to cancel when he fell ill with the flu. To accommodate Frank, the date was changed to April 16, and the Hollywood music community showed up for an evening titled "A Tribute to Nelson Riddle."

At the last minute, Frank sent Gregory Peck to take his place as the presenter of the award. "Nelson was justifiably livid at being snubbed," said Peter Levinson. Nelson told his son, "I'll never work for that man again, ever!"

Nelson went on to do excellent things, including three landmark albums with Linda Ronstadt, but no more recordings with Frank. Then, early one morning in December 1984, Nelson's phone rang. "I'm sorry," said Frank, from whatever time zone he was in. "I forgot what time it was for you."

"That's all right, Frank," said Nelson. "I had to get up to answer the phone anyway."

Frank wanted Nelson to be musical director for the second Reagan inaugural. After the January 1985 concert, they met at the Madison Hotel for a late dinner. Frank had a list of standards he had sung over the years, but never recorded, and he wanted Nelson to do the arrangements for a three-CD set. A musical hatchet was buried.

As Nelson started work on the project, his health began to fail. When trumpet player Eddie Bailey saw him backstage at a concert, he was shocked at Nelson's appearance. Riddle explained that he was suffering from hepatitis. "How could that be?" said Bailey. "In the old days you never even drank!"

"Eddie, you never had to work for Frank Sinatra!"

On September 29, Nelson checked into Cedars-Sinai Medical Center. Frank called to see how he was doing. "It might be a few months before I'll be in any condition to record, Frank," he said.

"Don't worry, Nelson," said Frank. "Get your strength back. I don't care how long it takes. The next album is with you."

At 8:30 P.M. on Sunday, October 6, 1985, Nelson Riddle died of cardiac and kidney failure. He was sixty-four.

Frank Sinatra, in New York to see his close friend Yul Brynner, who was dying of lung cancer, called Nelson's son Chris, saying he would be unable to attend the funeral. Sinatra asked his son, Frank, who had also recorded with Nelson, to attend on his behalf. At the funeral, a trombone choir composed of Nelson's old musicians played a tribute to the great arranger.

When Frank Sinatra, Jr., entered the chapel, Nelson's widow, Naomi, asked him to leave. "If his father can't attend, I don't want him here," she said. That night, when junior told his father what had happened, Frank shrugged it off. "A bad broad," he said.

. . . .

In 1985, at the age of sixty-two, Ava made her TV debut on a prime-time soap called *Knots Landing,* an evening serial drama, where she would be playing a sleek, villainous woman, a throwback to her days as a femme fatale. To some, it seemed a sad comedown from the great years at MGM. To Ava, it was three months' work and some most welcome loot, fifty thousand dollars an episode.

"Oh, television," she said, smiling at Peter Kaplan of the *New York Times* in Frank's Waldorf Towers suite. "It's awfully small, isn't it? Tatty."

"With her green eyes and shaken-out auburn coif, Miss Gardner did not look so very different from the way she looked in *The Barefoot Contessa, On the Beach* and *Mogambo,*" said Kaplan. "She sat with a bottle of spring water and chain-smoked, talking in a low voice that carried tones of North Carolina, where she was born, and London, where she lives." Later in the interview, she switched to scotch.

Ava kept a diva's perfectly straight face as she told Kaplan she loved another popular evening soap, called *Dallas,* and that she had recently met Larry Hagman, who played the infamous J.R. on the program, "and I was just as excited as I was the first time I met Clark Gable."

"One of the things that I loved about Ava is that she was a broad," said Donna Mills, the star of *Knots Landing*. "She was just very easy, and very down and dirty. She was very much her own woman. She knew who she was. She was still an incredibly beautiful woman."

When Mills made this observation to Ava, however, the actress demurred. "Oh no no no," she said. "I used to be. Not anymore."

. . . .

Life, which can be merciful, did not take pity on Ava. The years of heavy drinking and hard living had taken a toll on her greatest asset, her beauty. Perhaps—like Greta Garbo and Marlene Dietrich, who never appeared anywhere—she had decided to do her aging in private.

"Ava became very reclusive," said Stephen Birmingham. "When I'd go to see her in London, I'd try to make her get dressed up and go out, but she wouldn't leave the apartment. I think she felt that without her looks she was a nothing."

"Frank was still so protective of Ava, not least because she'd frequently call him up and tell him what was going wrong in her life," said Barbara Marx Sinatra. "Once, she was badly bitten breaking up a fight between her dogs, so Frank offered to pay her medical bills. Another time she called to tell him she had pneumonia and needed to go to Barbados to recuperate, so he arranged it. He was always sending her money; that was the type of heart he had. He took care of people he loved. I never minded a bit; I knew Ava Gardner wasn't a threat anymore."

. . . .

In 1986, Ava began experiencing serious respiratory problems and chest pains. Her London physician suggested testing for lung cancer. Frightened, on October 6 she flew to Los Angeles on a commercial flight, which became an ordeal, as her temperature started to rise and she collapsed in her seat. Passengers vacated the back row and Ava was able to lie across three seats beneath blankets.

"I just wheezed until my head was pounding, my body felt like jelly inside, and I thought, baby, you've made a big mistake getting on this plane," she said. "I must have shivered halfway across the Atlantic."

At LAX, she was on oxygen, and Bappie took her directly to St. John's Hospital and Health Center in Santa Monica. Her temperature soared to 105. Cortisone brought it down. The diagnosis was pneumonia. No cancer. There were flowers and calls from Frank, checking on her. Within a week, she was moving about.

After ten days, Ava was released to Bappie's house, where, after dinner that first night, she felt a tingling sensation in the palm of her left hand, which gradually became a needles-and-pins feeling, the avatar of a stroke. The left side of her body was paralyzed. "The only thing I could move was my big toe. The leg was gone. The arm was gone. . . . My mouth wasn't working. My speech was slurred. My damn tongue was like it had been injected with Novocaine," Ava later recalled. "I wasn't frightened. I wasn't depressed. Which was very strange, but that's the way the brain works, it protects you from the horror of the situation."

She spent the next two months in therapy at the hospital, with no visitors—including the *Knots Landing* cast, many of whom were calling. When Frank called, the nurses would hold the phone to her ear, said Ava's biographer Lee Server. "She tried to speak, but it was hard to make herself understood, and so she just listened to his voice. 'I love you, baby,' he told her. 'It stinks, getting old.'"

Finally, walking with a cane, she returned home to Bappie's. That November, Frank fell ill himself. He entered the Eisenhower Medical Center in Palm Springs with "a case of acute diverticulitis and, barely escaping death, underwent an eight-hour operation during which twelve feet of infected intestine were removed from his body," said Lee Server. "By the end of the month, he was performing again in Las Vegas."

Ava and Frank didn't meet face-to-face. In 1987, she returned to London for a year of rehab, including three months of bed rest for broken vertebrae after she toppled off a trampoline during one of her therapy sessions.

In January 1988, Ava returned to St. John's for a checkup and tests, with weekends spent at the Westwood Marquis. She was still numb on the left side and walked with a limp, but her speech wasn't slurred. She had been in conversations with British journalist Peter Evans and started work on her memoirs. "I'm broke, honey," she laughingly said to Evans. "I either write the book or sell the jewels. And I'm kinda sentimental about the jewels." The project fell apart after Gardner discovered that Evans had once angered Frank Sinatra.

In Los Angeles she called on Lawrence Grobel, whom she had met in 1986, when he was doing interviews in London for his biography *The Hustons*. Ava was a good source for Grobel. She had acted with Walter Huston in *The Great Sinner* in 1949 and she was directed by John Huston in *The Night of the Iguana, The Bible,* and *The Life and Times of Judge Roy Bean.* She liked Grobel, and invited him to play tennis with her.

When they met in the hotel, where Ava had registered as Ann Clark, it was like a reunion. "You're looking good," said Grobel, lying. "Oh, please, can the flattery," said Ava. "We must be honest with each other. I look like shit. It's the worst period of my life. Can't move my fucking arm—I'd like to cut the damn thing off. I'm barely alive since I had my stroke."

Grobel asked her why she wanted to work with him on her memoirs. "Because if you're good enough for John Huston, you're good enough for me," she replied. They spent time together at the hospital in Santa Monica, at Bappie's house, at Grobel's house, and at the Westwood Marquis, where Ava was staying. She brought Reenie Jordan (who now lived in Sacramento) in for several days, and another old friend, Roddy McDowall, to help refresh her memory.

One afternoon, Ava asked Grobel to take her to Bappie's, where she wanted to do a load of laundry; she had thrown the clothes into a large plastic trash bag. As Grobel walked through the lobby carrying the bag, he turned and saw Ava standing between the elevator and the entrance to the dining room, where a young newlywed couple were posing for pictures.

"I turned back to try to protect her from having her picture taken once the photographer recognized her," said Grobel, "but it wasn't necessary."

Ava looked at the young man with the camera. "Excuse me . . . ma'am," he said. "Would you mind moving just a bit? You're in the picture."

In the car, Grobel said, "That wedding photographer could have made more money today with just that one shot than he will make working that entire wedding, had he known."

"Well, two cheers for his not knowing, then," said Ava. "Thank fucking God for small favors."

. . . .

On February 25, Ava's manager, Jess Morgan, called Grobel. Ava was ready to make a deal. "She wants at least a million dollars," Morgan said. "So that means I won't accept anything less than a million and a quarter, which will guarantee you $250,000. And anything more than that, she will split with you 80-20."

Ava wanted Grobel to come to London, but the money wasn't right. "At that time, writers were getting fifty percent, but Ava's manager was firm—even for serial rights, 80/20," said the writer. "When I said no, Ava was furious. She thought she had found her writer. I always felt regretful. She and I got along very well. It would have been a great book."

Morgan approached other writers with his deal. He also got in touch with Sinatra's attorney, who had indicated that Frank wanted to help with the cost of the chartered jet that Ava used, and the medical expenses. There had been no calls or messages from Frank this trip. When Morgan told her that a check for fifty thousand dollars had come through, Ava was angry. "She didn't think it was enough," Morgan told Lee Server. "It's that fucking wife of his," said Ava.

. . . .

Ava became a total recluse when she returned to London in 1989. Her health began to fail. Mickey Rooney, who had come to town with Ann Miller for an extended tour of *Sugar Babies,* wanted to visit his former wife. In 1962, when Rooney declared bankruptcy after a series of hard falls, Ava had written out a check to him, leaving the amount blank.

He called her and though her voice sounded croaky, Ava seemed happy to hear from him. She told him about her strokes, and said she wasn't feeling well. "Don't be surprised if someday soon you hear that I've blown my fuckin' brains out," she said.

"Awww, Ava," Rooney said. He tried to soothe her, saying he had lost too many friends to suicide over the last few years. Did she know God?

"I—don't—know—God," she said, haltingly.

"Fortunately, Ava, God knows you," said Rooney.

They agreed to have dinner at her apartment on Sunday evening, but Mickey failed to show. "I just couldn't go—I was afraid to," he said. "I had had fantasies—that I might fall in love with her again, and she with me—and, shoot, I was married. . . . I'd heard that she was just as beautiful as she'd ever been, and I knew she was twice as salty."

. . . .

In the fall, Reenie visited Ava and thought the apartment damp and drafty, even when the heat was on. She lined the doors and windows to keep Ava from feeling the chill.

In October, Ava sold some jewels at a Sotheby's auction in New York. For Christmas, high bidder Jack Nicholson gave his girlfriend, Angelica Huston, an extraordinary pearl and diamond bracelet that Frank had once given Ava. "The card said he hoped I would not find it overbearing," said the daughter of Ava's favorite director.

. . . .

On Christmas Eve, a coconut cake arrived from Bappie, as always. A framed photograph of Frank and Ava in the early days was on Ava's bedside table. "Sometimes she would lie in bed and take out the letters from Frank," said Lee Server. "They were all sorts and sizes, from all over the world, notes, postcards, and long letters of many pages. She would take out each one and read it from start to finish, then put it back in the envelope and go on to the next one. She would read one and it would make her feel misty, then another that would have her laughing or cursing him on the page. Then she would pack them up again and put them away."

....

With her bad arm, Ava had difficulty turning over in bed. On a Thursday evening in late January, her maid, Carmen, thought she heard a sound from the bedroom. She went in and put her arm around Ava to make her more comfortable as Ava gave a sigh and her body relaxed.

"When I go, it won't be quiet," she had told friends. "I'll be going in a storm."

That night a chilling, unanticipated storm swept through Great Britain and Europe, leaving a near apocalyptic trail of devastation and killing sixty people. The Burns Day Storm, as it would be known, knocked down walls and blew off roof tiles. More than a million trees were uprooted, including many in the square across from 34 Ennismore Gardens, where the lift stopped between floors, and the lights went out, and Ava Gardner died one month past her sixty-seventh birthday, on January 25, 1990.

⊰ 14 ⊱

The Final Curtain

Ava's death was front-page news around the world. It was the cover story—"The Last Goddess"—for *People* magazine. In Europe, *Paris Match* published a retrospective of the goddess's life and times that ran forty-two pages. In death as in life, Ava remained controversial. "My heart is broken with the loss of my first love," said Mickey Rooney. "Ava died of confusion," said Artie Shaw, sanctimonious to the end. "Her beauty ruled her." "Ava was a great lady, and her loss is very painful," said Frank, speaking via his publicist.

"He was distraught, barely audible," wrote Tina Sinatra in her memoir. "My heart broke for him." "He wanted to go to the funeral but he feared Barbara's wrath," said Tony Consiglio. "He paid for Ava's entire funeral. He had the money funneled through Jilly Rizzo so Barbara wouldn't get upset."

. . . .

In Smithfield, North Carolina, Ava's body was received at the Underwood Funeral Home in a shipping coffin with a small metallic label on which her name was misspelled "Gardener." The body was transferred to a polished cherry casket, where Ava was laid out in a flowing pink gown for a private family viewing. At that service, her sister Myra wept. Bappie, seriously ill in California, could not make the trip.

That evening, some three thousand friends and fans paid their respects, passing by Ava's closed coffin. The next morning, January 29, 1990, about five hundred fans gathered beneath the stately magnolias in tiny Sunset Memorial Park for the grave site service. As a cold, light rain started to fall, umbrellas opened and someone said, "It's just like the opening scene in *The Barefoot Contessa*."

"She was no saint," said the Reverend Francis Bradshaw. "If we were all saints, then this whole God thing would not be necessary." At the evening service, the Methodist minister said, family members had "talked about her authenticity, her genuineness. They talked about her love for her home, for its realism, for its gentleness, for its roots, for its family."

Ava's maid, Carmen Vargas, sat with family members under a tent, weeping. In December, Ava had given her a wrapped package, saying, "If something happens to me, I want you to destroy it. I don't want anyone to open it or see inside." Carmen thought there were letters inside. "I respected her wishes," she said. "She trust me fully. I did what she asked."

A small array of bouquets marked the grave, including a wicker basket of yellow roses, with a card—"I love you"—from Lena Horne. There was also a large wreath of mixed flowers—red roses, asters, Fuji mums, and daisies—which Frank's secretary Dorothy Uhlemann had ordered, and a card, "With my love, Francis." It was the largest wreath order ($100) Twigg's Flowers & Gifts had ever filled, and Barbara Twigg, owner of the little country shop who designed the wreath, kept a copy of the check for years afterward.

When a black limousine with tinted windows pulled into the cemetery and parked a short distance from the crowd, there was a buzz. Was Sinatra in the car?

"No celebrities came to Ava's funeral," said local journalist Doris Rollins Cannon. "The occupants of the limousine turned out to be a hairdresser and several friends from Fayetteville who wanted to attend the funeral of a Hollywood legend in a style they deemed fitting." As the casket was lowered into the Gardner family plot, the sun broke through the clouds and umbrellas were closed.

1990

....

On January 30, the residents of Albany, New York, were eagerly awaiting the opening of the Knickerbocker Arena in the heart of downtown, where Frank Sinatra would be the inaugural act. The news of Ava's death, though, led to rumors that Sinatra was devastated and would be unable to perform; that he had to be hospitalized; that Liza Minnelli was going to sub for him.

Sinatra had pulled himself together by Tuesday morning. He flew into the Albany airport in the late afternoon and went directly to the Knick. Barbara, Frank Sinatra, Jr., Bill Miller, and a few sidemen came with him.

"The excitement was palpable," said Ed O'Brien. The arena was filled to capacity—eighteen thousand. "When he came on stage there was thunderous applause. He was not in great voice but it didn't matter. He went through his usual playbook and the audience loved every minute of it." A bottle of Jack Daniel's sat atop Bill Miller's piano. After doing "The Best Is Yet to Come" and "Mack the Knife," Frank informed the audience it was "about time to have a drink." He opened the bottle and took a swig. No glass.

"What happened next was unforgettable," said O'Brien. Frank introduced "one of the greatest saloon songs anybody ever wrote," Johnny Mercer and Harold Arlen's "One for My Baby." He did his obligatory buildup, setting the stage for the audience to be the bartender. But he went off-script, telling the audience that the poor soul "takes a walk, walks the whole day and the whole night." O'Brien had seen this acting out of the "saloon song" many times. Usually, Frank would stand in one spot, feigning the movements of a drunk as the sad story was told at the bar. This night was different. He was holding the bottle of Jack by the neck as Miller's piano guided him into the first lines of Mercer's lyrics. He took a gulp of the whiskey and started to sing. He moved around the stage, swaying, drinking from the bottle, and the pain in his voice was almost unbearable. As he sang "Let's make it one for my baby and one more for the road," you could hear the whispering start: "He's dancing with Ava." "She is up there with him." "Oh my God, you can almost *see* her."

When he reached "I've got a lot of things I want to say," the syllables were extended in a detached staccato as he continued dancing around the stage, and a little cry came out when he sang "Thanks for the cheer." The audience held its collective breath as he finished. Then the place exploded with rapturous applause and a standing ovation. "A great artist had shared with them what may have been the most desolate moment in his life," said O'Brien. "He had channeled his pain into magnificent artistic expression."

"That was the moment everyone was waiting for—no, make that *hoping* for—the moment when the Sinatra of the past, the Sinatra that raised the hair on the back of your neck, showed his hand and tore out our hearts," wrote critic Michael Eck in the *Albany Times Union* the next day. "If the Knick never hosts another show, it made its mark in entertainment history when one man connected with 18,000 in the beat of a heart."

. . . .

Frank was in his seventy-fifth year when he sang his farewell to Ava. He would continue to perform for another five years. Like any great fighter, he made adjustments as he aged; yet his vocal powers and memory for lyrics began to desert him. His mood swings were more erratic than ever. In the recording studio, for one final attempt at Reprise, Frank became upset with his son—who was producer on the album—when an arrangement was in the wrong key. He walked out, head down, avoiding eye contact. He just couldn't do studio recordings anymore.

In his absence, the band laid down tracks for several songs, and junior did the vocal on a few to test the arrangements. He took a tape of his recordings to play for his father in the Springs. This angered Frank even more. Was junior trying to show him up? Eventually, Frank returned to the studio for some overdubbing on the taped arrangements. As he came into the building for the third time, he said, "Have I ever been in this studio before?" The project collapsed.

In 1990, Frank returned to his old label, Capitol, where he (and producer Phil Ramone) created two *Duets* albums, which were considered gimmicky by Sinatra connoisseurs, but they sold by the millions to a vast audience turned on by the contemporary singers Frank collaborated with. The *Duets* concept took the burden of carrying a whole project off his weary vocal cords. Frank laid down the vocal for many of his longtime standards, and these tracks were merged with other voices—those of Gloria Esteban, Natalie Cole, Bono, Willie Nelson, et alia—for what would become the most commercially successful albums of his career. It looked like Frank was going out at the top.

Yet he continued to perform, using teleprompters for lyrics he had sung a thousand times. Frank Sinatra, Jr., who was now conducting the band and steering his father through the program, thought it would be easier (and less unsightly) if the ol' man could be fed the vocal through an in-ear monitor to keep him on the lyric. Impressions were made of Frank's ears, and the Mechanic Theatre in Baltimore was rented, with a full orchestra, one day prior to a concert at the Merriweather Post Pavilion. Finally, the ear monitors were ready; but when his son showed them to him in the dressing room, Frank said, "What the hell is this?"

"We are trying to create less of a need for you to use the prompters," said junior.

"I am doing the best I can," said Frank Sinatra, "and if you need another singer, I heard Vic Damone isn't working too much."

. . . .

The eighties and nineties had become sad because of the many farewells for Frank, who abhorred attending funerals . . . Buddy Rich . . . Count Basie . . . Gordon Jenkins . . . Jimmy Van Heusen . . . Orson Welles . . . his longtime drummer Irv Cottler . . . his right-hand man Irv "Sarge" Weiss . . . Sammy Davis Jr. . . . Dean Martin—all gone. Frank was even honorary pallbearer for the funeral of Greg Bautzer, the lawyer that "Big Nancy" sicced on him, and whom he befriended after the divorce settlement back in the Ava days.

The most devastating loss, however, was that of Jilly Rizzo, Frank's longtime travel companion and go-to guy, in 1992. When Frank was told that Jilly, 75, was killed in a fiery hit-and-run car accident, he fell to his knees. The brother Frank never had, he was buried in the Sinatra family plot, with Frank's parting inscription on Jilly's tombstone: "He was the best." "After Jilly's death, Barbara traveled with Frank to just about every performance," said Tony Consiglio. By now, Frank was battling Alzheimer's, and Barbara ran the show. Bill Miller said that by 1994 Frank had become an annoying pet to the lady. She loved parties, galas, and any festivity available. Frank, by then, hated them. The life of the man who liked to do everything his way was now in turnaround: He did it *her* way.

"I remember one time at dinner, Barbara tapped Frank's hand," said Tony. "With that, Frank got up and said it's time to go. Like maybe around nine o'clock. When did Frank *ever* call it a night at nine o'clock?" And so, as his health and well-being diminished, Frank became captive to a woman who was more than willing to tell him—not suggest, *tell* him—what to do.

On March 2, 1994, Frank received a lifetime achievement award at the thirty-sixth annual Grammy telecast. All the stars were there. In accepting the award, he started to free-associate and glided into some of his nightclub shtick—"That was more applause than Dean got in his entire career." When it looked like he was settling in for one of those long, meandering acceptance speeches, he was cut off. The camera went to a long shot of the stage, with a voice-over announcing other winners that night as, presumably, Frank was led from the stage by presenter Bono. "How long should he continue to be showcased in public when he clearly is not in full tune with what's going on around him?" asked David Hinckley of the New York *Daily News*. "His rambling raises the question whether there's a point where that faraway look in his eyes could start to erode his dignity."

The following week, at the Mosque Auditorium in Richmond, Virginia, the heat got to him. Frank performed sitting on a stool. Two songs from the end, in the middle of "My Way," he collapsed. He was rushed by ambulance to the Medical College of Virginia Hospitals, where he strode out after three hours. "He decided he wanted to leave and he left," said a hospital spokesman. The next day, from Palm Springs, he said it was "very, very good to be home." His publicist said Frank would resume his tour in a few weeks.

In August, Pete Caldera of the *Times Herald-Record* attended one of Frank's last concerts at the Garden State Arts Center in painful disbelief. "This was Sinatra now fighting the songs as much as singing them," he wrote. "He was lost somewhere inside the first eight bars of 'Come Fly With Me,' the band long since sailing past him as he strained back toward his son, the conductor, in search of the next line." Toward the end, he would often cry while doing encores, blowing kisses, telling the audience he loved them, being led from the stage, saying, "Think of me once in awhile."

Natalie Cole was the opening act for Frank's final concert at the Fukuoka Dome in Tokyo, in late December 1994. Before the performance, over dinner in his hotel suite with some members of his entourage, Frank sat at the head of a long table and talked with Natalie about her father, Nat King Cole. "Your dad was just cool," he said. "He was a man *and* a gentleman."

"It was the gentleness and the reverence that Frank held in his voice that I remember most of all," said Natalie in her memoir. Later, because he'd been so eloquent over dinner, "It was a shock when I saw Frank falter onstage. It was all he could do to get through 'My Way,' and I couldn't believe that he was losing the lyrics to signature songs like 'The Lady Is a Tramp' and 'New York, New York.' He had a teleprompter that was as big as a giant TV screen, but it was as if he didn't know how to read it. I could tell that it was really tough on him—it seemed to me that he knew what was going on, but couldn't do anything to help himself. He just stood there blankly while the music kept going. Finally he turned his back to the audience and glowered at Frank Junior, who was conducting, like it was *his* fault."

"It was terrible, it was sad, he couldn't remember one fucking lyric," said Bill Miller. "Not one tune could he do without asking for help. He was apologizing. That's when I think he and his old lady decided to knock it off. That was the end of his career right there."

Two months later, on February 25, 1995, at the charity Golf Tournament at the Marriott Desert Resort Hotel, Frank sang his final song. "He had five tunes to do, that's all," said Bill Miller. "He called me, wanted to warm up at the house. Well, we never did. They drove me to the house and we sat around. He had a drink. I had a half a drink. He had part of another drink. We went over, took our places, and comedian Tom Dreesen introduced Frank and he did 'I've Got the World on a String,' 'You Make Me Feel So Young,' 'Fly Me to the Moon,' 'Where or When' and 'My Kind of Town.' He sang *every tune* without the aid of a monitor. Dreesen came out to get him off, but Frank wanted to do one more. And he did, an encore, the last song he would sing in public, 'The Best Is Yet to Come.' Now, figure that one out. We were all looking at each other. We thought a miracle had happened. He got his brain back, his memory back. Isn't that amazing? But he still stuck to his guns. No more."

. . . .

In March 1995, the Compound was sold for just under five million dollars. Frank "was grieving as though someone had died," said Tina. The new owner allowed Frank and Barbara to stay on as guests for two months. In late May, they made their exit. They moved to a big house on Foothill Road in Beverly Hills, purchased in 1986 for six million dollars after Frank sold his old Japanese-modern bachelor pad overlooking downtown L.A. Thereafter, Frank was disoriented. At the new house, he couldn't understand why they weren't back in the desert, often asking, "When are we going home?"

Little that Frank had collected had been preserved; instead, most everything would be broken up and sold. On Friday, December 1, 1995,

Christie's conducted an auction in New York that would net $1.9 million for the Sinatras.

In the catalog was a letter from Barbara and Frank: "We have always loved beautiful things—it's as simple as that." And here's a sampling of what was up for bid: eleven snuffboxes; a record collection, assorted vinyl—classical and popular box sets and individual albums; goblets; silver-plated white wineglasses (one inscribed "Blondie"; the other, "Blue Eyes"); crystal bowls; paperweights; cut-glass decanters; mirrors; Frank's personalized mailbox ("A metal outdoor mailbox in the shape of a house; brass colored box features a front open flap with chain hinges . . . with stencil on glass lettering, F. SINATRA"); a 1976 Jaguar XJS two-door sports coupe (approximately 9,500 miles), British racing green, a wedding gift from Barbara to Frank in 1976, with a custom-fitted Panasonic audio system; Victorian card cases; a gold-plated cigarette lighter from Arnold Palmer; a silver and gold cigarette case from Jule Styne and Sammy Cahn; a Mathey-Tissot open-face stainless-steel pocket watch inscribed "To Charley Shoulders Thanks Smokey the 'B'" (Charley Shoulders was Sammy Davis, Jr.'s nickname for Frank, who called Sammy Smokey the B.); a French gold and gem-set shoehorn, a 1976 birthday gift, inscribed "To Francis Happy Birthday Love Gene and Mike Romanoff"; a casino slot machine ("can be played with or without coin") that featured a ringing bell on payoff; a bronze figure of John Wayne, cast from a model by Corsut; paintings by Andrew Wyeth (watercolor and pencil), Grandma Moses (one from 1943, the other done in 1955), Guy Wiggins, Max Kuehne, William Merritt Chase, Ernest Lawson; a painting of Jack Daniel with the inscription "To Francis Albert Sinatra from your good friends at Jack Daniel Distillery 1994"; *Village Protégé,* a 1974 oil painting (24 by 30 inches), by actress Elke Sommer (wife of hated journalist Joe Hyams), estimated value $200–$300; the Bosendorfer black grand piano ("a centerpiece in the Sinatra Palm Springs residency, this grand piano was used by Mr. Sinatra to rehearse prior to touring and for special intimate concerts for friends and family"); a landscape painting from Jaime McEnnan, a seven-year-old who read about the auction and added a note to

Ms. Sinatra: "My mom said the pictures were donated by actors. Since I am an actor, I would like to donate a picture too," estimate $20–$50. All going, going . . . gone.

. . . .

On Thursday morning, May 14, 1998, Frank Sinatra arose quiet and withdrawn. He had slept poorly. The day turned sunny and Barbara coaxed him to have some lunch near the pool. Frank was in his wheelchair. He ordered his favorite—a grilled cheese sandwich—but didn't finish it. He returned to his room in a state of growing agitation.

Frank's health had been in steady decline for nearly two years. On November 1, 1996, he was hospitalized for pneumonia and heart problems. Two months later, he suffered a heart attack, and he had been reclusive for the past fifteen months.

Visitors were few. Jerry Lewis called Frank regularly, and they talked and laughed over old times. Tony Oppedisano, Frank's road manager, told Peter Bogdanovich about the time Lewis sent Frank a note, with a check for $27.50 enclosed. He wanted Frank to buy "something special" for Barbara and himself. Frank broke up. Barbara wanted him to endorse the check so that she could cash it. Tony had it framed.

Barbara often invited Bill Miller over to keep him company: "Why don't you come over. Drop by, any day. Six, six-thirty, a perfect time." "It was just he and I and Vine, his housekeeper, who sat down and had dinner with us," said Miller. "Barbara wasn't there. The time before she didn't want to come down from her room, and he'd call her on the phone from the den. 'Are we still married?' he said. 'Where the hell are you?' He was pretty alert at that point.

"Another time I had dinner there one night, and I wasn't sure Frank knew who I was. He was sitting across from me, and every once in awhile he would give me this look, as if to say, who the hell is he? I was watching him with curiosity more than anything: What's wrong with this poor man? 'Oh, we're having ice cream,' he said. 'That's good, that's good.' Finally, he got up from the table and kind of shuffled away with one of the nurses right alongside him, shuffling, not walking, like doing an imitation of an old man."

On Thursday evening, May 14, Barbara was dining at Morton's with Harriet and Armand Deutsche (Ardie, as he was called). At home, Frank was in his room. There was a nurse on hand, and Vine, the longtime housekeeper, had all of the emergency numbers, just in case.

An hour later, Frank started experiencing chest pain and difficulty breathing—another heart attack. He sat up and screamed. His lips turned blue. Vine called 911. Then she called Barbara at the restaurant. "You'd better come right away," she said. "The paramedics are here. They're going to take Mr. S to the hospital."

"What happened?" asked Barbara.

"They can't find a pulse."

As the ambulance rushed him to the ER at Cedars-Sinai, Frank Sinatra spoke his final words. "I'm losing it," he said.

When Barbara arrived at the ER, Frank was barely alive, beyond talking. Three doctors, led by Rex Kennamer, worked on him for ninety minutes with intravenous medication. Frank Sinatra was formally pronounced dead at 10:50 P.M.

············

After a tiring day, Tina Sinatra had watched the TV finale of *Seinfeld* and was getting ready for bed when the phone rang at 11:10. "I have bad news," said Rex Kennamer. "We lost him."

"Lost who?" she said.

"Your father," he said. "I'm sorry."

In shock, Tina drove to her sister's, where Nancy, who had also watched *Seinfeld* that night, was waiting outside the house. They drove to the Cedars emergency room, where Scoop Marketing publicist Susan Reynolds was working the phone at the nurses' station. Tony Oppedisano was there. He had held Frank's hand in the final minutes. Barbara sat in a chair next to Frank's body, which lay on a gurney, his eyes closed, his hands on his chest.

The news reports would mention that Barbara was at Frank's side when he died, and that family members arrived later. Barbara had been out for dinner with friends for a fourth consecutive night, according to Tina's memoir. "The pity was that she didn't feel the necessity to phone Nancy or me to stay with him in her stead," said Tina. "Of all the nights for none of us to be there, this was the worst." Frank remained alive at Cedars "for more than eighty minutes," said Tina. "There was ample time to notify his children and get them to their father's bedside. I believe the omission was deliberate. Barbara would be the devoted wife, and then the grieving widow, *alone* at her husband's side." Regrets, there were more than a few.

....

At the Church of the Good Shepherd in Beverly Hills, a trio of Frank's wives was present—Nancy, Mia, and Barbara. "If Ava had been alive, she would have been here too," said Tina. "I can't remember how many times Frank said that when he died he wanted to be buried next to Ava," said Tony Consiglio. "She was his one love."

In an anteroom, as four hundred invited guests entered the church, pianist Bill Miller, guitarist Ron Anthony, and bassist Chuck Berghoffer played songs from *In the Wee Small Hours,* "the Ava album," and other songs for lovers.

Frank was dressed in one of his finest navy blue suits and a striped tie. In his coffin were some of his favorite things: cherry Life Savers, Tootsie Rolls, a roll of dimes, a pack of Camels, a Zippo lighter, small dog biscuits (he loved dogs), and a small bottle of Jack Daniel's—one for the road on the long journey. Barbara slipped a gold Bulgari medallion she had given Frank for one of his birthdays into his pocket. The wording, translated into Italian, was "You still give me a thrill."

Near the closed casket, on an easel to the right of the altar, was the Paul Clemens oil portrait that Ava had given Frank. "It was strange to see Dad before us with that lonely, faraway look," said Tina.

"When I finished Frank's portrait I found I had painted a man withdrawn into himself, thinking private thoughts," said Paul Clemens. "It is not the face of an extrovert; that face appears when the music and the fun start and he bares himself in song . . . never all of himself, but enough to captivate several generations and still remain an enigma to them and, perhaps, himself."

. . . .

"All stories, if continued far enough, end in death," wrote Ernest Hemingway in *Death in the Afternoon,* his 1932 book about the ceremonies of bullfighting and the rituals of life. Accordingly, "If two people love each other," and one dies before the other, "there can be no happy end to it."

As Hollywood endings go, Frank and Ava's was tinged with sadness and pain. They were both deeply flawed, highly ambitious icons on a big stage in a business that, as the songwriters like to say, eats them up and spits them out.

"They loved each other as if love were a battle to the death," said Ava biographer Lee Server. Neither was prepared to make a life for the other. They were too busy living lives of their own. When it wasn't love, it was war.

They lived large—life was a long-run happy hour—and they gave each other tremendous sexual satisfaction. It was like an addiction. "The problems were never in bed," Ava said famously. "Our fights began on the way to the bidet." Or to the bar. Alcohol—what director Preston Sturges called "man's worst friend"—became another addiction.

The inability of Frank and Ava to make it together certainly wasn't about "being a couple," as though they had some pesky lifestyle divergence: He's a slob; she's a neatnik. Each had much more than a need for doing it "my way." Each had a need to be free, and a profound resistance to being submerged and ultimately drowned in passion that made them feel trapped, owned, obligated, which prevented them from being free— the very thing completely mitigated by love and marriage. It was the *needing* each other that they both loved and feared, that held them together and drove them apart.

In the end, they arrived at a deep friendship, the relationship that most couples come to value above all others. It must have been like a bond that had formed before they decided to call it a day, an old affinity rising again and again, holding them, so that they came away speaking of each other with great respect and affection, sharing the special compassion of two people who, once, long ago, had been in a bad accident together and had survived.

It was not unlike the sad yet stoical closing scene of Hemingway's *The Sun Also Rises,* when Lady Brett and Jake Barnes, in a taxi in Madrid, speak of things that might have been and accept unfulfilled yearning as one of the conditions of life.

"Oh, Jake, we could have had such a damned good time together," says Brett.

"Yes," he replies. "Isn't it pretty to think so?"

⤙ ACKNOWLEDGMENTS ⤚

I am indebted to the following people for providing answers, opening doors, and easing the way for my research. My thanks to Pete Johnson and the late Stan Cornyn for bringing me aboard to assist with the comeback of Ol' Blue Eyes at Warner/Reprise back in the mid-1970s; to Marilyn Greenwald, my fellow biographer and sounding board from Scripps School of Journalism; to coconspirator Douglass Daniel for sharing wit, intelligence, and strategies that enabled me to overcome obstacles; to Lilia F. Brady for a meticulous first reading, as always; to the fabulous John Christie for proofing an early draft with his customary touch of style; to Ed O'Brien for straightening out misinformation and for keeping all of the details of the Sinatra story accurately on track; to Kate Broughton for coordinating photo research; to Jim Perikli for assisting me at Ava's museum in North Carolina, where it all began, and for pestering me until it was finished; to Linda Parent Spikol, who is magical, for insight at the final bell; to Michael K. Cantwell for his wise counsel; to my editor, Peter Joseph, for his patience and perseverance steering these pages into final form; and to the late Jack Nessel for introducing me to my agent, Julia Lord, without whose support and guidance this book would not have been possible.

John Brady
Newburyport, Massachusetts
May 2015

⪦ SOURCES ⪧

All direct quotes are from print or interview sources; no scenes or conversations are fabricated. Among those who provided me with interviews were Franz Douskey, Scott Eyman, Mary Edna Grantham, Lawrence Grobel, Lee Herschberg, Ed O'Brien, Jim Ritz, Ric Ross, and Terry Woodson. I also interviewed Jim Bacon, Bob Thomas, Lee Solters, Billy May, Bill Miller, Al Viola, and Jill Weiss, who have since passed on.

When more than one source has been available, I have combined or merged details and dialogue for completeness while maintaining narrative flow. In general, I have tried to give credit where credit is due in the text by attributing quotes to sources by name. Full information for sources in the text and those cited hereafter can be found in the bibliography.

1. She Can't Act, She Can't Talk, She's Terrific

Grabtown Girl, by Doris Rollins Cannon, is a key source for understanding Ava's background and her early years. The cover story in *Time* magazine— "The Farmer's Daughter," September 3, 1951—provides further background and insight. For an understanding of MGM and how the factory system worked, Elia Kazan's *A Life* is an exceptional memoir that doesn't sugarcoat studio monsters and methods. *The Fixers*, by E. J. Fleming, explains how the publicity machine created stars and handled damage control when the stars misbehaved. To understand MGM is to attempt to understand L. B. Mayer. The best biography is Scott Eyman's *Lion of Hollywood: The Life and Legend of Louis B. Mayer.*

Ava's marriages are chronicled in her memoir, *Ava: My Story,* published in the year after her death. Mickey Rooney's memoir, *Life Is Too Short,* provides the Mick version. Arthur Marx's *The Nine Lives of Mickey Rooney* fills many gaps. The brothel that Mickey frequented—T&M Studios, with its look-alike vixens—may have been the inspiration for the Kim Basinger character in 1997's *L. A. Confidential,* in which Kim was cast as a hooker made up to look like Lana Turner.

For the life and hard times of starlets, I drew on memoirs by Esther Williams, Lana Turner, Evelyn Keyes, Betty Garrett, John Huston, and Jerry Lewis. Mearene ("Reenie") Jordan's memoir—*Living With Miss G*—is a recent addition to the stack of books on Ava, and it is valuable for its authenticity. Reenie served Ava from the mid-1940s to the end. She died at ninety-two in 2014.

Ava came to Hollywood on the same train as Hedy Lamarr, who acquired a reputation for being hard to work with, and who gradually faded at the studio. When she departed, Ava was given her dressing room.

2. Frankie Comes to Hollywood

George Evans's original Sinatra biography is from *Legend: Frank Sinatra and the American Dream,* edited by Ethlie Ann Vare. Another recent publication, Tony Consiglio's *Sinatra and Me: The Very Good Years,* as told to Franz Douskey, is rich in anecdotes and details from the early formative years when he was Frank's traveling companion. Like Reenie Jordan's remembrances, Tony Consiglio's are credible because he had no vested ego in the Sinatra story—he paid attention to what was happening, and he didn't drink. The pigeon episode is from Tony Consiglio's memoir. The Richard Sudhalter quote is from Peter Levinson's *Tommy Dorsey: Livin' in a Great Big Way*. How big did Tommy live? After selling the Tall Oaks mansion in November 1944, he resided in Miami long enough to purchase a ninety-eight-foot yacht, which he dubbed *The Sentimentalist*. Shortly afterward, he relocated to Los Angeles, and the yacht, with its nine-man crew, including a cook—and silverware inscribed with a trombone—sailed through the Panama Canal and up to Santa Monica to meet the bandleader. That's big.

Robin Douglas-Home's *Sinatra,* published in 1962, is a good source for Frank's recollections of the Dorsey days. Sinatra opened up to the young British writer, who hung out with him for about six months and was working toward an authorized biography with photos. The story of Frank and Tommy Dorsey on the golf course is from his book. When Robin committed suicide, Frank gave up any thoughts he may have had about doing an autobiography.

Tom Nolan's *Three Chords for Beauty's Sake: The Life of Artie Shaw* is the source for Artie Shaw's interaction with Frank at the Palladium. Earl Wilson's *Sinatra* includes numerous exchanges with George Evans. Earl knew him well from the New York club scene. E. J. Kahn Jr.'s famous 1946 profile of Frank for *The New Yorker* introduces the Sinatra mantra—"Don't tell me what to do. *Suggest.*"—and stresses the importance of not crowding Frank. "Bill Miller tipped me off," said Billy May during our interview. "'Those that are successful friends of Sinatra never try to get too close to him,' he said. I didn't. I always kept busy doing something else. And Bill didn't. But there were guys who were successful with him, and then they'd smother him: 'Here's my wife' . . . and after a while they'd be gone."

Insights to Marty Sinatra are from the memoirs of granddaughters Tina and Nancy Sinatra.

3. The Education of a Femme Fatale

Ava told coauthor Peter Evans about someone using her douche bag in *Ava Gardner: The Secret Conversations,* published in 2013, long after those conversations were held and both were dead. Ava's recollections of Howard Hughes are from *Conversations with Ava Gardner,* by Lawrence Grobel, and from *The Man Who Seduced Hollywood,* the biography of Hughes's lawyer Gregson Bautzer.

One background source for Artie is Liz Smith, the gossip columnist, who said that Shaw once put the moves on her. "Come on, girl, you're going home with me," he said, and she was sorely tempted. "He was damned sexy. But then I thought about Ava and Lana and Kathleen Winsor and Evelyn Keyes. They hadn't been good enough for Artie Shaw so how could I possibly measure up to those goddesses?"

Sources for the Mark Hellinger story are George Frazier and Jim Bishop; the latter was the columnist's secretary. Mark Hellinger had lyrics for a song that Ava was to sing in *The Killers,* but there was a dispute about the words being off-color. "We want Crosby and Sinatra to sing it on the air, sweetheart," said Hellinger. It all ended on the cutting room floor.

The source for Mel Torme's adventure is the singer's memoir, *It Wasn't All Velvet.* The early Palm Springs descriptions are from George Jacobs, Frank's longtime valet, and Frank Rose's book *The Agency.*

4. More Stars Than There Are in Hoboken

Frank's infamous checklist of starlets he planned to bed appears in Robert Reisner's 1958 *Playboy* profile of the philanderer. When Frank was escorting Joan Blackman, an attractive eighteen-year-old starlet, around town, he introduced her to inquisitive reporters as "Ezzard Charles," the heavy-weight boxer.

The source for the Kern tribute episode is Beverly Linet's *Star-Crossed: The Story of Robert Walker and Jennifer Jones.* The FBI *Sinatra Files* have Bugsy in L. A. on December 18, 1946 "to contact Lana Turner, Jimmy Durante, and Frank Sinatra for the purpose of having these individuals attend the opening of the Flamingo Hotel operated by Siegel." Shirley MacLaine, in her memoir *My Lucky Stars,* tells us that in the pit opening night, dealing blackjack, was Dean Martin.

In *Living with Miss G,* Reenie provides a credible version of Frank and Ava's first real date, something that biographers have often disagreed about. Betty Garrett visited Frank's place in Holmby Hills, a home that she and her husband yearned for. While shooting *On the Town,* Garrett tried to give Frank a friendly pat on the behind. "Don't do that!" he said very sharply. What's the matter with him? Betty wondered. "Don't you know?" said Gene Kelly. He told her about symmetricals, which Shakespearean actors used in their tights so that their calves looked bigger. Frank needed some padding in the rear. "If I were you," said Kelly, "I wouldn't pat Frank on the behind while he's wearing his sailor suit."

The description of Walt Disney and Holmby Hills neighbors is from Tina Sinatra's memoir, *My Father's Daughter,* which is painful but poignant reading. Tina tells of her mom's Tuesday ritual tea with "Missy" Stanwyck. The infamous Indio episode (which Jim Bacon confirmed to me in conversation) is reconstructed here from several sources, including Kitty Kelley's version of the dialogue when Frank called for help from George Evans's associate Jack Keller, who later provided an oral history of his adventures.

5. Hollywood Department of Public Affairs

Ezra Goodman's *The Fifty-Year Decline and Fall of Hollywood* is a key source for understanding the trustbuster backdrop to the demise of the studios. You can Google and view video excerpts of the MGM twenty-fifth anniversary lunch—with snippets of Ava and Frank—where L. B. Mayer attempted to sell the sales staff on the bright future of the studio. No worries. It was Mayer's indomitable spirit to battle anything that threatened the moviemaking business. Mayer sided with William Randolph Hearst in trying to stop the screening of *Citizen Kane,* offering $805,000 to rival RKO chief George Schaefer before the movie's opening if he would burn the master print and all copies of the film. Schaefer stood firm. Mayer warned director Elia Kazan, "We are in the business of making beautiful pictures of beautiful people, and anyone who doesn't go with that has no place here." After Mayer saw *Sunset Boulevard* at a screening, he accused director Billy Wilder of biting the hand that feeds Hollywood. Wilder told the old lion, "Fuck you."

The Ingrid Bergman source is her autobiography, plus David Thomson's *Showman: The Life of David O. Selznick*. Ingrid and Roberto Rossellini would always have Paris, where it all began in September 1948, when they met to discuss a movie they would make together. Louella frightened everyone on her radio show, observed Jesse L. Lasky, Jr., in his memoir. And the gossipist could be unintentionally funny, as when, after the affair with Roberto Rossellini, she asked, "But tell me, Ingrid, what everyone wants to know, is *whatever* got *into* you?" Bergman returned to Hollywood (and to forgiveness from her fans) in 1956, winning the Oscar for *Anastasia,* and divorcing Rossellini in 1957.

Earl Wilson's *Sinatra* is the source for Frank's battle with Hal Swisher. Reenie Jordan's *Living with Miss G* is the source for Ava's putting pressure on Frank to get a divorce, dump George Evans, and marry up. When Ava returned to Los Angeles for the last time, a year before her death, she invited Reenie—who operated a beautician shop in Sacramento—to join her discussions with Lawrence Grobel. Ava and Grobel searched for the little pink stucco house that was the original love nest for her and Frank in Nichols Canyon, in the Hollywood Hills, but they couldn't find it. "Too many houses," said Ava.

6. America's Original Reality Show

Charles Champlin, writing in *Architectural Digest,* is the source for George Sidney's comments on casting Ava in *Show Boat*. James Gavin's biography of Lena Horne tells her side of the story. Ava often vented her frustrations with Sinatra to Lena, whom Frank saw as an accomplice in Gardner's rejection of him. "Ava was one of the only women who told Sinatra to go fuck off," said Ray Ellis, Horne's conductor. "She'd say, 'Ah, you dumb fucking guinea'—she'd put him down all over the place." In *Life* magazine, Sinatra dismissed Lena as "a beautiful lady but really a mechanical singer. She gimmicks up a song, makes it too pat." "We don't like each other personally," said Lena in 1972. "It started with Ava Gardner."

Earl Wilson is the source for Frank's encounter with Mitch Miller. Nicolas Gage is the source for Willie Moore's telegram to Frank with some marital advice.

Sources for Ava's affair with Robert Taylor are Reenie Jordan and George Jacobs. Taylor was married to Barbara Stanwyck when he succumbed to Ava's charms in 1948.

It has often been taken for granted that Frank put all his grief over Ava Gardner into his recording "I'm a Fool to Want You." It became one of his all-time classics. "The story of Frank walking out of the studio, in tears, after one take is apocryphal," says Ed O'Brien, who has reviewed the Columbia recording session work sheets for March 27, 1951. "Mitch Miller told me 'Mama Will Bark' was the A side of the single. "Sinatra drew the line at barking like a dog and Miller had to hire someone else to do that, but it was this record more than anything else that Sinatra held against Miller," says Donald Clarke in his Sinatra biography.

7. A Star Is Reborn

In *King Cohn,* Bob Thomas characterizes Harry Cohn, the ogre who ran Columbia Pictures, as a sheep in wolf's clothing. "Frank Sinatra and Harry Cohn became good friends during the years when Sinatra was enjoying his initial burst of fame in Hollywood," writes Thomas. "Cohn, who preferred to seek favors of no one, made a request of his friend Frank Sinatra."

The biographer (and veteran AP reporter) then tells the story of Cohn's asking Frank to take a Columbia picture—*Miss Grant Takes Richmond,* starring Lucille Ball and William Holden—with him for a four-week engagement at the Capitol Theatre in New York. Sinatra did so, but he fell ill during the third week, stricken with strep throat. Frank took to bed at the Gotham Hotel apartment of his friend Manie Sacks. Cohn flew to New York, according to Thomas, and spent mornings with Frank. "Cohn read to the patient, reminisced of his early days in films, told jokes and delivered numbers recalled from his days as a song plugger. Cohn continued the daily routine until Sinatra recovered. Cohn's parting remark was in character: 'You tell anybody about this, you son of a bitch, and I'll kill you!'"

This story does not hold together. *Miss Grant* premiered on September 20, 1949—long after Frank's "initial burst of fame in Hollywood," and the movie never appeared on a Capitol bill. Nor was Frank Sinatra at the Capitol that year. Instead, Bob Thomas may have been thinking of Frank's well-known, ominous November 1947 appearance at the Capitol— when the movie was *Her Husband's Affairs,* with Lucille Ball and Franchot Tone. The engagement was a harbinger of things to come. After the first week, the bobby-soxers stayed away. The adult crowd wasn't interested and quite a few nights the house was filled to only 40 percent of its capacity. Sinatra was still selling records, but the teenage girls were moving away from him. No strep throat or confinement to bed.

Is the Cohn story true? Unlikely. One of Thomas's sources for the book was Sinatra, whom he interviewed—and who, presumably, told him this tall tale. When I spoke with Thomas years afterward, he conceded that he did not like Sinatra, and that he had turned down several requests to do a biography of Frank for that reason. Perhaps the feelings were mutual.

In 1954, artist Paul Clemens, who befriended Ava and Frank, married actress Eleanor Parker, who appeared with Frank in *Man with a Golden Arm.*

There are many versions of the Palm Springs encounter of October 1952. According to Lana, none of the principals ever referred to that evening again. "It was as though it hadn't happened, except that a lot of sick rumors grew out of it. One particularly vile rumor had it that Ava had walked into the house and found Frank and me in bed together. Another one suggested that it was Frank who walked in to find Ava and me in bed. There was even a third version that Ava and I had gotten mad at Frank, picked up a strange man, and shared him between us—and Frank had walked in on that scene. So much for Hollywood Babylon. Their marriage was a dreadful fiasco, and believe me, I did my best not to get involved in their domestic quarrels, whatever the consequences. I stayed fairly close to Ava in Hollywood, but after she moved to Europe I gradually lost touch with her." The version of events in this book is based upon AP news stories of the day, and Ava's final reflections on the episode in Lawrence Grobel's *Conversations with Ava Gardner.*

How much of a financial struggle did they have? Ava said that their troubles began after Frank had "gone and gotten successful again and become his old arrogant self. We were happy when he was on the skids." Actually, the skids weren't all that bad. Sinatra never had a really tough year financially. In 1954, *Billboard* profiled the hottest acts, including Frank's. A first-rate club paid him between ten and fifteen thousand dollars per week. If you add to that his TV work, recordings, other club work, and deferred pay, Frankie pulled in about $800,000. Not bad for a has-been; though, with Nancy's divorce settlement, plus other expenses and the high style Frank maintained, he was probably operating in the red. Ava talked variously about paying the bills during this period, which is probably part of the reason he continued to pay *her* bills in the late innings when he was flush and she was down and out in London.

Sources for the George Wood and Frank Costello material include Frank Rose's *The Agency* and Sandra Lansky's memoir, *Daughter of the King: Growing Up in Gangland.*

8. The Barefoot Diva

The recipe for Ava's coconut cake can be found in the *Ava Gardner Museum Cookbook,* available from the museum, 325 E. Market Street, Smithfield, NC 27577. The cookbook also includes a recipe for Southern Fried Chicken, Gardner Style, and contributions from friends and fans for dishes that Ava surely would have enjoyed: Judge Roy Bean Delight, Mogambo Gumbo, Earthquake Cake, The Bun Also Rises, One Touch of Beanus, Rice Vaquero, and The Diet of the Iguana Salad. (Ava probably had no problems with gluten.) Ava shared her famed martini recipe with David Hanna and Reenie Jordan, however, with slight variations. She made them eight parts gin to one part vermouth. "It's got to be bone dry," she said. "Just show the bottle of vermouth to the gin." She plopped ice into a glass shaker, stirring with her fingers for twenty or thirty seconds. "Never use metal," she said. "Never bruise the gin." After wiping the rim of the chilled martini glass with lemon, she poured the cocktail straight up.

The source for exchanges between Hemingway and Ava is A. E. Hotchner's *Papa Hemingway.* David Hanna's *Ava: A Portrait of a Star* is also a source for Dominguín observations, plus Ava's comments to Lawrence Grobel. In 1954, Hemingway was in Spain following the mano a mano between the two great matadors, Luis Miguel Dominguín and Antonio Ordóñez. In order to learn whom the winner was, you might read Hemingway's *The Dangerous Summer.* Or (spoiler alert), you may read on here: Dominguín was the loser.

9. Of Rats and Men

Sources for the early days of the Rat Pack and the Fourth of July regatta include Richard Burton's diary, David Niven's *The Moon's a Balloon,* Nathaniel Benchley's *Humphrey Bogart,* Stefan Kanfer's biography *Tough Without a Gun,* Graham Lord's *Niv: The Authorized Biography of David Niven,* and George Jacob's memoir.

The source for Ava's revolt on the set of *The Sun Also Rises* is Robert Evans's memoir *The Kid Stays in the Picture.* The story of emerging songwriter Sadie Vimmerstedt is from Philip Furia's *Skylark: The Life and Times of Johnny Mercer.*

10. Top of the Heap

Another significant and much-honored album from the Capitol years was *Frank Sinatra Sings for Only the Lonely,* recorded in early summer 1958. "For my money, this is the greatest blues album that was ever made," said Frank Sinatra, Jr. "This album should be available in drugstores by prescription only—because this is *death,* this record." Among the noteworthy songs were "Angel Eyes," "What's New?" (an Ava favorite), and Frank's classic rendering of "One for My Baby (and One More for the Road)." In 2007, journalist David McClintick, who won a Grammy for his liner notes on Frank's *Trilogy* album, conducted a "brackets" tournament in *The Enlightened Bracketologist: The Final Four of Everything,* to determine the greatest Sinatra recording ever. The competition started with thirty-two of Frank's best recordings, and then McClintick reduced them in a series of playoffs (with textual notes explaining winners and losers), down to the final two: "I've Got You Under My Skin," and, from *Only the Lonely,* "Blues in the Night," which McClintick declared the winnah. A gutsy—and highly controversial—call by the ref.

In her 2013 memoir, Shirley Jones wrote that she learned, at a press conference, from "an old-time journalist at the back of the room," the "real reason" Frank walked out on *Carousel.* "According to the journalist, at the time Frank was due to start filming *Carousel,* his grand passion, Ava Gardner, was shooting another film and was getting lonesome for Frank. She called him, and, according to the journalist, said, 'You better get your ass down here, Frankie, otherwise I'm going to have an affair with my costar.' Poor Frank didn't know that another actress on the shoot was already having an affair with the costar, and that Ava was making an empty threat to

Frank. But because Ava was his dream girl, the woman he would love for the rest of his life, Frank dropped everything, walked out of *Carousel,* and flew to be with Ava, to prevent her from having an affair she probably wasn't going to have anyway. Mystery solved."

Shirley made the talk-show rounds promoting her book and repeating this bogus tale. Let the record show that Ava and Frank split in late 1953. The marriage was over, and both had moved on to various other lovers. *Carousel* started shooting nearly two years later, in August 1955. Why would Frank be so distracted by Ava's threat of infidelity, if you want to call it that, some two years after he'd made his exit? Answer: He wouldn't. But for Shirley on the talk show and bookselling circuit, that's infotainment.

Andy Rooney's quote is from the November 16, 1965, CBS TV profile of Sinatra at fifty, which Rooney wrote, narrated by Walter Cronkite.

The source for the closing saloon scene is Pete Hamill's homage, *Why Sinatra Matters.* Frank's drink for the cameras, of course, was Jack Daniel's, on the rocks (three cubes), with water, just a splash. "Water rusts you," he said. In private, Frank often drank vodka; he loved a big Italian red with a meal. During the 1970 gathering at Clarke's, according to Hamill, someone asked, "Who is the worst living American?" Frank's nominee was boxer Jake LaMotta. "He dumped the fight to Billy Fox, and *never told his father,* who bet his life savings on Jake," said Sinatra. "Lower than whale shit."

11. Twilight of the Goddess

In 1959, director Stanley Kramer stipulated that Ava was to wear no makeup for *On the Beach*—a requirement she had happily met for *The Killers* in 1946. After watching some rush scenes, though, Kramer was certain the makeup artists had done things impossible to detect. Also, Ava's right cheek had been damaged in 1957, and there were stories of her using special makeup to cover a scar. In a restaurant one evening, Kramer said, "Remember the promise you made when you signed your contract? That you would use no makeup in the picture?" "I haven't forgotten it," replied Ava. "What do you think of the makeup I'm wearing tonight?" She took the director's hand and guided his index finger around the contours of her face, then showed him the finger. No makeup. Later, Kramer said, "I was amazed."

In the early 1960s, during her flamenco madness period, Ava visited Grace Kelly in Monaco, where the Hollywood escapees shared some laughs and memories. "I was staying at Grace's house—sorry, *palace*—with Prince Rainer, the family, the whole lot," said Ava. After a few drinks, Grace suggested a visit to Aristotle Onassis on his yacht in the harbor. "His guest is Winston Churchill," said Her Highness. "Would you like to meet him? I think he usually stays up pretty late polishing off a few brandies."

Off the gals went, and there was Sir Winston, in a white Panama hat and cruising suit, an honored (and frequent) guest aboard the *Christina*. "It wasn't a boat. It was a mansion. Everybody seemed to like the idea of two ancient ex–movie stars joining the party," said Ava. "Churchill was, to put it mildly, perhaps a teeny-weeny bit tipsy, but as we were too, that made us level. We sat across the dinner table, me looking at Churchill through a haze of my cigarette smoke, and he looking at me through a haze of his cigar smoke." Afterward, back to the palace.

Ava returned to Madrid, and Onassis called. "Ava, we're going to go on a voyage, a tour through the East Indian islands, stopping where we please, and then finally heading across to the East Coast of the States and up to New York," he said. "It's going to take six weeks. Aboard there is going to be only Sir Winston, Lady Churchill and Winston's private secretary. Nobody else. Sir Winston has asked personally if you would care to go with us."

Ava had nothing coming up, no movie in progress, and no love affair under way, nothing. But she felt shy and just a bit frightened. "I didn't want six weeks with Onassis on that yacht," she told Reenie. "I was sure the man wasn't going to rape me, but I thought it might be a tricky situation." Ava begged off, saying she couldn't go. She had things coming up.

A few weeks later, Onassis called from the Canary Islands. "Ava, the invitation is still open," he said. "I'll send my private plane to Spain to pick you up, so that you can join us here." Ava said no again.

Onassis called one more time. These Greek billionaires are nothing if not persistent. It was still no. Years later, though, Ava would regret a lost opportunity. "Winston Churchill was one of the great men of our time," she told Reenie. "There was no reason on earth why I shouldn't have gone and had that wonderful experience. I was a stupid little girl who had nothing to do except sit around Madrid and go out to flamenco every night."

Sources for *55 Days at Peking* are Bernard Gordon and Charlton Heston, who kept journals. Regarding sex on location, Heston said there is value for filmmakers in the old maxim, "Don't fuck the talent—it's distracting and counterproductive." He adds that it is true, for both men and women, that sex establishes a certain power. Another old maxim applies: "Get hold of a man's balls, and his heart and mind will surely follow."

Sources for Ava's relationship with George C. Scott include Ava's memoir, John Huston's memoir, *Ava Gardner: The Secret Conversations,* by Peter Evans, and Ava's conversations with Lawrence Grobel. Grobel interviewed George Scott for *Playboy* in 1980 at the actor's house in Connecticut, where he drank a full pitcher of Bloody Marys as they talked. When Grobel brought up Ava's name, Scott cut him off. "I never talk about Ava," he said. "That was a very, very low point in my life. Don't ask me anything about her." Scott, in a later discussion of leading ladies, told actor Frank Langella, "I had 'em all. Ava about killed me."

The portrait of Ava that Rex Reed wrote for *Esquire* was a breakthrough for the young writer. His mentor, Liz Smith, describes it in her memoir, *Natural Blonde*: "One night he went out with Ava Gardner and a beau and slipped into the bathroom every few minutes to jot down notes. When he told me of the experience, I said, 'Write this exactly as you told it to me and let me send it to *Esquire*.' He did. I did. And Rex became an enormous byline. Ava never forgave him for spending a social evening with her and writing it up when she didn't know he was a journalist."

The "Rex Reed treatment" became "one of the hallmarks of success for an actor or director," said *New York Times* book critic Henry Flowers. "I give people the benefit of the doubt and if they hang themselves, that's their problem," Reed told a *Newsweek* interviewer. "The old broads are the ones who interest me the most." *Newsweek* called the Ava profile in *Esquire* "a poignant glimpse of a sex goddess for whom life has been one supreme swindle." Afterward, Ava said Reed crucified her. "Did she say I misquoted her?" Reed replied to your author in correspondence. "No. Every word of it is true and it was written in as flattering a way as it is possible to write something when the subject will not let you ask questions, take notes or give any semblance of a dignified interview. Also, she was completely drunk."

12. There Are No Third Acts in American Lives

All Paul Anka quotes are from his memoir, entitled, yes, *My Way*. Paul also did his own "duet" with Frank's original recording for his *Duets* album.

The source for Frank's phone-ripping adventure in Miami is Tony Consiglio. Bill Zehme caught the Tony Rome line—"I used to know a broad who collected bullfighters"—for his *The Way You Wear Your Hat,* a real gasser.

Ava's tax predicament in Spain was captured by Stephen Birmingham and included as a cameo in her posthumous memoir, *Ava: My Story.*

13. Down and Out in London

Ava's apartment search and description is from Reenie's memoir, *Living with Miss G.* The Judge Roy Bean scene is from Lawrence Grobel's *The*

Hustons, and John Huston's memoir, *An Open Book.* The *Earthquake* source, once again, is Charlton Heston.

On March 21, 1987, Dean Paul Martin, the thirty-five-year-old son of Rat Packer Dean Martin, died when his air force F-4C Phantom jet slammed into mount San Gorgonio at 5,500 feet during a snowstorm. It was a death eerily similar to Dolly's ten years earlier, when Dean Paul said, "That mountain shouldn't be there. It should be moved. It's a hazard to all pilots." In conversation, Frank referred to San Gorgonio, the tallest peak in the San Bernardino Mountains, as "Mama's mountain."

The Ava and Lena scene in London is from Lena's biography, by James Gavin. Apart from Frank, Lena was the only celebrity to send flowers to Ava's funeral. "She sort of destroyed herself," said Liz Smith. "It was really drink. I would say in a way she was a tragic actress, but my God she was an incredible presence on the screen."

14. The Final Curtain

Buddy Rich, Frank's old antagonist, died on April 2, 1987, at the age of sixty-nine. During his final illness, Frank brought chicken soup. They would sit and talk for hours, reminiscing about the days with Dorsey. Frank hated funerals, yet he delivered the eulogy at Buddy's, where many of the old gang paid their respects.

Irv "Sarge" Weiss was a longtime assistant who dedicated his life to Frank, driving him to and from everywhere while running Frank's music-publishing company, Sergeant Music (thus the nickname). As Sarge started to lose his battle with Alzheimer's, his job became more of a challenge. "Sarge always drove Frank to the recording studio," recalled Lee Herschberg, "but the last time I saw him, Sarge was in the passenger seat and Frank was behind the wheel." Frank had introduced Sarge to his wife, Jill, a former showgirl from the Copa in the old days—whom Frank dated (when Nancy wasn't looking). Frank called Jill to inquire about Sarge after he retired, and she brought him up-to-date. "Well, don't let it bother you," said Frank, "because I had dinner last night with some very good friends and I couldn't remember their names."

In 1995, Nancy Sinatra's homage to her father, *Frank Sinatra: An American Legend,* established her as keeper of the family flame. In the album-size book, she recalled meeting Ava for the first time in 1950. "She was just the most beautiful creature I had ever seen in my life," wrote Nancy. "I couldn't stop staring at her. At last, in my pre-teenage wisdom, I had some understanding of why Daddy left us. In 1984, I asked him if, given the choice again, he would have left us, and he said, 'No.'" On March 29, 2015, on the CBS TV *Sunday Morning* program, Nancy reiterated her exchange with Dad, but the topic now was not abandonment; it was Ava. "What was Ava Gardner like?" asked interviewer Mo Rocca. "She was fantastic," said Nancy. "I met her when I was eleven, and I could see it. She was on the fast track, and he wanted to be on the fast track, and he usually got what he went after. My mom had one great love of her life, and that was my dad. To this day, she still loves and adores him. I asked him once, if he had it to do again, would he leave Mom for Ava, and he said 'No.'"

It is hard to imagine a different response from a father, especially at that stage in Frank's life.

In the final years at the Compound, Frank liked to retreat to his "caboose"-style building, put on his railroad cap, sit by the controls, and play with his trains for hours.

At Frank's funeral, Bill Miller, plus guitar and bass (no drums), played his final accompaniment as people walked into the church. "I played songs that seemed appropriate," he said. "About fifteen or so . . . 'I'll Be Seeing You' . . . 'All the Way' . . . 'Too Marvelous for Words' . . . 'Put Your Dreams Away' (played late in the medley) . . .'Nancy' . . . 'All My Tomorrows' . . . 'All or Nothing at All' . . . 'Night and Day' . . . 'Young at Heart' (on guitar) . . . 'You Make Me Feel So Young' . . . 'Emily' (because I know he liked the tune) . . . 'Moonlight in Vermont' . . . 'Don't Worry About Me' . . . He hated 'Strangers in the Night' . . . didn't do that."

Eydie Gormé approached Bill afterward. "Very nice," she said. "You did it just right." She noticed the chord changes, and, approvingly, that he did not play "My Way." "I didn't like 'My Way,' either," said Miller.

The Sinatra family chose just one recording to be played toward the end of the service—the Nelson Riddle arrangement of "Put Your Dreams Away," a wistful little waltz that Frank had commissioned Ruth Lowe to write in 1943, when he'd been given his own radio show by CBS—"Songs by Sinatra"—and he sang it as his closing theme. He sang it on radio for decades, and it was his closing theme on the popular "A Man and His Music" TV specials. It was a song he had kept in his book virtually until the end. When Frank's voice filled the church with those heartbreaking opening lines—"Put your dreams away for another day, and I will take their place in your heart . . ."—"there wasn't a dry eye in the house," said Barbara.

As the funeral party departed the church, a small plane overhead did intricate loops, skywriting Frank's initials, then encircling them with a smoke ring in the shape of a heart.

Kirk Kirkourian's private plane took the casket and family to Palm Springs, where the air-traffic controller said, "You're clear for landing—and welcome home, Mr. Sinatra." As Frank's casket came down the conveyor belt, workers on the tarmac stood, caps in hand. Hundreds lined the route to Desert Memorial Park, saluting, waving, throwing flowers, and crying, "Good-bye, Frank," "Welcome home, Blue Eyes."

The first line on Frank's gravestone is the title of the last song he sang in public, all caps: THE BEST IS YET TO COME.

The Paul Clemens oil portrait of Frank, commissioned by Ava, was also used as cover art for the final album released during Frank's lifetime, *Everything Happens to Me*. The last selection on the nineteen-song album is "Put Your Dreams Away," the same Nelson Riddle version that was played at Frank's funeral. When your author requested permission to reproduce the album cover in these pages, he was advised, "Frank Sinatra Enterprises does not generally permit the use of its materials in connection with third-party creative projects as a matter of policy. Accordingly, we must respectfully decline permission." Readers who wish to view the portrait may Google the album on the Internet.

The concluding lines of *The Sun Also Rises* are from the novel by Ernest Hemingway, not from the Zanuck movie version, where Ava, as Lady Brett, says, "Darling, there must be an answer somewhere." And Tyrone Power, as Jake, says, "I'm sure there is."

That is not Hemingway. That's entertainment.

⊰ BIBLIOGRAPHY ⊱

Books

Anka, Paul. *My Way.* New York: St. Martin's Press, 2013.

Bacall, Lauren. *By Myself.* New York: Alfred A. Knopf, 1979.

Baker, Carlos. *Ernest Hemingway: A Life Story.* New York: Charles Scribner's Sons, 1969.

Bart, Peter. *Fade Out: The Calamitous Final Days of MGM.* New York: William Morrow, 1990.

Behlmer, Rudy, ed. *Memo from David O. Selznick.* New York: Viking, 1972.

Benchley, Nathaniel. *Humphrey Bogart.* Boston: Little, Brown, 1975.

Berg, A. Scott. *Goldwyn.* New York: Alfred A. Knopf, 1989.

Bergman, Ingrid. *Ingrid Bergman: My Story.* New York: Delacorte, 1980.

Birmingham, Nan Tillson. *Store.* New York: G. P. Putnam's Sons, 1978.

Birmingham, Stephen. "Stephen Birmingham," afterword in *Ava: My Story,* by Ava Gardner. New York: Bantam Books, 1990.

Bishop, Jim. *A Bishop's Confession.* Boston: Little, Brown, 1981.

———. *The Golden Ham.* New York: Simon & Schuster, 1956.

———. *The Mark Hellinger Story.* New York: Appleton-Century-Crofts, 1952.

Blair, Betsy. *The Memory of All That.* New York: Alfred A. Knopf, 2003.

Bloom, Ken. *The American Songbook.* New York: Black Dog & Leventhal, 2005.

Bogdanovich, Peter. *Pieces of Time.* New York: Arbor House, 1973.

———. *Who the Hell's in It.* New York: Ballantine Books, 2004.

Brown, Peter Harry, and Pamela Ann Brown. *The MGM Girls: Behind the Velvet Curtain*. New York: St. Martin's Press, 1983.

Bushkin, Henry. *Johnny Carson*. Boston: Houghton Mifflin, 2013.

Cahn, Sammy. *I Should Care: The Sammy Cahn Story*. New York: Arbor House, 1974.

Caldera, Pete. "The Voice." *Times Herald-Record Sunday Magazine,* December 10, 1995, 3.

Cannon, Doris Rollins. *Grabtown Girl*. Asheboro, NC: Down Home Press, 2001.

Carpozi, George, Jr. *Poison Pen: The Unauthorized Biography of Kitty Kelley*. Fort Lee, NJ: Barricade Books, 1991.

Catalog 8228: *Sinatra Christie's Collection of Mr. and Mrs. Frank Sinatra*. New York: Christie's, 1995.

Champlin, Charles. "Where the Elephants Go to Die." In *A Day in the Life of Hollywood*. New York: Collins, 1992.

Chandler, Charlotte. *Nobody's Perfect: Billy Wilder, a Personal Biography*. New York: Simon & Schuster, 2002.

Clarke, Donald. *All or Nothing at All: A Life of Frank Sinatra*. New York: Fromm International, 1997.

Cole, Natalie, with Digby Diehl. *Angel on My Shoulder: An Autobiography*. New York: Warner Books, 2000.

Coleman, Ray. *Sinatra: A Portrait of the Artist*. Nashville, TN: Turner Publishing, 1995.

Consiglio, Tony, with Franz Douskey. *Sinatra and Me: The Very Good Years*. Old Saybrook, CT: Tantor Media, 2012.

Cornyn, Stan, with Paul Scanlon. *Exploding: The Highs, Hits, Hype, Heroes, and Hustlers of the Warner Music Group*. New York: Rolling Stone Press, 2002.

Cramer, Richard Ben. *Joe DiMaggio: The Hero's Life*. New York: Simon & Schuster, 2000.

Curtis, Tony, with Peter Golenbock. *American Prince: A Memoir*. New York: Harmony Books, 2008.

Dardis, Tom. *Keaton: The Man Who Wouldn't Lie Down*. New York: Charles Scribner's Sons, 1979.

———.*Some Time in the Sun*. New York: Charles Scribner's Sons, 1976.

Douglas-Home, Robin. *Sinatra*. New York: Grosset & Dunlap, 1962.

Duchin, Peter. *Ghost of a Chance*. New York: Random House, 1996.

Dunne, Dominick. "Afterword." In *Vanity Fair's Hollywood,* edited by Graydon Carter and David Friend. New York: Viking, 2000.

Dwiggins, Don. *Frankie: The Life and Loves of Frank Sinatra*. New York: Paperback Library, 1961.

Eames, John Douglas. *The MGM Story*. Rev. ed. New York: Crown, 1979.

Ephron, Henry. *We Thought We Could Do Anything*. New York: W. W. Norton, 1977.

Epstein, Edward Z. *Portrait of Jennifer: A Biography of Jennifer Jones*. New York: Simon & Schuster, 1995.

Evans, Peter, and Ava Gardner. *Ava Gardner: The Secret Conversations*. New York: Simon & Schuster, 2013.

Evans, Robert. *The Fat Lady Sang*. New York: HarperCollins, 2013.

———. *The Kid Stays in the Picture*. New York: Hyperion, 1996.

Eyman, Scott. *Lion of Hollywood: The Life and Legend of Louis B. Mayer*. New York: Simon & Schuster, 2005.

Farrow, Mia. *What Falls Away: A Memoir*. New York: Doubleday, 1997.

Fisher, Eddie. *Been There, Done That*. New York: St. Martin's Press, 1999.

———. *Eddie: My Life, My Loves*. New York: Harper & Row, 1981.

Flamini, Roland. *Ava: A Biography*. New York: Coward, McCann & Geoghegan, 1983.

Fleming, E. J. *The Fixers*. Jefferson, NC: McFarland & Company, 2005.

Florida, Richard. *The Rise of the Creative Class*. New York: Basic Books, 2002.

Forbes, Malcolm, with Jeff Bloch. *They Went That-a-Way*. New York: Simon & Schuster, 1988.

Fountain, Charles. *Another Man's Poison: The Life and Writing of Columnist George Frazier*. Chester, CT: Globe Pequot Press, 1984.

Frazier, George. *The One with the Mustache Is Costello*. New York: Random House, 1947.

Friedrich, Otto. *City of Nets: A Portrait of Hollywood in the 1940s*. New York: Harper & Row, 1986.

Friedwald, Will. *Sinatra!: The Song Is You*. New York: Charles Scribner's Sons, 1995.

Furia, Philip. *Skylark: The Life and Times of Johnny Mercer*. New York: St. Martin's Press, 2003.

Gage, Nicholas. "Frank Sinatra Is a Pal." In *Mafia, U.S.A.*, edited by Nicholas Gage. Beverly Hills, CA: Playboy Press, 1972.

Gardner, Ava. *Ava: My Story*. New York: Bantam, 1990.

Garner, James, with Jon Winokur. *The Garner Files*. New York: Simon & Schuster, 2011.

Garrett, Betty, with Ron Rapoport. *Betty Garrett and Other Songs*. Lanham, MD: Madison Books, 1998.

Gavin, James. *Stormy Weather: The Life of Lena Horne*. New York: Atria Books, 2009.

Gehman, Richard. *Sinatra and His Rat Pack*. New York: Belmont Books, 1961.

Giddins, Gary. *Bing Crosby, A Pocketful of Dreams: The Early Years, 1903–1940*. Boston: Little, Brown, 2001.

Gladstone, B. James. *The Man Who Seduced Hollywood*. Chicago: Chicago Review Press, 2013.

Goodman, Ezra. *The Fifty-Year Decline and Fall of Hollywood*. New York: Simon & Schuster, 1961.

Gordon, Bernard. *Hollywood Exile, or How I Learned to Love the Blacklist*. Austin: University of Texas Press, 1999.

Graham, Sheilah. *Confessions of a Hollywood Columnist*. New York: William Morrow, 1969.

———. *Hollywood Revisited*. New York: St. Martin's Press, 1985.

Greenberger, Howard. *Bogey's Baby*. New York: St. Martin's Press, 1976.

Griffith, Richard. *The Talkies: Articles and Illustrations from a Great Fan Magazine, 1928–1940*. Mineola, NY: Dover, 1971.

Grobel, Lawrence. *Conversations with Ava Gardner*. New York: HMH Press, 2014.

———. *Conversations with Capote*. New York: New American Library, 1985.

———. *The Hustons*. New York: Charles Scribner's Sons, 1989.

Guilaroff, Sydney. *Crowning Glory*. Los Angeles: General Publishing Group, 1996.

Hall, Carolyn. *The Forties in Vogue*. New York: Harmony Books, 1981.

Hamill, Pete. *Why Sinatra Matters*. Boston: Little, Brown, 1998.

Hanna, David. *Ava: A Portrait of a Star*. New York: G. P. Putnam's Sons, 1960.

———. *Sinatra: Ol' Blue Eyes Remembered*. New York: Gramercy Books, 1997.

Harmetz, Aljean. *The Making of the Wizard of Oz*. New York: Alfred A. Knopf, 1977.

Haver, Ronald. *A Star Is Born: The Making of the 1954 Movie and Its 1983 Restoration*. New York: Alfred A. Knopf, 1988.

Hayes, Helen. *Helen Hayes: My Life in Three Acts*. New York: Harcourt, Brace, Jovanovich, 1990.

Heston, Charlton. *The Actor's Life: Journals 1956–1976*. New York: E. P. Dutton, 1976.

———. *In the Arena: An Autobiography*. New York: Boulevard Books, 1995.

Higham, Charles. *Ava: A Life Story*. New York: Delacorte, 1974.

———. *Celebrity Circus*. New York: Delacorte, 1979.

———. *Merchant of Dreams: Louis B. Mayer, M.G.M. and the Secret Hollywood*. New York: Donald I. Fine, 1993.

Hirsch, Foster. *Film Noir: The Dark Side of the Screen*. New York: A. S. Barnes, 1981.

Horton, Robert, ed. *Billy Wilder Interviews*. Jackson: University Press of Mississippi, 2001.

Hotchner, A. E. *Papa Hemingway*. New York: Random House, 1966.

Huston, Anjelica. *Watch Me: A Memoir*. New York: Scribner, 2014.

Huston, John. *An Open Book*. New York: Alfred A. Knopf, 1980.

Hyams, Joe. *Mislaid in Hollywood*. New York: Peter H. Wyden, 1973.

Jablonski, Edward. *Harold Arlen: Happy with the Blues*. New York: Doubleday, 1961.

Jacobs, George, with William Stadiem. *Mr. S: My Life with Frank Sinatra*. New York: HarperCollins, 2003.

Johnson, Dorris, and Ellen Leventhal, eds. *The Letters of Nunnally Johnson*. New York: Alfred A. Knopf, 1981.

Jones, Shirley, with Wendy Leigh. *Shirley Jones: A Memoir*. New York: Simon & Schuster, 2013.

Jordan, Mearene. *Living with Miss G*. Smithfield, NC: Ava Gardner Museum, 2012.

Kahn, E. J., Jr. *The Voice: The Story of an American Phenomenon*. New York: Harper & Brothers, 1946.

Kanfer, Stefan. *Tough Without a Gun: The Life and Extraordinary Afterlife of Humphrey Bogart*. New York: Alfred A. Knopf, 2011.

Kanin, Garson. *Tracy and Hepburn: An Intimate Memoir*. New York: Viking, 1970.

Kaplan, James. *Frank: The Voice*. New York: Doubleday, 2010.

Kazan, Elia. *Elia Kazan: A Life*. New York: Alfred A. Knopf, 1988.

Keith, Slim, with Annette Tapert. *Slim: Memories of a Rich and Imperfect Life*. New York: Simon & Schuster, 1990.

Kelley, Kitty. *His Way: The Unauthorized Biography of Frank Sinatra*. New York: Bantam, 1986.

———. *Nancy Reagan: The Unauthorized Biography*. New York: Simon & Schuster, 1991.

Keyes, Evelyn. *I'll Think About That Tomorrow*. New York: E. P. Dutton, 1991.

———. *Scarlett O'Hara's Younger Sister*. New York: Lyle Stuart, 1977.

Kinn, Gail, and Jim Piazza. *The Academy Awards: The Complete History of Oscar*. New York: Black Dog & Leventhal, 2002.

Kramer, Stanley. *A Mad, Mad, Mad, Mad World*. New York: Harcourt, Brace, 1997.

Kuntz, Tom, and Phil Kuntz, eds. *The Sinatra Files: The Secret FBI Dossier*. New York: Three Rivers Press, 2000.

Lambert, Gavin. *On Cukor*. New York: Rizzoli, 2000.

Lansky, Sandra, with William Stadiem. *Daughter of the King: Growing Up in Gangland*. New York: Weinstein Books/Perseus, 2014.

Lasky, Jesse, Jr. *Whatever Happened to Hollywood?* New York: Funk & Wagnalls, 1973.

Lawrence, D. H. "The Phenomenal Growth of the Movies." In *Vanity Fair's Hollywood*, edited by Graydon Carter and David Friend. New York: Viking, 2000.

Leff, Leonard J., and Jerold L. Simmons. *The Dame in the Kimono: Hollywood, Censorship and the Production Code from the 1920s to the 1960s.* New York: Grove Weidenfeld, 1990.

Leigh, Janet. *There Really Was a Hollywood.* New York: Doubleday, 1984.

Levinson, Peter J. *Tommy Dorsey: Livin' in a Great Big Way.* Boston: Da Capo Press, 2005.

———. *September in the Rain: The Life of Nelson Riddle.* New York: Billboard Books, 2001.

Levy, Shawn. *Rat Pack Confidential.* New York: Doubleday, 1998.

Lewis, Jerry, with James Kaplan. *Dean & Me (A Love Story).* New York: Doubleday, 2005.

Linet, Beverly. *Star-Crossed: The Story of Robert Walker and Jennifer Jones.* New York: G. P. Putnam's Sons, 1986.

Lord, Graham. *Niv: The Authorized Biography of David Niven.* New York: St. Martin's Press, 2003.

Loren, Sophia. *Yesterday, Today, Tomorrow: My Life.* New York: Atria Books, 2014.

MacLaine, Shirley. *My Lucky Stars: A Hollywood Memoir.* New York: Bantam Books, 1995.

Malden, Karl. *Karl Malden: When Do I Start.* New York: Simon & Schuster, 1997.

Maltin, Leonard, ed. *Leonard Maltin's Movie Encyclopedia.* New York: E. P. Dutton, 1994.

Marx, Arthur. *The Nine Lives of Mickey Rooney.* New York: Stein & Day, 1986.

Marx, Harpo, with Rowland Barber. *Harpo Speaks!* New York: Bernard Geis Associates, 1961.

McClintick, David. *Indecent Exposure.* New York: William Morrow, 1982.

McMahon, Ed, with David Fisher. *For Laughing Out Loud: My Life and Good Times.* New York: Warner Books, 1998.

Munn, Michael. *David Niven: The Man Behind the Balloon.* Grand Rapids, MI: JR Books, 2009.

Murray, Lyn. *Musician: A Hollywood Journal.* New York: Lyle Stuart, 1987.

Niven, David. *Bring on the Empty Horses.* New York: G. P. Putnam's Sons, 1975.

———. *The Moon's a Balloon.* New York: G. P. Putnam's Sons, 1972.

Nolan, Tom. *Three Chords for Beauty's Sake: The Life of Artie Shaw.* New York: W. W. Norton, 2010.

O'Brien, Ed, and Scott P. Sayers, Jr. *Sinatra: The Man and His Music: The Recording Artistry of Francis Albert Sinatra, 1939–1992.* Austin: Texas State Directory, 1992.

———. *The Sinatra Sessions 1939–1980.* Dallas: Sinatra Society of America, 1980.

O'Brien, Ed, with Robert Wilson. *Sinatra 101*. New York: Boulevard Books, 1996.

O'Neill, Terry. *Sinatra: Frank and Friendly*. London: Evans Mitchell Books, 2007.

Parish, James Robert. *Hollywood Divas*. Chicago: Contemporary Books, 2003.

Randall, Stephen, ed. *The Playboy Interviews: Larger Than Life*. Milwaukie, OR.: M Press, 2006.

Reed, Rex. "Ava: Life in the Afternoon." In *Smiling Through the Apocalypse,* edited by Harold Hayes. New York: Dell, 1969.

————. *Big Screen, Little Screen*. New York: Macmillan, 1971.

Reiter, Mark, and Richard Sandomir. *The Enlightened Bracketologist: The Final Four of Everything*. New York: Bloomsbury Books, 2007.

Richmond, Peter. *Fever: The Life and Music of Miss Peggy Lee*. New York: Henry Holt, 2006.

Rooney, Mickey. *Life Is Too Short*. New York: Villard Books, 1991.

Rose, Frank. *The Agency*. New York: HarperBusiness, 1995.

Rozsa, Miklos. *Double Life*. New York: Midas Books, 1982.

Schulberg, Budd. *Moving Pictures: Memories of a Hollywood Prince*. New York: Stein & Day, 1981.

Seebohm, Caroline. *No Regrets: The Life of Marietta Tree*. New York: Simon & Schuster, 1997.

Server, Lee. *Ava Gardner: "Love Is Nothing."* New York: St. Martin's Press, 2006.

Shaw, Arnold. *Sinatra: Twentieth-Century Romantic*. New York: Holt, Rinehart and Winston, 1968.

Shearer, Stephen Michael. *Beautiful: The Life of Hedy Lamarr*. New York: St. Martin's Press, 2010.

Sheed, Wilfrid. *The House That George Built*. New York: Random House, 2007.

Sheldon, Sidney. *The Other Side of Me*. New York: Warner Books, 2005.

Sheward, David. *Rage and Glory: The Volatile Life and Career of George C. Scott*. Milwaukee: Applause Books, 2008.

Simon, George T. *The Big Bands*. New York: Macmillan, 1967.

Sinatra, Barbara, with Wendy Holden. *Lady Blue Eyes: My Life with Frank*. New York: Random House, 2011.

Sinatra, Nancy. *Frank Sinatra: An American Legend*. Los Angeles: General Publishing Group, 1995.

————. *Frank Sinatra, My Father*. New York: Doubleday, 1985.

Sinatra, Tina, with Jeff Coplon. *My Father's Daughter*. New York: Simon & Schuster, 2000.

Smith, Liz. *Natural Blonde: A Memoir.* New York: Random House, 2000.

Smith, Sally Bedell. *Reflected Glory: The Life of Pamela Churchill Harriman.* New York: Simon & Schuster, 1996.

Spada, James. *Grace: The Secret Lives of a Princess.* New York: Doubleday, 1987.

———. *Peter Lawford: The Man Who Kept the Secrets.* New York: Bantam, 1991.

Spoto, Donald. *Madcap: The Life of Preston Sturges.* Boston: Little, Brown, 1990.

Sturges, Preston, with Sandy Sturges. *Preston Sturges.* New York: Simon & Schuster, 1990.

Summers, Anthony, and Robbyn Swan. *Sinatra: The Life.* New York: Alfred A. Knopf, 2005.

Sunshine, Linda. "On the Backlot with a Sony Walkman." In *A Day in the Life of Hollywood.* New York: Collins, 1992.

Taraborrelli, J. Randy. *Sinatra: Behind the Legend.* Secaucus, NJ: Birch Lane Press, 1997.

Thomas, Bob. *King Cohn: The Life and Times of Harry Cohn.* Rev. ed. Beverly Hills, CA: New Millennium Press, 2000.

Thompson, Charles. *Bing.* Philadelphia: David McKay, 1975.

Thompson, Verita, with Donald Shepherd. *Bogie and Me.* New York: St. Martin's Press, 1982.

Thomson, David. *Marlon Brando.* New York: DK Books, 2003.

——— *Showman: The Life of David O. Selznick.* New York: Alfred A. Knopf, 1992.

Torme, Mel. *It Wasn't All Velvet.* New York: Viking, 1988.

Turner, Adrian. *Hollywood 1950s.* New York: Gallery Books, 1986.

Turner, Lana. *Lana: The Lady, the Legend, the Truth.* New York: E. P. Dutton, 1982.

Van Dyke, Dick. *Dick Van Dyke: My Lucky Life in and out of Show Business.* New York: Crown, 2011.

Vare, Ethlie Ann, ed. *Legend: Frank Sinatra and the American Dream.* New York: Boulevard Books, 1995.

Vidal, Gore. *Screening History.* Cambridge: Harvard University Press, 1992.

Wagner, Robert, with Scott Eyman. *Pieces of My Heart: A Life.* New York: HarperCollins, 2008.

———. *You Must Remember This: Life and Style in Hollywood's Golden Age.* New York: Viking, 2014.

Walls, Jeannette. *Dish: The Inside Story on the World of Gossip.* New York: Avon Books, 2000.

Weintraub, Jerry. *When I Stop Talking, You'll Know I'm Dead.* New York: Grand Central Publishing, 2011.

Wiley, Mason, and Damien Bona. *Inside Oscar.* New York: Ballantine, 1986.

Williams, Chris, ed. *The Richard Burton Diaries.* New Haven: Yale University Press, 2012.

Williams, Esther, with Digby Diehl. *The Million-Dollar Mermaid.* New York: Simon & Schuster, 1999.

Wilson, Earl. *Sinatra.* New York: Macmillan, 1976.

Wilson, John S. "Guide for the Great Bands." In *The Story of the Great Bands, 1936–1945.* White Plains, NY: Reader's Digest Association, 1980.

Winters, Shelley. *Shelley: Also Known as Shirley.* New York: William Morrow, 1980.

———. *Shelley II: The Middle of My Century.* New York: Simon & Schuster, 1989.

Wright, William. *Lillian Hellman: The Image, the Woman.* New York: Simon & Schuster, 1986.

Young, Jeff. *Kazan: The Master Director Discusses His Films.* New York: Newmarket Press, 1999.

Young, Toby. *How to Lose Friends and Alienate People.* Boston: Da Capo Press, 2001.

Zehme, Bill. *The Way You Wear Your Hat.* New York: HarperCollins, 1997.

Periodicals

Bogdanovich, Peter. "Ava's Allure." *The New York Times Book Review,* April 23, 2006.

Brody, Richard. "The Shadows of Lauren Bacall." *The New Yorker,* August 13, 2014.

Brooke, Geoff. "Ol' Blue Eyes and Me." *The Age* (Australia), May 15, 2000.

Buckley, Reid. "Ave *Ava.*" *The National Review,* April 16, 1990.

Champlin, Charles. "Hedda Hopper and Louella Parsons: Private Lives of Hollywood's Powerful Columnists." *Architectural Digest,* April 1990, 114–126.

Collins, Amy Fine. "Idol Gossips." *Vanity Fair,* April 1997.

Curran, Bob. "Has Frankie Had It?" *Motion Picture and Television,* July 1952, 50–51, 64.

DeWolf, Rose. "Frank & Ava: An Unforgettable Day." *Philadelphia [Daily News] Online,* August 13, 2001. Available at http://phillyonline.com.

Douskey, Franz. "The Man Who Knew Everyone." *Yankee,* July/August 2000, 66–70, 133–134.

"The Farmer's Daughter." *Time,* September 3, 1951.

Flint, Peter B. "Lana Turner Is Dead at 75; 'Sweater Girl' and Sultry Star." *New York Times,* July 1, 1995.

"Frank Talk on FS Liner." *Billboard,* October 8, 1962.

Gates, David. "Voices of the Century: America Goes Hollywood." *Newsweek,* June 28, 1999, 34–80.

Gehman, Richard. "The Hollywood Horrors." *Cosmopolitan,* November 1958, 38–42.

Gibbons, Ed. "Ava Gardner: Beauty and the Bullfighters." *Climax,* March 1961, 13–17, 69–71.

Grove, Lee. "Last Night, When We Were Young." *Boston Magazine,* November 1974, 74–77, 129–142.

Hartford, Bob. "Why Ava Gardner Is Afraid to Come Back to Hollywood." *Police Gazette,* August 1957, 3–4.

"How a New Actress Sees Hollywood: Marta's Eyes on Hollywood." *Life,* June 13, 1949, 103–107.

Howell, M. "Forever Frank: James Isaacs Celebrates Sinatra." *Boston Phoenix,* December 7, 1990.

Kaplan, Peter W. "Gable to J.R. with Ava Gardner." *The New York Times,* February 25, 1985.

Kashner, Sam. "Here's to You, Mr. Nichols: The Making of *The Graduate,*" *Vanity Fair,* March 2008.

Kendall, Robert. "Superstar Ava Gardner: Her Last Years in London." *Classic Images,* July 2002, 6–11.

"The Kid from Hoboken." *Time,* August 29, 1955, 52–59.

Lancaster, Burt. "Now I Know." *Motion Picture,* November 1949, 65–67.

"Last Year's Movies," *Life,* March 8, 1948, 58–64.

"Louis B. Mayer: MGM's Archetypal Studio Head at Home." *Architectural Digest,* April 1990, 144–145, 284.

Nelson, Michael. "Frank Sinatra: The Loneliness of the Long Distance Singer." *The Virginia Quarterly Review,* 75, no. 4 (1999).

Pleasants, Henry. "Frank Sinatra: A Great Vocal Artist Retires." *Stereo Review,* November 1971, 59–74.

Reid, James. "I Don't Want to Be a Career Girl!" *Motion Picture,* August 1940, 22–23, 70–73.

Reisner, Robert George. "Sinatra." *Playboy,* November 1958, 62–63, 84–88.

Rizzo, Johnna. "A Brush-Off With Greatness." *Frank Sinatra: The Man Behind the Voice,* a *TV Guide* Special Edition, 2014.

Rothman, Cliff, and Peter Scallion. "Notorious! The Ingrid Bergman/Roberto Rossellini Affair." *Memories,* March 1989, 46–52.

Shaw, Arnold. "Sound Scene: The Aura of an Era." *Cavalier,* February 1968, 12–14.

Sinatra, Frank. "Frankie Says . . ." *Motion Picture,* December 1949, 10.

Sinatra, Nancy (Sands). "That Restless Soul, My Father." *Modern Screen,* February 1961, 30–31, 69–70.

"Sinatra's Secrets: How Frank Did It His Way." *National Enquirer,* Special Anniversary Issue, June 2013.

"Starlets Are World's Most Envied Girls." *Life,* January 29, 1940, 37–39.

Sufrin, Mark. "Frank Sinatra: He Still Does It His Way." *Saga,* November 1974, 35–37, 50–54.

Surmelian, Leon. "Can Women Be Friends in Hollywood?" *Motion Picture,* August 1940, 29, 88–89.

"Texas Monthly Talks: Liz Smith." *Texas Monthly,* May 2005, 112–122.

"A 200,000-Product Company: General Electric Manufactures Something for Everybody." *Life,* October 4, 1948, 80–89.

Waterbury, Ruth. "Ava Gardner's Dry Tears." *Photoplay,* April 1957, 60–61, 112–113.

Young, Tom. "My Thoughts on In-Ear Monitors." *ProAudio Review,* September 2006, 33.

Videos and TV Programs

"Ava Gardner." *E! Mysteries & Scandals: AVA.* E (Entertainment) channel television broadcast. Produced by Danny Schwartz, Alison Martino, and Michael Danahy. November 2012.

MGM: When the Lion Roars. Television broadcast miniseries. Point Blank Productions, Turner Pictures, 1992.

Rat Pack's Las Vegas. Travel Channel television broadcast. White Star Studio, 2002. DVD.

Sinatra: All or Nothing at All. HBO Documentary Films. Directed by Alex Gibney. April 2015.

Sinatra: Off the Record. 1965 CBS news special. Written by Andy Rooney; host, Walter Cronkite. CBS News video 7557.

Recordings

Artie Shaw: A Legacy. Camp Hill, PA: Book-of-the-Month Records, 1984. Vinyl sound recording, monaural 33 1/3 rpm. Issue #71-7715.

Frank Sinatra. *Everything Happens to Me*. Reprise Records 9-46116-2, 1996.

Frank Sinatra. *Sinatra—The Great Years*. Capitol WCO/SWCO 1792, released October 1962.

Show Boat: Original MGM Soundtrack, CBS Special Products AK 45436, released 1990.

☙ INDEX ❧